The Indian Social Sector

Published by
ACADEMIC FOUNDATION
in association with

Institute of Public Enterprise

The Indian Social Sector

Trends and Issues

Editors

R.K. Mishra and Anand Akundy

ACADEMIC FOUNDATION
NEW DELHI

www.academicfoundation.org

First published in 2015
by

ACADEMIC FOUNDATION
4772-73 / 23 Bharat Ram Road, (23 Ansari Road),
Darya Ganj, New Delhi - 110 002 (India).
Phones : 23245001 / 02 / 03 / 04.
Fax : +91-11-23245005.
E-mail : books@academicfoundation.com
www.academicfoundation.org

in association with
Institute of Public Enterprise (IPE), Hyderabad.

Disclaimer:
The findings/views/opinions expressed in this book are solely those of the authors and do not necessarily reflect the views of the publisher.

Cataloging in Publication Data--DK
Courtesy: D.K. Agencies (P) Ltd. <docinfo@dkagencies.com>

The Indian social sector : trends and issues / editors, R.K. Mishra and Anand Akundy.
pages cm
Contributed articles.
Includes bibliographical references.
ISBN 9789332701946

1. Social planning--India. 2. India--Social policy. I. Mishra, R. K., 1948-, editor. II. Akundy, Anand, editor.

DDC 361.610954 23

Typeset by Italics India, New Delhi.

Printed and bound by The Book Mint, New Delhi.
www.thebookmint.in

Contents

List of Tables, Figures and Boxes

Tables

Figures

Boxes

About the Editors/Contributors

Editors:

R.K. Mishra, Senior Professor and Director of the Institute of Public Enterprise (IPE), Hyderbad, is a graduate of International Management Programme, SDA Bocconi, Milan, Italy. He has been a Fellow of British Council and Commonwealth Secretariat, He has been awarded Fellowships by UNDESA, ICSSR and UGC. He has had research stints at London Business School and Maison Des Sciences De L' Hommes, Paris. He has taught at the University of Bradford, United Kingdom and was a visiting Professor at Maison Des Sciences De L' Hommes, Paris. He has handled assignments for the Ministry of Finance, Ministry of Power, Ministry of Heavy Industries, Ministry of Trade and Commerce, Ministry of Heavy Industry and Public Enterprises, and Ministry of Disinvestment. He has been a Management Consultant to organisations including PWC and Adam Smith Institute, London, and the Asian Development Bank. He has been a member of the Planning Commission Study Group on Restructuring of SLPEs. He has also been a researcher for Planning Commission, Finance Commission, Prime Minister's Economic Advisory Council, OECD, United Nations University-World Institute for Economic Development Research, International Civil Service Consortium, State Bureaus of Public Enterprises, financial institutions and banks. His current interests include: economic reforms, privatisation and restructuring, finance, poverty management and good governance.

Anand Akundy is currently a Senior Faculty Member at IPE, Hyderabad. In a long academic and research career, he had worked with prestigious international projects, including as an Advisor to a project funded by the Economic and Social Research Council of U.K.; his immediate past stint was with the Administrative Staff College of India (ASCI), Hyderabad, where he was Director of the Centre for Human Development and an Associate Professor, during which time he directed training programmes for the Planning Commission and Ministry of Statistics and Programme Implementation, Government of India. He had also carried out several studies prominent among which is the Assessment of Development Results: India (along with a team), which is Evaluation of the India Country Programs of UNDP during 2007-2012, commissioned by the Evaluation Office of UNDP–New York. He led an ASCI team in the IDRC sponsored project called Teaching Evaluation in South Asia (TESA) and developed curriculum for teaching evaluation, along with a South Asian team. He was member of an ASCI team that provided support to the DFID-FHI funded project, the A.P. Health Sector Reforms Project during 2008-2010. He had led the UNDP commissioned Impact Assessment Study of R&R in Orissa and the UNICEF–ASCI partnered advocacy initiative, Promoting Quality Education among Children Belonging to Tribal Communities in Andhra Pradesh. He has authored several chapters in edited books and articles in academic journals among which a chapter for a book published by the Routledge is noteworthy.

Contributors:

S. Mahendra Dev is currently Director and Vice Chancellor, Indira Gandhi Institute of Development Research (IGIDR), Mumbai. He was Chairman, Commission for Agricultural Costs and Prices (CACP), Government of India, Delhi (2008-2010) and Director, Centre for Economic and Social Studies (CESS), Hyderabad (1999-2008). He is member of the Board of Trustees of International Food Policy Research Institute (IFPRI), Washington, D.C. He is also member of National Statistical Commission in the rank of

Secretary to Government of India. Prof Dev has more than 100 research publications in national and international journals and has published 15 books. He has been a consultant and adviser to many international organisations, such as UNDP, World Bank, IFPRI, ILO, FAO, and ESCAP. He is the Chairman of the Committee on Terms of Trade on Agriculture constituted by the Ministry of Agriculture, Government of India. He is also member of the newly constituted Expert Panel on Poverty Estimates chaired by Dr C. Rangarajan. He has been a member of several government committees including the Prime Minister's Task Force on Employment and Rangarajan Commission on Financial Inclusion.

S. Galab, a Development Economist, is currently Director, CESS, Hyderabad and is also leading the Young Lives—an International Longitudinal Project in Andhra Pradesh, on Childhood Poverty. He has carried out research in the broad field of rural development on various aspects like rehabilitation and resettlement of project affected people, natural resource management, solid waste management in urban areas, handloom and power loom sector, agrarian distress and farmers' suicides, rural indebtedness, MGNREGS, dry land agriculture. He also worked on the effectiveness of public policies related to poverty alleviation including social capital, women empowerment, child labour and livelihoods. Besides conducting research, he also does teaching and supervising MPhil and PhD students. He was a member of Farmers Welfare Commission—a commission appointed by the Government of Andhra Pradesh in response to the agrarian crisis in the united state of Andhra Pradesh. He is presently a member of the Commission on "Sustainable Agricultural Development of Andhra Pradesh". He is one of the co-editor of the book "On Joint Forest Management in Andhra Pradesh" and "Organizing Poor Women: The Andhra Pradesh Experience".

Binoy Goswami is currently serving as an Assistant Professor of Economics, South Asian University, New Delhi. His broad areas of research interest include: agricultural economics and issues in development economics. He has already published a dozen of articles which have appeared in journals like *Economic and Political Weekly, Bangladesh Development Studies, Indian Journal of Human Development, Man Power Journal, Indian Journal of Regional Science* and *ICFAI Journal of Industrial Economics*.

R.S. Goyal is a development scientist with specialisation in empirical and operations research, programme evaluation, policy and strategy formulation, networking, training and capacity building, and institution building. His areas of special interest include: dynamics of population change, population and health care management, disaster management, water and sanitation, ageing, disability, gender, social development and related issues. He is presently working as Senior Adviser and Regional Director, Ramana Group at Dehradun, and serves as Senior Adjunct Professor, TALEEM Research Foundation, Ahmedabad. Prior to it, he has served as the Professor and Dean, Himgiri Zee University, Dehradun. Earlier, he served as the Dean, Institute of Health Management Research (IIHMR), Jaipur; Senior Faculty at Panjab University, Chandigarh; TN Medical College, Mumbai and WHO Human Reproduction Research Unit at KEM Hospital, Mumbai.

Hemnath Rao Hanumankar presents a distinctive blend of professional exposure to both business and development management that complements his outstanding academic background. His work experience over the last quarter century has involved senior management responsibilities in organisations across the private, public and cooperative sectors. Actively associated with the formulation of corporate and competitive strategies for large and small businesses, he has significantly contributed to strategic restructuring/repositioning of various departments/institutions of Government of India and states. He has designed and delivered programmes in strategic management, agribusiness strategies, rural management and advanced general management for senior and top management of large public and private sector enterprises, senior civil servants, technocrats, owner-managers and entrepreneurs from within India, South Asia, Pacific Region and across Continental Africa. He has been lecturing at leading management institutions across the country and abroad, and is a Visiting Professor at IPE, Hyderabad and at the University of Ljubljana, Slovenia. While on the faculty of ASCI since 1996, he served as Head, Tata Management Development Centre, Jamshedpur for a year (2003-04). He has also researched and published papers in many refereed journals. His widely read book, "Tryst With Global Competition" analyses the strategic response of Indian businesses to the forces of global competition and globalisation while his book "Study of MGNREGA: A Case in Implementation of an Anti Poverty Programme in A.P." captures the strategic issues in implementing India's flagship programme for alleviating rural poverty. His areas of interest include: strategic management, agribusinesses and rural management, rural co-operatives, small and medium enterprises (SMEs), strategic leadership, good public governance and strategic management of change.

Nazmul Ahsan Kalimullah,[1] is currently a Professor in the Department of Public Administration, University of Dhaka, Bangladesh. He is the founder and Chairman of JANIPOP (National Election Observation Council), Bangladesh. He has a PhD and Post-doctoral research experience from the universities of Birmingham and Bath in the United Kingdom. He has published 60 research articles and books on NGOs, international development and tourism management. Prof Kalimullah is the President of BEN (Bangladesh Evaluation Network). He is a life member of Sri Lankan Evaluation Association (SLEvA) and is a member of Community of Evaluators (CoE), American Evaluation Association (AEA). He is involved in evaluation and monitoring

1. Prof Kalimullah's profile is taken from Rugh, Jim and Marco Segone (eds.) (2013). *Voluntary Organizations for Professional Evaluation (VOPEs): Learning from Africa, Americas, Asia, Australasia, Europe and Middle East.* Published by UNICEF, EvalPartners and IOCE in partnership with Cooperacion Espanola, Ministry for Foreign Affairs of Finland, United Nations Evaluation Group and UN Women.

for nearly three decades. Moreover, Prof Kalimullah is involved in election monitoring and assessment.

N.J. Kurian is currently President of Indo-Global Social Service Society (IGSSS), a Delhi based NGO and also Visiting Professor at IPE, Hyderabad. He was formerly Director, Council for Social Development, Sr. Advisor (Financial Resources), Planning Commission, Economic Advisor, Ministry of Finance, Director, Dept. of Rural Development. He also served as Consultant to Asian Development Bank, United Nation's Development Programme, Food and Agricultural Organisation and United Nation's Children's Emergency Fund. He has published over 30 research articles in journals of international repute. His latest publication is an edited book.

Prajna Paramita Mishra is Assistant Professor at the School of Economics, University of Hyderabad. Her main research interest is in the area of mining, livelihoods and economic valuation of environmental impacts. Currently, she is working on coal mining and livelihoods issues in the Indian state of Jharkhand and Chhattisgarh. She teaches Microeconomics Theory and Environmental Economics. Prior to joining University of Hyderabad, she worked as an Assistant Professor in the Research Unit for Livelihoods and Natural Resources (RULNR), Centre for Economic and Social Studies (CESS), Hyderabad.

Sripad Motiram is an Associate Professor at the IGIDR, Mumbai. He has worked on poverty, interpersonal and group-based inequality, and provision of basic goods (e.g. education, water) in India. He has also worked on agricultural labour markets in India. His work has been published in reputed journals like *Economic Development and Cultural Change, Review of Development Economics, Feminist Economics* and the *Economic and Political Weekly*.

P. Prudhvikar Reddy has rich experience in field survey methods, using both quantitative and qualitative techniques including for longitudinal studies. He gained a wealth of experience in the areas of the multi-dimensions of poverty and rural development. His areas of research interests include: agriculture, poverty, rural development, irrigation management, health, credit and handloom sector. Some of his recent works include Co-editor of CESS published book on agriculture; co-author of four published reports brought by CESS on rural poverty in Andhra Pradesh, rural indebtedness in Andhra Pradesh, impact, issues and challenges of MGNREGS in Andhra Pradesh; three papers as a joint author on rural poverty published in an edited book "Organising Poor Women: The Andhra Pradesh Experience", apart from CESS working papers, papers in edited books and several journal articles.

Bhanoji Rao is currently Hon/Adjunct Professor, ASCI and ICFAI Business School (IBS), Hyderabad, and Member, Governing Board, GITAM University. His teaching and research career spans five decades and included assignments at National University of Singapore, the World Bank and TISCO. He was associated with the Centre for Public Policy at IIM-B, GITAM Institute of Foreign Trade, the ASCI and the Sri Sathya Sai University. Dr Rao's consultancy clientele included Singapore Airlines, IBM-Singapore, IDRC–Canada, UNESCAP, the World Bank and most recently the Asian Development Bank, Manila. His publications include 18 books, 40 chapters in books, 62 papers in refereed journals and 14 monographs.

M. Gopinath Reddy is Professor of Political Science and Public Policy at the Centre For Economic and Social Studies (CESS) Hyderabad and also Principal Coordinator for the Division for Sustainable Development Studies (DSDS) at CESS. He was Principal Coordinator for the recently concluded Research Unit for Livelihoods and Natural Resources (RULNR), supported Jamsetji Tata Trust (JSTT, Mumbai), and brought a number of monographs/working papers under Forest Ecosystem spanning across major forest states of India. He has published articles relating to forest governance and livelihoods and natural resources in the journals of *Development and Change*, *The Small*

Scale Forestry Journal, *Economic and Political Weekly* (EPW) and written chapters in the book titled "Forests, People and Power: The Political Ecology of Reform in South Asia". He has written two books: "Political Economy of Watershed Management: Policies, Institutions, Implementation & Livelihoods" (co-authored with Prof Ratna Reddy and Prof John Soussan) and "A Study of Redistributive Politics and its Impact on PRIs: A Case of Assembly Constituency Development Programme (MLA LADS Scheme in Andhra Pradesh)".

Shaheen is currently an Assistant Professor in the faculty of Information Technology at IPE, Hyderabad. She has published a number of papers in refereeed journals and has also presented various academic as well as research based papers at several national and international conferences. A statistician by interest and technologist by qualification, Shaheen has 2 years of research experience. Her research activities are currently twofold: while the first research activity is related to the study of problems using Statistical Process Control (SPC) techniques for monitoring software reliability, the second major research theme that she is currently focusing on is related to the religious minorities of India. Currently, she is associated with a research study on "The Study of Socio-Economic Conditions of Minorities in India" sponsored by ICSSR.

Suman Sahai, who has had a distinguished scientific career in the field of genetics, was awarded the Padma Shri in 2011. In 2004, she received the Borlaug Award for her outstanding contribution to agriculture and the environment. Dr Sahai has served on the faculties of the University of Alberta, University of Chicago, and the University of Heidelberg. She was appointed Knight of the Golden Ark (Netherlands) in 2001 for generating awareness about the importance of genetic resources to food security. She is Founder Chairperson of the Gene Campaign (GC) which is a leading research and advocacy organisation, working on issues relating to food, nutrition and livelihoods, and has played a key role in formulating the Biodiversity Act as well as the Farmers

Rights in the Indian legislation. She is a member of several national policy forums on scientific research and education, biodiversity and environment, biotechnology and bioethics as well as intellectual property rights.

Shulagna Sarkar is an Assistant Professor, IPE, Hyderabad. She is also the Jt. Coordinator, Center for Corporate Social Responsibility at IPE. She has worked in the areas of corporate social responsibility, baseline surveys, impact assessment and green HRM in India. Her areas of interest include:CSR, green HRM, and environmental competencies. She has published several books and papers in her interest areas and has also organised a number of conferences in the area of CSR and HR.

Soma De Silva is a former Regional Monitoring and Evaluation Officer UNICEF Regional Office for South Asia. She is a founder member and two times past president of the Sri Lanka Evaluation Association, the immediate past president of the International Organisation for Collaboration in Evaluation (IOCE) and founder co-chair of EvalPartners. She has initiated and coordinated the project "Teaching Evaluation in South Asia" which was designed to establish evaluation training at post graduate diploma level in academic institutions in South Asia, sponsored by the International Development Research Centre. For nearly 20 years she has worked in the field of evaluation, commissioning, organising and supporting evaluations of national development programmes. She initiated and coordinated the South Asia Evaluation volume published in 2008 and was instrumental in initiating and setting up the United Nations Development Evaluation Group in Asia and the Pacific (UNIDAP). Prior to moving into the development field, she was a senior Government official who carried primary responsibility for the population census and demographic surveys of the Government of Sri Lanka. Her current interest is psychology, especially counselling and research. She has completed an MSc degree in psychology and is currently engaged in a PhD research related to mindfulness

Chhattisgarh, Madhya Pradesh and Uttar Pradesh. Slowest reduction of poverty in these states is attributable to their sluggish growth rate and poor public delivery systems during the post–reform period. There is also very low flow of private investment into these states due to their low levels of physical and social infrastructure. What is of more concern is the regressive nature of the flow of formal credit to these states. Secondly, poverty is also concentrated among scheduled communities. In the developed states of Punjab, Haryana and Himachal Pradesh, Scheduled Caste (SC) households represent highly disproportionate share of poor. In these states, absolute and relative poverty are becoming more of a sociological phenomenon making the economic instruments weak in the reduction of poverty. In the states of Chhattisgarh, Rajasthan and Odisha, Scheduled Tribe (ST) households account for more than 40 per cent of the poor. These states are facing double burden i.e., low growth and high incidence of poverty. Their per capita development expenditure as well as per capita social expenditure is low. Thirdly, with reduction of income poverty, the remaining poor are hardcore poor who suffer from multiple deprivations.

While India succeeded in income poverty reduction, it has not been very successful in reducing malnutrition. The rate of reduction of the incidence of malnutrition has been slow. A sizeable section of population, especially children and women belonging to the vulnerable groups, suffer from various forms of malnutrition, including micronutrient deficiency. Malnutrition seriously retards improvements in human development and further reduces child mortality. The economic costs of the current scale of malnutrition are high. Apart from low income and cultural factors, poor supply of environmental and health services are found to be the causes of malnutrition.

In the successive development plans, basic education has been considered a public good and a key instrument for reducing inequalities in the process of development. The outcomes of the Indian educational system are mixed in nature. Universal enrolment as well as gender equality has been achieved at the primary level. However, dropping rate in secondary education is very high.

Moreover, quality of education leaves much to be desired. Despite a significant expansion of higher education, the gross enrolment ratio in higher education is very low at 13 per cent, which is half of the world's average. Way back in 1966, the Kothari Commission recommended for public expenditure on education at 6.0 per cent of GDP, which was about 3.2 per cent even in 2008. What is worse, the interstate variations in public expenditure on education are substantial. The per capita public expenditure on education in Bihar is only one-fourth of that in Kerala; and in Madhya Pradesh, Uttar Pradesh and Jharkhand, it is less than half of that in Kerala. Admittedly, this contributes inequality in opportunities in education, and children of marginalised groups will be at a disadvantage. Due to lack of relevance and poor quality, the spread of education does not enhance the capabilities of a larger section of population.

India's poor performance on social development gets reflected on its international ranking. It ranked 102 among 132 countries on Social Progress Index which is lowest among the BRIC countries. India fared worse on parameters of access to basic knowledge, information and communications, health and wellness, ecosystem sustainability, and on opportunity dimensions such as personal rights, freedom and choice, tolerance and inclusion and access to education. Most of the health and education indicators of India were worse than that in China and Sri Lanka. The UNDP Report (2010) shows that infant mortality rate (IMR) in India at 50 was three times more than that of China and four times more than that of Sri Lanka; maternal mortality rate (MMR) at 450 was about 10 times more than that of China and Sri Lanka. Life expectancy at birth at 64 years was about 10 years less than that of China and Sri Lanka. Mean year of schooling of adults at 4.4 years was merely half of that in China and Sri Lanka. What is worse, India fared badly on health and education indicators even compared to some of the less developed countries. Bangladesh with less than half of the per capita income improved its position on some of the development indicators and reported better outcomes than that of India. It had higher life expectancy at birth, higher mean years of schooling and lower gender inequality.

"The Indian Social Sector: Trends and Issues" is a comprehensive and contemporary treatment of the major challenges confronting India. It highlights proximate and structural factors underlying the poor progress of India on social development and suggests pathways for achieving the same. It also deals with emerging concerns in farming. It argues that market-oriented reforms are sufficient for improving the livelihoods of small farm holders and suggests policies to integrate them with the development process. This volume provides valuable resource material for the researchers and policy makers.

— R. Radhakrishna
Chairman, Centre for Economic and Social Studies, Hyderabad; former Chairman, National Statistical Commission, Government of India.

Preface

At a time when social sector programmes in the past decade have shown skewed results across sectors, it is strongly speculated that one of the important reasons for this poor performance could be the absence of a robust critique of policy. Admittedly, a number of studies and evaluations on flagship programmes of governments in India have been carried out, but in silos. This suggests the need for a concerted effort at streamlining of different studies, given that there are very few publications on Indian social sector that address issues in multiple sectors. The *Indian Social Sector: Trends and Issues* is one such focused effort in this direction. Institute of Public Enterprise (IPE) has forayed into rendering policy advisory on public enterprises during the last few decades and established a niche for itself. Today, IPE is well poised to delve into the issues of social sectors too, on the strength of its credentials in social science research through affiliation with Indian Council of Social Science Research (ICSSR). It is this institutional vigour coupled with its potential to contribute to the discourse on social sector, and in view of the fact that public enterprises are a part and parcel of the social sectors that renders it befitting to bringing out a volume on the Indian social sector.

This book's relevance stems from two key factors—firstly, the complex issues that this book is engaging with, and secondly, the need to keep revisiting social issues, given the fact that society advances more rapidly than the knowledge about it. No sooner had IPE shared this idea with the contributors to this volume, whose eminence in their respective fields has long been established, quickly came forward and contributed essays and papers and supported IPE's endeavour. IPE is greatly indebted to all the contributors many of whom have also spoken in the International Seminar on Social Sector Development (ICSSR sponsored) that IPE had organised during November 27-28, 2014, an event that appropriately became a curtain-raiser to the releasing of this volume. IPE thus wishes to place on record that without the unflinching support it received from all the contributing authors it could not have brought out this volume. Prof R. Radhakrishna, Chairman, Centre for Economic and Social Studies (CESS), who is also the former Chairperson of National Statistical Commission, Government of India, wrote the Foreword for this volume which has greatly enhanced the value of this publication. We hope the reader shall find this book a good source for triggering policy suggestions that could potentially benefit the social sector programmes in general.

— R.K. Mishra and Anand Akundy

Acknowledgements

We are extremely grateful to Prof. R. Radhakrishna, Chairman, Centre for Economic and Social Studies (CESS), and all the contributors for engaging with us in publishing this book. We are also thankful to the Institute of Public Enterprise (IPE) community for supporting us in our efforts towards publishing this volume. We would like to sincerely recognise the valuable inputs of Prof Bhanoji Rao and Sri Phaneendra Vinnakota.

R.K. MISHRA AND ANAND AKUNDY

Introduction

From United Nations Development Programme's (UNDP) Human Development Index (HDI) to the more recent Multidimensional Poverty Index (MPI), there have been conceptualisations and frameworks towards understanding social development. However, there have not been consistent efforts by governments, multilateral agencies, NGOs (non-governmental organisations) and disciplinary leaders in academia towards contextualising the different concepts and frameworks for addressing social development. With a view to aggregate the various strands of discourse relating to social sector development from the academic and practitioners' world, the Institute of Public Enterprise (IPE), Hyderabad and Academic Foundation, New Delhi, are bringing out this volume "The Indian Social Sector: Trends and Issues".

The main theme of this volume is social sector development in India. Social sector issues are not limited to health, education and housing, but encompass concerns relating to agriculture, food security, rural development, gender and livelihoods. Within that broad canvas, the objective of this collection of papers is to assess performance and analyse the challenges of social sector programmes, policies and remaining issues.

The papers in this volume are written by specialists in diverse fields such as agriculture, health, education, nutrition, gender, food security, agrobiodiversity, poverty, minorities, rural development and livelihoods. Several of these relate to the debate about economic growth and social development, elegantly articulated by Dreze and Sen (2013): "Why has growth not produced commensurate social development or has done so with poor results?" Overall, these papers attempt to bring social development to centre stage and make inclusive growth a visible reality.

committees and community volunteers to promote family planning (Bang, 1986) and social accountability strategies such as community scoring of local health facilities where the performance of a PHC (primary health care centre) is monitored by an Advisory Committee at the block level, by the DM&HO (District Medical and Health Officer) at the district level, and by the Director of Health and Commissioner of Family Welfare at the state level. The advisory committee, whose meetings are seldom held, includes Gram Panchayat members and eminent local citizens and is the only mode of downward accountability (World Bank, 2007).[5]

The Present Volume: Highlights

The overarching aim of the contributions in the present volume is bridging the gap between research and policy.

"Towards Understanding Poverty in India" (Sripad Motiram and Vamsi Vakulabharanam) deals with debates on the conceptualisation and measurement of poverty in India. It provides an overview of the problems that have plagued the assessment of poverty in the Indian context and suggests some directions to move forward in a meaningful manner. The writers contend that there are opposing views on poverty reduction and the policy reforms leading to it. The paper is motivated by the need for getting a genuine picture of poverty in India in order to address larger questions of human/economic development in the country.

The paper, in large parts, examines the concepts propounded by Prof Amartya Sen about poverty identification and aggregation; it further looks at problems of measurement—both unidimensional and multidimensional.

In "Challenges and Opportunities for Small Farmers", S. Mahendra Dev contends that there are significant land inequalities in India and sets out to examine the challenges and opportunities for smallholding agriculture in achieving agricultural growth, food security and livelihoods in India. The paper also shows that market-oriented reforms are not sufficient and government intervention and other support are needed

---

5. *http://siteresources.worldbank.org/INTSOCACCDEMSIDEGOV/Resources/Case1AndhraPradeshSAcCSCealthAugust2007.pdf*

for smallholdings to achieve the above goals. He makes a case for small farmers to have a level playing field with large farms in terms of accessing land, water, inputs, credit, technology and markets.

Suman Sahai in "Gene Campaign" pitches strongly for agrobiodiversity as the key to sustainable food production, especially in the context of climate change induced by global warming. Efforts at creating food security are faulted for resorting to high-tech approaches, ignoring the need for integrating genetic diversity into farming systems of all kinds—traditional, conventional or even based on genetic engineering. The author claims that good management and deployment of agricultural biodiversity will allow production systems to adapt to changing conditions, maintaining productivity at the same time, while being effective as a risk reduction strategy.

In "Livelihoods and Indigenous People: A Case of Mining Project in Odisha", M. Gopinath Reddy and Prajna Mishra argue against the universality of the benefits of the relationship between mineral extraction and economic development. Mining, it is argued, profoundly impacts local communities in several ways: it affects jobs, migrant workers and land and water resources; it produces air and noise pollution; and it also results in the loss of wildlife habitat. The authors contend that the local community bears the negative impact, while all benefits accrue to the mining industry and its workforce. The study focuses on analysing the socio-economic and livelihood impacts and challenges of bauxite mining, and the environmental effects of the mining project on the region.

In "Addressing Social Sector Issues in India: Collaborative Approach to Corporate Social Responsibility", R.K. Mishra, Punam Singh and Shulagna Sarkar aim to study the changing phases of corporate social responsibility (CSR) in India, identify the social sector issues in India that can be addressed through CSR, and discuss the collaborative approach as a tool for inclusive growth. The paper highlights the roles of government, corporates and the civil society in India in initiating structured format for CSR. The paper discusses a few case studies of the PPP (public-private partnership) model of CSR as well as highlights some of the issues and provides solutions in the areas of education, health, sanitation, and skill development. The authors claim that CSR in a collaborative form can make a significant impact on addressing the social sector issues in India.

In "Social Sector Expenditures by Governments and their Impact on Health and Educational Attainments: An Investigation across Indian States", Binoy Goswami proposes an exercise of inter-state comparison of governmental spending in the social sector in general and health and education in particular and their outcome in terms of health and educational attainments of the states, with the objective of understanding the correspondence between the two in the context of Indian diversity.

In "Equitable and Inclusive Health Care in India", N.J. Kurian presents an in-depth commentary on the issues around achievements and inequity in the health care sector in India. He proposes that there are four types of disparities/imbalances: (1) between regions, (2) between urban and rural areas, (3) between social classes and (4) between males and females.

He contends that public expenditure based on government budget support is not commensurate with the declared objectives and most of the medical expenditure is borne by the households themselves. Indeed, National Sample Survey Organisation (NSSO) surveys indicated that one of the major reasons for continuing high level of poverty in the country is the burden of expenditure on health care.

The author further says that immediately after independence, along the lines of National Health Services (NHS) of UK, India also attempted to build a national health service on the basis of the recommendations of Bhore Committee. However, on account of resource constraints, only a watered-down version of the recommended model was implemented. Over the years, instead of strengthening the system with additional resources and manpower, the system got weakened. This is especially true since the economic reform process was initiated in 1991. Implicitly, the private sector was assigned to play the dominant role. Of late, our planners have been modelling a new health care system along the lines of the 'failed US health care model' based on private health care providers and health insurance companies. He concludes that commitment to provide universal health care based on public funding is the only way to ensure inclusive and equitable health care in India.

In "Patterns and Determinants of Transition in Stunting among Younger Children in Andhra Pradesh: An Analysis Based on Longitudinal Data", S. Galab and P. Pruthvikar Reddy propose to fill the gaps in terms of improving understanding on the mobility in nutritional status of younger children (pre-school going) by drawing the data from the Young Lives project that provides longitudinal database. The authors focus on the stunting (stunted or short children are those who are more than two standard deviations below the median of the reference population in terms of height-for-age as a measure of linear growth retardation) dimension of the mobility in nutrition as stunting enables to capture chronic under-nutrition that reflects a failure to receive adequate nutrition over a long period of time. They adopt the UNICEF conceptual framework for the causes of (mal) nutrition in young children. The framework enables to capture the multiple causes that operate at the immediate (individual) level, at the underlying (household/community) level and at the basic (societal) level. It links these levels of causation to the short and long routes to nutritional improvement.

In "High Yielding Seed for Inclusive Growth: 12 Years of Quality Schooling for All", Bhanoji Rao points out that achieving a high rate of economic growth is not difficult if a sound investment climate for both domestic and foreign investments is created by an appropriate policy framework. However, to achieve a trickle down of the fruits to the majority, entrepreneurs and employees need to participate in large numbers. Such involvement can only be achieved through good quality 12-year education for all. This paper outlines the way forward for India after a brief review of 12th Plan provisions and ground reality as it stands today.

In "Gender Inequality at Work: Case of a Mining Community", Prajna Paramita Mishra examines the gender inequality in workforce of a coal mining community in rural Odisha based on data collected using a structured questionnaire. A Herfindahl index of livelihoods diversification shows that women in control villages have more diversified livelihoods than the mining village women. The author attributes this to other social and economic factors like education, caste and household head's monthly income. She then argues for more focus to be placed on other socio-economic matters, which influence women's participation.

In "Millennium Development Goals and Muslim Minorities in India: A Status Report", Shaheen tries to assess the progress of marginalised Muslims in India against the millennium development goals. She reviews the work of a number of writers and thinkers on this subject to show how Muslims suffer from various infirmities, social exclusions, lack of growth, unemployment, etc. She goes on to measure performance of the signatory country India towards meeting Millennium Development Goals (MDGs) by the target date in 2015. She lists a detailed summary of the MDGs from the Millennium Declaration and a summary of the comprehensive analysis of progress of India with reference to the goals and targets. She also documents a review of performance of Muslim minorities in India against the targets identified in the MDGs.

In "Teaching Evaluation in South Asia: Collaboration among Voluntary Organisations for Professional Evaluation (VOPEs), Academia and Development Partners", Soma De Silva, R.S. Goyal, Nazmul Kalimullah and Anand Akundy propound the critical importance of professional evaluation in fostering accountability in development projects. Based on their experience and lessons learned from the programme "Teaching Evaluation in South Asia" (TESA), this paper tries to establish formal evaluation as a profession. The authors posit that in South Asia, as in many other regions, there has been an increasing demand, at various levels of government, for effective and focused evaluation of development efforts for accountability, performance management and organisational learning.

In "Converging a Wage Employment Based Anti-Poverty Programme with Natural Resource Management: A Holistic Case Study of the Kandhamal District in Odisha, India", H. Hemnath Rao attempts to examine how MGNREGA (Mahatma Gandhi National Rural Employment Guarantee Act) stands out for its emphasis on development of natural resources and assets at community and household levels through a process of participatory decision-making in Gram Panchayats (GPs) for strengthening the livelihood resource base of the rural poor. His study analyses how a partnership of the Kandhamal district Administration with an NGO helped promote Integrated Natural Resource Management (INRM) in the course of implementation of the MGNREGA and contributed to an enhanced credibility of the NGOs with district and state administrations. The case study seeks to document how socio-economic status and human development had improved in villages where the pilot projects for innovative livelihoods were implemented.

In Conclusion

Research on social sector development, however comprehensive the coverage and in-depth the investigations, cannot produce easily replicable and universally valid models. With actors of infinitely varying backgrounds, goals and attitudes, societies and their problems will not respond to one–size–fits–all diagnostics and solutions. This volume is just one tiny step in the vast ladder that one needs to climb to understand and tackle the problems of social sector development in India.

IPE and all of us involved in the organisation of this volume are grateful to the authors and the publisher for their unstinted cooperation and understanding.

References

Agarwal, S. and I. Sarasua (2002). "Community-Based Health Financing: CARE India's Experience in the Maternal and Infant Survival Project", *Research in Healthcare Financial Management* 7(1): 85-94.

Bang, A. (1986). "Community Participation in FP (Family Planning) Programme: A Report", *Economic and Political Weekly* 21(32).

Chambers, Robert (1997). *Whose Reality Counts? Putting the First Last.* London: Intermediate Technology Publications.

Cooke, B. and U. Kothari (eds.) (2001). *Participation: The New Tyranny?* New York: Zed Books.

Dreze, Jean and Amartya Sen (2013). *An Uncertain Glory: India and its Contradictions.* London: Allen Lane, Penguin Books Ltd.

Eliason, R.N. (1999). "Towards Sustainability in Village Health Care in Rural Cameroon", *Health Promotion International* 14 (4): 301-06

Flynn, B. (1995). "Measuring Community Leaders' Perceived Ownership of Health Education Programs: Initial Tests of Reliability and Validity", *Health Education Research: Theory and Practice* 10.

Hunt, S. (1990). *Building Alliances: Professional and Political Issues in Community Participation—Examples from a Health and Community Development Project.* Health Promotion International.

Murty, R. and B. Klugman (2004). "Service Accountability and Community Participation in the Context of Health Sector Reforms in Asia—Implications for Sexual and Reproductive Health Care Services", *Health Policy and Planning* 19(1): i78-i86.

Pellissery, Sony and Sylvia I. Bergh (2007). "Adapting the Capability Approach to Explain the Effects of Participatory Development Programs: Case Studies from India and Morocco", *Journal of Human Development* 8(2).

Rifkin, S.B. (1985). *Health Planning and Community Participation: Case Studies in South East Asia.* London: Carom Helein.

————. (1990). *Community Participation in Maternal and Child Health/Family Planning Programmes.* Geneva, Switzerland: World Health Organization.

Stone, Linda (1989). "Cultural Cross-roads of Community Participation: A Case from Nepal", *Human Organization* 48.

WHO (2002). *The World Health Report 2002: Reducing Risks, Promoting Healthy Life.* Geneva: WHO.

World Bank (2007). "Case Study 1: Andhra Pradesh, India: Improving Health Services through Community Score Cards", *Social Accountability Series* Note No. 1. World Bank South Asia Sustainable Development Department.

1

SRIPAD MOTIRAM AND VAMSI VAKULABHARANAM

Towards Understanding Poverty in India[1]

Introduction

This paper deals with debates on the conceptualisation and measurement of poverty in India. It provides an overview of the problems that have plagued the assessment of poverty in the Indian context and suggests some directions in which we could move forward in a meaningful manner. In recent times, there has been considerable controversy and debate over poverty estimates and trends.[2] This debate is highly polarised: on the one hand is the Planning Commission (Planning Commission, 2012; 2013) which has presented a highly optimistic picture of poverty reduction in the past two decades, whereas on the other hand are critics of the Planning Commission who have questioned the official methodology and thereby the estimates, with some (e.g., Patnaik, 2013) arguing that poverty has actually increased. The extent of poverty and its rate of reduction are of course important, but much more is at stake in this debate. An optimistic picture vindicates the policy reforms that have been adopted since the early 1990s and the growth process that India has been experiencing in the past two decades. A modest or negative picture does the opposite. It is therefore important to analyse this

---

1. *Acknowledgement:* We acknowledge the contributions of participants of the workshop, Capabilities Approach and the Indian Poverty Debates, August 2013, held at the University of Hyderabad and Hyderabad Urban Lab.

2. In 2011, the recommendations of the 2009 expert group appointed by the Planning Commission (Tendulkar Committee) were severely criticised by both scholars and the media. More recently, the Planning Commission released poverty estimates based upon the Tendulkar committee poverty line and data from the National Sample Survey (NSS) on consumption expenditure for the year 2011-12. This has reignited the debate. We discuss the scholarly work and provide the references below; some references on the media coverage of this issue are: Ghosh (2011), Parsai (2011 a; b), Patnaik (2011; 2013), Shah (2013) and Rama Kumar (2013).

debate carefully—what are the similarities and differences among various positions? What are the issues that are highlighted and obscured? How do we take this debate forward, to get a more realistic assessment of poverty in India? Without getting a genuine picture of poverty in India, it is hard to address larger questions of human/ economic development in the country. This paper is motivated by these considerations.

Much of what we say below is an attempt to synthesise various strands of the relevant literature in a coherent way. We draw upon two different sets of literature. The first set that we examine focuses upon poverty measurement in India. This comprises scholarly work elucidating issues that are relevant for the Indian context and assessing various policy proposals and documents. As is well known, following the seminal work of Sen (1976), the problem of poverty measurement can be divided into two parts—identification and aggregation. The former is concerned with the issue of identifying who the poor are and the latter is concerned with the problem of arriving at a measure of poverty at the aggregate level desired (e.g., for the country, region etc.). In the Indian context, there has been considerable debate on the identification problem, in particular on the specification of a poverty line in monetary terms which can then be used to identify the poor. We will therefore be largely concerned with this issue. There are two different traditions in poverty measurement—unidimensional and multidimensional. In the former, one focuses on poverty on a single dimension (usually income or expenditure in monetary terms[3]), whereas in the latter, one focuses on multiple dimensions (e.g., income, health, education).[4] In the Indian context, the unidimensional tradition has been the more dominant one, although there has been some recent work in the multidimensional tradition. Hence, we focus mostly on

3. This is the reason why the term 'money-metric' has been used to refer to such poverty and we retain this terminology.

4. For a recent discussion of the conceptual issues involved in poverty measurement (uni-dimensional or multidimensional), see Chakravarty (2009: Chapters 2 and 6) and the references therein.

unidimensional poverty, but we also look at the few studies that exist on multidimensional poverty.

We believe that the capability approach holds considerable promise for the conceptualisation and measurement of poverty in the Indian context. Hence, the second literature that we focus on deals with this approach. This literature is vast, multidisciplinary and still evolving; so rather than presenting an exhaustive survey, we will be selective and present basic concepts. We believe that a careful institutional analysis that identifies the deeper causal structures in our development process dovetailed with a rigorous exercise of measuring poverty is essential to make any further meaningful contributions given the series of problems that have beset poverty measurement in India in recent times—termed in the literature (e.g., Deaton and Kozel, 2004; Reddy, 2007; Subramanian, 2005) as the "Great Indian Poverty Debate", "Conceptual Muddle", etc. In this broad sense, at the present moment, we are still at an early stage in both understanding the nature and extent of poverty in India, and finding effective ways to counter it.

The remaining part of the paper is organised into three sections. The next section presents a summary of the debates on poverty measurement in India, the third section discusses the capability approach and the final section concludes with a discussion of our broad policy suggestions.

Debates on Poverty in India

Poverty has been a salient issue in India since colonial times[5] and at the time of independence, it was deemed to be an important problem that India had to address.[6] In our discussion below, we will focus on attempts since independence to set a money-metric poverty line and to measure poverty. A fine account of this process has

5. See e.g., the work of Dadhabhai Naoroji, particularly Naoroji (1901) which deals with the drain of wealth from India.

6. In his famous "Tryst with Destiny" speech, Nehru had remarked that: "...The future beckons to us. Whither do we go and what shall be our endeavour? To bring freedom and opportunity to the common man, to the peasants and workers of India; to fight and end poverty and ignorance and disease; to build up a prosperous, democratic and progressive nation, and to create social, economic and political institutions which will ensure justice and fullness of life to every man and woman."

been given in Subramanian (2012) which also presents the relevant conceptual issues and debates surrounding poverty lines from other contexts (US and the international poverty line of the World Bank). In our discussion below, we draw heavily upon this work (particularly, Chapter 3 on India) and partly on some other recent studies.[7]

Early attempts to set a poverty line in India were made in the 1960s by the Planning Commission, possibly based upon the recommendations of a nutrition advisory committee of the Indian Council for Medical Research (ICMR). This committee's recommended balanced diet, combined with consumption of other items, cost ₹35 per person per month at 1960-61 prices, which would have resulted in 80 per cent of the population being classified as poor. The Planning Commission deemed this estimate of poverty too high (i.e., unaffordable) and therefore used a lower norm of ₹20 per person per month for the country. Since the urban areas required a higher standard, it set the urban norm at ₹25 per person per month, which, given the overall norm and the rural and urban population shares, yielded a rural poverty line of ₹18.90 per person per month. In our view, from this exercise, one can already get a glimpse into the arbitrariness that has characterised the setting of poverty lines in India, and the role played by extraneous (political) calculations—something that has lasted till today. Even this meagre and arbitrary norm of ₹20 resulted in an estimate as high as 60 per cent of the country being poor. The next significant (and highly influential) step was taken by Dandekar and Rath, who in 1971 set the precedent for using nutrition-based norms, They used a norm of 2250 kcal per person per day and the NSS data on consumption expenditure and calories, to arrive at rural and urban poverty lines of ₹15 and ₹22.50 per person per month (at 1960-61 prices), respectively. Actually, the norm of 2250 kcal was met at ₹14.20 and ₹22.60 per person per month (at 1960-61 prices) in rural and urban areas, respectively; but given the earlier higher poverty line of ₹18.90 in rural areas (discussed above), the rural poverty line was adjusted to ₹15 and

7. The discussion draws mostly from Subramanian (2012: Chapter 3) and we do not cite this explicitly again. Where we use other studies, we cite them.

the urban poverty line was rounded off to ₹22.50. The 1970s saw considerable debate and controversy, although the ₹15 norm of Dandekar and Rath achieved widespread acceptance.

We skip the developments in the 1980s and discuss the recommendations of the expert groups set up by the Planning Commission in 1993 and 2009, since most recent controversies are centred on these. However, two important developments need to be highlighted. First, a task force of the Planning Commission was set up as a part of the Sixth Five Year Plan to project effective consumption demand and minimum nutrition. This task force employed norms of 2400 and 2100 kcal per person per day in rural and urban areas, respectively. Using linear interpolation and consumption and calorie data from the 1973-74 NSS consumption expenditure survey,[8] the task force estimated the consumption expenditure that satisfies these calorie norms—₹9.09 and ₹56.06 per person per month at 1973-74 prices, for rural and urban areas, respectively. Second, given the discrepancy between estimates from National Accounts and the NSS (the former being higher), for poverty estimation, the Planning Commission adjusted the NSS consumption distribution by multiplying it by a factor.[9] To examine poverty estimation, the government appointed an expert group in 1993 which recommended that the above adjustment process be discontinued. The other important recommendations were as follows: the above task force's poverty lines (₹49.49 and ₹56.56 per person per month at 1973-74 prices) should be used; 1973-74 should be treated as the base year and poverty lines should be updated regularly using price indices; new poverty lines should not be specified for every NSSO consumption expenditure survey, so that the basket on the basis of which the poverty line is computed remains the same (i.e., use of an invariant Poverty Line Bundle [PLB]); state-specific poverty

8. The NSS presents grouped data for Monthly Per Capita Expenditure (MPCE). For each sise class, the average MPCE, the proportion of people, and the quantity and value of food/non-food items consumed are presented. These can be used to estimate the average value of calorific consumption for each sise class.

9. This factor was the average consumption from National Accounts divided by the average consumption from NSS.

lines should be obtained by using state-specific price indices. There is a major problem with the 1993 expert group's methodology, and we have discussed this elsewhere (Vakulabharanam and Motiram, 2012). Suppose one accepts this methodology, since it is based upon shortfalls from a calorie norm, there is no solid rationale for using 1973-74 as the base year. One could use different base years and adopt the same procedure; one could even use each year as the base year, i.e., for every year, find the proportion of individuals who fall short of the calorie norm. The choice of the base year dictates the trend of poverty and the rate of poverty reduction. For example, if one chooses the official base year, then one finds a decline in poverty during 1983 to 2004-05 (Himanshu, 2006); whereas if one chooses the current year as the base year (i.e., looks at the calorie shortfall), then one finds an increase in poverty during the same period (Patnaik, 2007; 2010; 2013). Patnaik's findings have to be seen in light of the observation (made by other scholars too, based upon the NSS data) that there has been a divergence between the proportion of the population that has been falling below the official poverty line and the proportion of population that has been falling short of the calorie norms. This divergence has been growing over time.[10]

The government appointed another expert group in 2009 (i.e., the Tendulkar Committee) to examine the issue of setting a poverty line. Like the 1993 expert group, this committee also believed in an invariant PLB. The bundle was identified as the one corresponding to ₹578.8 per person per month at 2004-05 prices in urban India. This was nothing but the urban poverty line according to the 1993 expert group methodology (i.e., with base year as 1973-74) if it were updated using 2004-05 prices. This was inconsistent with the committee's claims that they broke with past practice and attempted to move away from calorie-based norms. The rationalisation offered for this poverty line was quite vague and circular. Essentially, the committee wanted to specify a poverty line that would yield a poverty rate that was neither too low nor too high, to avoid controversy.

10. This phenomenon has been referred to as 'calorie drift' and can be predicted on the basis of elementary consumer theory as shown in Subramanian (2012: Chapter 3, Appendix A2).

Using the 1993 methodology, the urban poverty in 2004-05 was 25.7 per cent, whereas the rural poverty was 28.3 per cent. The committee deemed the urban poverty rate as acceptable (not too controversial) but the rural poverty rate as too low (controversial). It therefore took the urban poverty line as dictated by the 1993 methodology at 2004-05 prices as the urban poverty line for 2004-05. To calculate the rural poverty line, it took the urban PLB and evaluated it at rural prices to get a rural poverty line of ₹446.7 per person per month. It then recommended 2004-05 to be chosen as the base year and regular updating of the poverty lines (as earlier). Essentially, the poverty line was determined from the idea of a plausible Head Count Ratio (HCR), which is a reverse of what we are taught to do (i.e., HCR from the poverty line). While we have drawn upon the discussion in Subramanian (2012, Chapter 3) and focused on the process of setting of the poverty line, several scholars have highlighted other problems with the recommendations of the committee, e.g., Suryanarayana (2011) has argued that the committee has used the median without a proper justification for doing so and has in fact used it inappropriately. He has also highlighted that the committee relied on the 2004-05 NSS consumption expenditure survey which has major problems, e.g., more than half of the poorest four MPCE classes (accounting for 30% of the population) do not have Antyodaya or Below Poverty Line (BPL) cards.[11]

After coming under serious criticism, the government appointed yet another committee last year, with Dr Rangarajan as the chairman, to arrive at a new poverty line. This committee is yet to submit its report and is expected to do so in 2014 (Planning Commission, 2013). The Planning Commission has created a new round of controversy recently by publishing poverty estimates (Planning Commission, 2013) based upon the Tendulkar committee poverty lines and data from the latest (2011-12) NSS survey on consumption expenditure. These estimates provide a highly rosy picture of poverty reduction in the past two decades and have immediately attracted the charge of political opportunism. Critics have questioned the reliance

11. Also see the critique of Swaminathan (2010).

of well-being, e.g., commodities, income and utility. Commodities and income are only means and may not be valuable in themselves; utility is too crude, being unable to distinguish between different kinds/sources of pleasure and pain and characterised by problems with interpersonal comparability. The capability approach helps us reconceptualise the basis of well-being. At the heart of this approach is the idea of a 'functioning'—a person's achievement, 'being or doing', e.g., being well-nourished. A person's achievement depends not only upon commodities that he/she has access to, but also his/her personal characteristics. The notion of capability combines the idea of functioning with that of freedom; it is the ability to achieve a functioning. A capability set (or opportunity set) is a set of functionings that an individual can choose from.

A simple example can be used to clarify the above notions. Consider a situation characterised by one commodity (a newspaper) and two individuals, one educated and the other illiterate. The first individual can be in two different states (functionings)—being aware of world events, or being unaware of them; whereas the second can only be unaware. Even if both the individuals have the same functioning, their situations could be different—e.g., both have access to the newspaper and both are unaware, but the first individual has chosen to be unaware, whereas the second individual does not have this choice.

Although the capability approach is intuitively appealing, there are several philosophical problems that have been raised in the literature; e.g., how do we rank various capability sets, e.g., do we rank them on the basis of the best element or the number of elements? There are also practical problems that one encounters in applying this approach, e.g., what are the functionings that are relevant? Should we consider the most basic ones (e.g., being well-nourished) or should we be expansive (and consider for example political freedoms)?

In our opinion, in terms of the context that we are interested in, *viz.*, poverty measurement in India, two alternatives present themselves. First, we can continue with the money-metric approach, choose particular functionings and examine the amount in monetary terms that is required to achieve these functionings. Second, we can conceptualise poverty in a multidimensional manner. This is the approach that has been taken in the human development paradigm (albeit not in this explicit manner) and in the newer literature that has emerged recently. We have discussed these below.

The Human Development Index (HDI) pioneered by the United Nations Development Programme (UNDP) consists of three components, reflecting education, health and living standards.[16] The education component itself is a geometric mean of two components—the average years of schooling for adults 25 years of age and expected years of schooling for children (with an upper limit of 18). The health component is measured in terms of life expectancy at birth and the living standards component is measured in terms of the logarithm of the Gross National Income per capita (Purchasing Power Parity, PPP $). These three components are aggregated into a single index which is their geometric mean. More recently, the inequality adjusted HDI (IHDI) has been introduced which incorporates the idea that inequalities in each of the three components are harmful. The IHDI is arrived at by adjusting the HDI for inequality in each of the components. The IHDI falls below the HDI (unless there is no inequality) and as inequality rises, the value of the IHDI declines.

At the conceptual level, the HDI (and IHDI) recognise the idea that to assess development we need to move beyond income and consider achievements on other fronts—in this sense, it is broadly in the spirit of the capability approach. At an empirical level, countries that perform very well on the income dimension could perform badly on the other dimensions. At a conceptual level, the HDI is an improvement over simply focusing on incomes, e.g., GDP (gross domestic product). At an empirical level, incomes are highly correlated with achievements on other dimensions (Ray, 1998), but there are some important outliers. However, one problem with the HDI is that it is constructed by taking data from different sources; e.g., for health and education in a particular country, usually the individuals involved in the evaluation of these components are different. This raises some

16. This description of the HDI draws upon the material presented by UNDP available at *http://hdr.undp.org/en/statistics/hdi/*

theoretical problems, which have been highlighted in the recent literature on welfare economics (e.g., Pattanaik, 2012; Pattanaik *et al.*, 2012). There is also the pervasive problem in empirical research of poor quality of data, and inconsistencies and differences among data from different countries. Notwithstanding these problems, the HDI has been quite useful in tracking progress made by various countries and in making cross-country and within country comparisons.

Specifically for India, Human Development Reports (HDRs) have been released for different states and the components of the HDI have been presented over time (e.g., see the various Economic Surveys). Given the problems associated with money-metric poverty that we discussed above, these are useful, even if they come with their own problems of data quality, comparability, etc.

Although the debate on poverty has largely been about unidimensional poverty, more recently, there have been attempts to shift the focus towards multidimensional poverty. In the measurement of multidimensional poverty, one considers several dimensions apart from income (e.g., health, education). The problems of identification and aggregation are complicated because on each dimension, one needs to identify whether an individual falls short of a norm (or threshold) and aggregation has to be performed across dimensions for an individual and across individuals for a society. This is an evolving literature and in our reading, several issues and problems remain to be addressed.[17] One can of course present summary measures on various dimensions (e.g., average educational attainment) and proportion of individuals who fall short on these dimensions (e.g., individuals who do not have access to water), but the relevant question is whether such a 'dashboard' approach can be improved upon by aggregation into an index.

Among the studies on multidimensional poverty in India, two are worth discussing. Alkire and Seth (2013) use data from National Family Health Surveys (NFHS) in 1998-99 and 2005-06 and consider three broad dimensions—education, health and living standards.

---

17. For a succinct description of the basic ideas and literature, see Chakravarty (2009: Chapter 5) and the references therein.

Within these dimensions, they consider different indicators, e.g., schooling and attendance for school-age children. They develop an index of multidimensional poverty that can be compared over time. Their analysis reveals that deprivation has declined on each of these dimensions, e.g., the percentage of the population who have no access to electricity has reduced from 39.2 per cent to 32.8 per cent (Alkire and Seth, 2013: Table 5.1). Multidimensional poverty (as measured by the index) has also reduced from 0.300 in 1999 to 0.251 in 2006.

Jayaraj and Subramanian (2010) deal with a situation where purely ordinal data is available (e.g., whether a person has access to potable water or not) and where comparisons of deprivations across dimensions are difficult to make (e.g., it is difficult to argue that access to water is more or less important than access to schooling) so that one is forced to weigh these deprivations equally. In this context, they argue that one can make gradations in deprivation (e.g., none, mild, moderate, severe) based upon the number of dimensions on which an individual is deprived. Drawing upon the well-known Foster-Greer-Thorbecke family of poverty measures and the literature on social exclusion (in particular, Chakravarty and D'Ambrosio, 2006), they develop a family of indices of multidimensional deprivation. They also develop a graphical tool (deprivation-distribution profile or D-curve) that can be used to compare multidimensional deprivation across different regimes. They apply this methodology to data from the NFHS surveys in 1992-93 and 2005-06 and consider eight dimensions to show that multidimensional deprivation has declined at the all-India level and for all states. However, both the proportion and number of individuals who are severely deprived (deprived on seven or eight dimensions) continue to be large.

Discussion and Conclusions

Classical economists like Adam Smith, David Ricardo and Karl Marx have argued that the wages of workers typically correspond to a level of bare subsistence. According to these thinkers, in a capitalist society, there could be periods when the bare subsistence is not met in the prevailing wage regimes that exist on the ground; and in other periods, wages could be higher. But typically, wages tend to hover around the threshold of subsistence (a kind of a natural wage). But what is this level of subsistence? These classical economists argued that moral, historical and contextual considerations go into defining the minimum subsistence that is needed to reproduce a person or a household.[18] They were careful in identifying certain basic abilities (such as the oft-quoted "appearing in public without shame,"[19] or having adequate nourishment) that they then related to notions of subsistence. Amartya Sen, through his capabilities approach, broadens this scope by adding ideas of freedom and choice with notions of subsistence in the context of thinking about poverty. Connecting back to the classical economists through Sen's framework is the right way forward in understanding poverty (both identification and aggregation), if we wish to break free from the largely meaningless poverty computations that have emanated from the Planning Commission of India over the last few decades. This will also help us put the concept of human development on a much more solid footing.

Capabilities approach provides a way forward by identifying the anchors (which are absolute) through which we can define a basis for evaluating what a decent livelihood is, the characteristics of commodities and actual commodities that are consumed by people (the latter two are relative, so they can change with time, place and

18. See for example the discussion in Chapter 6 ("Buying and Selling of Labour Power") of Marx's *Capital* Vol. I, where he argues that: "His means of subsistence must therefore be sufficient to maintain him in his normal state as a labouring individual. His natural wants, such as food, clothing, fuel, and housing, vary according to the climatic and other physical conditions of his country. On the other hand, the number and extent of his so-called necessary wants, as also the modes of satisfying them, are themselves the product of historical development, and depend therefore to a great extent on the degree of civilisation of a country, more particularly on the conditions under which, and consequently on the habits and degree of comfort in which, the class of free labourers has been formed. In contradistinction therefore to the case of other commodities, there enters into the determination of the value of labour-power a historical and moral element."

19. See the discussion in the *Wealth of Nations,* Book V, Chapter II, e.g., "The Greeks and Romans lived, I suppose, very comfortably, though they had no linen. But in the present times, through the greater part of Europe, a creditable day-labourer would be ashamed to appear in public without a linen shirt, the want of which would be supposed to denote that disgraceful degree of poverty, which, it is presumed, nobody can well fall into without extreme bad conduct. Custom, in the same manner, has rendered leather shoes a necessary of life in England. The poorest creditable person, of either sex, would be ashamed to appear in public without them."

the larger moral/historical context). Figuring out poverty through the capabilities approach might be a slightly harder exercise to undertake, but it may be unavoidable if we wish to say something substantive or meaningful about poverty in any context, including the Indian one. If this exercise is conducted in close consultations with the communities on the ground, poverty computations (especially relative aspects) can be brought into an exercise that is conceptually rigorous as well as participative in taking people's own choices and notions of freedom into account.

However, the institutional, class, caste, gender or other axes that enter into causal structures of understanding poverty need to be researched simultaneously in order to understand the deeper structures that produce and perpetuate poverty. Otherwise, it would simply be an exercise of describing a certain aspect of the reality around us. A capabilities approach that pays close attention to the deeper institutional structures is essential in any kind of society (capitalist or non-capitalist) in order to think and act rigorously to achieve human development, or believe in the higher promise of achieving such a goal.

References

Alkire, S. and S. Seth (2013). "Multidimensional Poverty Reduction in India between 1999 and 2006: Where and How?", *Working Paper No.* 30. Oxford Poverty & Human Development Initiative.

Chakravarty, S. (2009). *Inequality, Polarisation and Poverty: Advances in Distributional Analysis*. New York: Springer.

Chakravarty, S.R. and C.D. Ambrosio (2006). "The Measurement of Social Exclusion", *Review of Income and Wealth* 52 (3): 377-98.

Clark, David (2005). "The Capability Approach: Its Development, Critiques and Recent Advances", *Working Paper* No. GPRG-WPS-032. Global Poverty Research Group.

Deaton, A. and V. Kozel (2004). *Data and Dogma: The Great Indian Poverty Debate*. New Delhi: Macmillan.

Ghosh, J. (2011). "India's Official Poverty Line Doesn't Measure Up", *The Guardian*, October 4.

Himanshu (2006). "Recent Trends in Poverty and Inequality: Some Preliminary Results", *Economic and Political Weekly* 42(6): 497-508.

Hindu (2011). "Rs. 32 a Day Poverty Line Not All That Ridiculous: Montek", *The Hindu*, October 12, 2011.

———. (2012). "Rangarajan to Head Panel for Reviewing Poverty Line", *The Hindu* 24 May.

———. (2013a). "Vanishing Poverty Trick", *The Hindu*, 25 July.

———. (2013b) "No Politics in National Sample Survey Round", *The Hindu* 6 August.

Jayaraj, D. and S. Subramanian (2010). "A Chakravarty-D'Ambrosio View of Multidimensional Deprivation: Some Estimates for India", *Economic and Political Weekly* XLV(6): 53-65.

Marx, K. (1861). *Capital: A Critique of Political Economy*. London: Penguin Classics.

Naoroji, D. (1901). *Poverty and Un-British Rule in India*, London: S. Sonnenschein.

Nussbaum, M. and A.K. Sen (1993). *The Quality of Life*. Oxford: Clarendon Press.

Parsai, G. (2011a). "Is Rs. 25 all that You Need for a Day?", *The Hindu*, September 21.

———. (2011b) "Tendulkar Poverty Line will Remain Reference Point," *The Hindu*, 4 October.

Patnaik, U. (2007). "Neoliberalism and Rural Poverty in India", *Economic and Political Weekly* XLII(30): 3132-50.

———. (2010). "Trends in Urban Poverty Under Economic Reforms: 1993-94 to 2004-05", *Economic & Political Weekly* XLV(4): 42-53.

———. (2011). "How little can a Person Live On?", *The Hindu*, September 30.

———. (2013). "The Dishonesty in Counting the Poor", *The Hindu*, July 30.

Pattanaik, P. (2012). "Economics, Individual Well-Being, and Social Welfare", *Distinguished Silver Jubilee Lecture*. Mumbai: Indira Gandhi Institute of Development Research.

Pattanaik, P., S.G. Reddy and Y. Xu (2012). "On Measuring Deprivation and Living Standards of Societies in a Multi-attribute Framework", *Oxford Economic Papers* 64: 43-56.

Planning Commission (2012). *Press Note on Poverty Estimates: 2009-10*. New Delhi: Government of India.

———. (2013). *Press Note on Poverty Estimates: 2011-12*. New Delhi: Government of India.

Rama Kumar, R. (2013). "Not a Straight Poverty Line", *The Hindu*, August 12.

Ray, D. (1998). *Development Economics*, Princeton: Princeton University Press.

Reddy, S.G. (2007). "The Great Indian Poverty Debate", *Development* 50(2): 166-71.

Sen, A.K. (1976). "Poverty: An Ordinal Approach to Measurement", *Econometrica* 44(2): 219-231.

———. (1980). "Equality of What?", in S.M. Mc Murris (ed.), *The Tanner Lectures on Human Values*. Salt Lake City: University of Utah Press.

Sen, A.K. (1983). "Poor, Relatively Speaking", *Oxford Economic Papers* 35(2): 153-169.

———. (1985). *Commodities and Capabilities*. Amsterdam: North-Holland.

———. (1992). *Inequality Reexamined*. Oxford: Clarendon Press.

———. (1999). *Development as Freedom*. New York: Knopf.

Shah, M. (2013). "Understanding the Poverty Line", *The Hindu*, 5 August.

Schokkaert, E. (2009). "The Capabilities Approach", in P. Anand, P. Pattanaik and C. Puppe (eds.), *The Handbook of Rational and Social Choice*. Oxford: Clarendon Press.

Smith, A. (1776). *An Inquiry into the Nature and Causes of Wealth of Nations*. An Electronics Classics Series Publication. Downloaded from *http://www2.hn.psu.edu/faculty/jmanis/adam-smith/wealth-nations.pdf* (accessed on August 31, 2013)

Subramanian, S. (2005). "Unravelling a Conceptual Muddle: India's Poverty Statistics in the Light of Basic Demand Theory", *Economic and Political Weekly* XL(1): 57-66.

———. (2012). *The Poverty Line*. New Delhi: Oxford University Press.

Suryanarayana, M.H. (2011) "Expert Group on Poverty: Confusion Worse Confounded", *Economic and Political Weekly* XLVI(46): 36-39.

Swaminathan, Madhura (2010). "The New Poverty Line: A Methodology Deeply Flawed", *Indian Journal of Human Development* 4(1): 121-25.

Vakulabharanam, V. and S. Motiram (2012). "Understanding Poverty and Inequality in Urban India Since Reforms: Bringing Quantitative and Qualitative Approaches Together", *Economic and Political Weekly* XLVII(47, 48): 44-52.

2

S. MAHENDRA DEV

Challenges and Opportunities for Small Farmers

Introduction

Smallholdings agriculture which is the focus of this paper is important for raising agriculture growth, food security and livelihoods in India. It may be noted that Indian agriculture is the home of small and marginal farmers (85%). Therefore, the future of sustainable agriculture growth and food security in India depends on the performance of small and marginal farmers. Agricultural Census data shows that there were about 138 million agricultural holdings in India in 2010-11. Around 117 million were small and marginal farmers. The average size of an agricultural holding has declined from 2.3 ha. in 1970-71 to 1.16 ha. in 2010-11. Although small and marginal farmers account for 85 per cent of total farm households (hhs), their share in operated area is around 44 per cent. Thus, there are significant land inequalities in India.

The role of small farms in development and poverty reduction is well recognised (Lipton, 2006). The global experience of growth and poverty reduction shows that GDP (gross domestic product) growth originating in agriculture is at least twice as effective in reducing poverty as GDP growth originating outside agriculture (World Bank, 2008). Smallholdings play an important role in raising agricultural development and poverty reduction.

The objective of this paper is to examine the challenges and opportunities for smallholding agriculture in achieving agricultural growth, food security and livelihoods in India. The paper also shows that market-oriented reforms are not sufficient and government intervention and other support are needed for smallholdings to achieve the above goals. It is known that small farmers face several challenges in the access to inputs and marketing. They need a level playing field with large farms in terms of accessing land, water, inputs, credit, technology and markets.

Smallholdings also face new challenges on integration of value chains, liberalisation and globalisation effects, market volatility, other risks and vulnerability, adaptation of climate change, etc. (Thapa and Gaiha, 2011). Recent "world-wide processes of farm change—commercialisation of increasing proportions of input and output: institutional developments such as super markets; privatisation of key aspects of technical progress, and of output and process grades and standards—now indicate large farm focus" (Lipton, 2006: 59). Therefore, support is needed for smallholdings in the context of these world-wide processes of farm change. There are also high returns from investments in agricultural research and development (R&D), rural roads and other infrastructure and knowledge generation.

The paper is organised as follows: section 2 examines the roles and challenges of smallholding agriculture in India and section 3 discusses about the opportunities for improving productivity and incomes of small farmers.

Role and Challenges for Small Farmers

The objective of this section is to examine the role and challenges of smallholding agriculture in achieving agricultural growth, food security and livelihoods in India.

Role of Small Farmers

Structure of land holdings: The share of small and marginal farmers in total holdings increased significantly in the last three decades. As shown in Table 2.1, the share of marginal and small farmers increased from 75 per cent in 1980-81 to 85 per cent in 2010-11. Thus, the smallholding character of Indian agriculture is much more prominent today than even before. It may be noted that 67 per cent of land holdings belong to marginal farmers with less than 1 ha. The average size of marginal holdings is only 0.38 ha. at all India level. The average size of smallholdings is 1.42 ha.

Table 2.1

Changes in Percentage Distribution of Operated Holdings and Operated Area

	Percentage of No. of Holdings		*Percentage of Operated Area*	
Land Class	*1980-81*	*2010-11*	*1980-81*	*2010-11*
Marginal	56.39	67.04	12.04	22.24
Small	18.08	17.93	14.14	22.07
Small & Marginal	74.47	84.97	26.18	44.31
Semi-medium	14.01	10.05	21.15	23.59
Medium	9.08	4.25	29.64	21.18
Large	2.44	0.73	23.03	10.92
Total	100.0	100.0	100.0	100.0

Note: Marginal 0.01 to 1.00 ha.; Small 1.01 to 2.00 ha; Semi-Medium 2.00 to 4.00 ha; Medium 4.01 to 10.00 ha; Large above 10 ha.

Source: *Agricultural Census* 1981, 2011, Directorate of Economics and Statistics, Ministry of Agriculture, Government of India.

Access to irrigation: The access to irrigation has increased for all categories of farmers. It is the highest for marginal farmers followed by small farmers. The percentage of area under irrigation for small farmers increased from 40 in 1980-81 to 51 in 2000-01. On the other hand, for large farmers it rose from 16 to 31 per cent during the same period. It may, however, be noted that large farmers capitalise on cheaper sources like canals while small farmers have to rent water. About 40 per cent of the irrigated area for large farmers was from canals while it was less than 25 per cent in the case of small and marginal farmers (NCEUS, 2008).

Access to fertilisers and area under high yielding varieties (HYV): The fertiliser per hectare is inversely related to farm size for both irrigated and unirrigated areas. It increased for marginal farmers in irrigated areas from 100 kgs in 1980-81 to 252 kgs in 2001-02. In fact, the per hectare consumption for all farm sizes was similar on irrigated areas in 1981-82, but it rose faster for marginal farmers and small farmers in 2001-02. This is true in the case of unirrigated areas also.

Similarly, the percentage of area under HYV is also inversely related to farm size. In the irrigated areas, the coverage of area under HYV was 89 per cent, 86 per cent and 78 per cent respectively for marginal, small and large farmers in 2001-02. In the case of unirrigated areas, the coverage was above 50 per cent for marginal, small and semi-medium farmers but it was only 30 per cent for large farmers in 2001-02 (NCEUS, 2008).

Cropping patterns: Do small and marginal farmers grow high value crops? Birthal *et al.* (2011) provide four conclusions for these cropping patterns: (a) small and marginal farmers allocate larger proportion of their cultivated land to high value crops like fruits and vegetables; (b) small and marginal farmers seem to have comparative advantage in growing vegetables than fruits because of quick returns in the former; (c) small and marginal farmers allocate larger proportion of land to rice and wheat than other farmers; (d) small and marginal farmers allocate lower proportion of land to pulses and oilseeds.

Farm size, output and productivity: The contribution to output is higher for marginal and small farmers as compared to their share in area. The share of these farmers was 46.1 per cent in land possessed but they contributed 51.2 per cent to the total output of the country (Table 2.2) at all India level in 2002-03. There are significant regional variations in their contribution to output. The share of output is less than the operated area in 10 states (Table 2.2). In rest of the states, the reverse was true. The contribution of small and marginal farmers to output ranges from 19 per cent in Punjab to 86 per cent in West Bengal. It is less than 50 per cent in 10 out of 20 states. In the Eastern states, the share of both area and output are high for these farmers. On the other hand, in some of the states in Central, Western and Northwestern regions, medium and large farmers still dominate in both area and output.

In terms of production, small and marginal farmers also make larger contribution to the production of high value crops. They contribute around 70 per cent to the total production of vegetables, 55 per cent to fruits against their share of 44 per cent in land area (Birthal, 2011). Their share in cereal production is 52 per cent and 69 per cent in milk production. Thus, small farmers contribute to both diversification and food security. Only in the cases of pulses and oilseeds, their share is lower than other farmers.

Table 2.2

Share of Small and Marginal Farmers in Land Possessed and in Crop Output

(Per cent)

States	*Share in Area (Land Possessed)*	*Share in Output*
West Bengal	83.0	86.2
Uttaranchal	81.4	46.7
Kerala	79.8	78.1
Himachal Pradesh	73.7	73.9
Orissa	73.2	72.5
Jharkhand	73.1	78.1
Assam	72.4	70.7
Bihar	67.2	69.2
Jammu and Kshmir	66.4	77.3
Uttar Pradesh	59.4	65.1
Tamil Nadu	54.4	51.7
Chattisgarh	49.4	46.1
Andhra Pradesh	47.5	46.7
Haryana	42.2	29.9
Karnataka	37.4	38.5
Madhya Pradesh	34.3	27.9
Gujarat	34.3	35.3
Maharashtra	31.7	35.2
Punjab	29.9	19.3
Rajasthan	22.6	33.2
All India	46.1	51.2

Source: NCEUS (2008).

There has been debate in India on the relationship between farm size and productivity. The results of NSS 2003 Farmers' Survey has empirically established that small farms continue to be produce more in value terms per hectare than the medium and large farms. Table 2.3 shows that value of output per hectare was ₹13,944 for marginal farmers as compared to ₹11,333 for medium and large farmers. It shows that from efficiency point of view, smallholdings are equal or better than large holdings. Table 2.3 indicates large regional variations in the value of output per hectare. For marginal farmers, it varies from ₹29,448 in Punjab to ₹7,177 in Rajasthan. This is also true for large medium and large farmers—it ranges from ₹28,983 in Punjab to ₹4,213 in Rajasthan. In many states, smallholdings have

Table 2.3

Value of Output Per Hectare

(in ₹)

State	*Marginal*	*Small*	*Marginal & Small*	*Medium & Large*	*All*
Punjab	29448	26120	27213	28983	28623
Kerala	26485	27576	26814	28655	27197
Jammu & Kashmir	26774	24768	26057	16914	23214
West Bengal	21065	20429	20874	19004	20594
Assam	18484	17370	17975	18296	18068
Haryana	17769	16872	17304	17541	17470
Uttaranchal	15405	12694	14859	69131	25536
Andhra Pradesh	14777	14849	14813	12886	13720
Uttar Pradesh	14442	14441	14442	15611	14826
Himachal Pradesh	12680	17650	14347	19198	15362
Tamil Nadu	15629	11353	13926	15799	14771
Bihar	14230	13184	13833	13847	13837
Jharkhand	14275	12457	13568	11420	13034
Maharashtra	13212	11350	12064	7140	8339
Karnataka	11727	12178	11962	10194	10809
Gujarat	12001	11656	11807	11504	11609
Chhattisgarh	8612	8128	8339	7953	8126
Madhya Pradesh	8543	7546	7927	8783	8526
Orissa	7207	6374	6870	6731	6831
Rajasthan	7177	5629	6330	4213	4739
All India	14754	13001	13944	11333	12535

Note: All India includes small states Goa, Delhi, Pondicherry, Northeastern States and UTs.

Source: Computed using NSS unit level data 59th Round on Situation Assessment Survey of Farmers, 2003.

higher value of output per hectare than large farms. However, in the case of states like, Kerala, Madhya Pradesh, Uttar Pradesh, Himachal Pradesh and Tamil Nadu, the large farms have higher productivity (in value terms) than marginal farmers. In the case of Punjab, the differences in productivity are not large across farm sises.

Small Holders and Livelihoods

We have mentioned above that 117 million out of total 138 million farm holdings are small and marginal farmers. The sustainability of these farmers is crucial for livelihoods in rural areas and for the entire country. It is true that smallholdings have higher productivity than medium and large farms. But, as our discussion below shows that it is not enough to compensate for the disadvantage of the small area of holdings. The cost of cultivation per hectare is also high on small and marginal farmers than medium and large farms. At the all India level, net farm income per hectare for smallholdings is higher than large holdings. The data at state level shows that in 9 out of 20 states, the reverse is true—net farm income per hectare in large holdings is higher than smallholdings.[1]

However, the monthly income and consumption figures across different size class of land holdings show that marginal and small farmers have dis-savings compared to medium and large farmers. The average monthly income of farmer households is comprised of income from wages, net receipts from cultivation, net receipts from farming of animals and income from non-farm business. The average monthly consumption of farmer households is comprised of total food and non-food expenditure. According to NSS 2003 data, large farmers have savings while small farmers have dis-savings (Figure 2.1).

Challenges

There are many issues and challenges for smallholding agriculture in India. They face several challenges in the access to inputs and marketing. They need a level playing field with large farms in terms

1. On returns to farming, see Sarthak and Mishra (2011). Also see Chand *et al.* (2011)

of accessing land, water, inputs, credit, technology and markets. Smallholdings also face new challenges on integration of value chains, liberalisation and globalisation effects, market volatility and other risks and vulnerability, adaptation of climate change etc. (Thapa and Gaiha, 2011).

Figure 2.1

All India: Income and Consumption

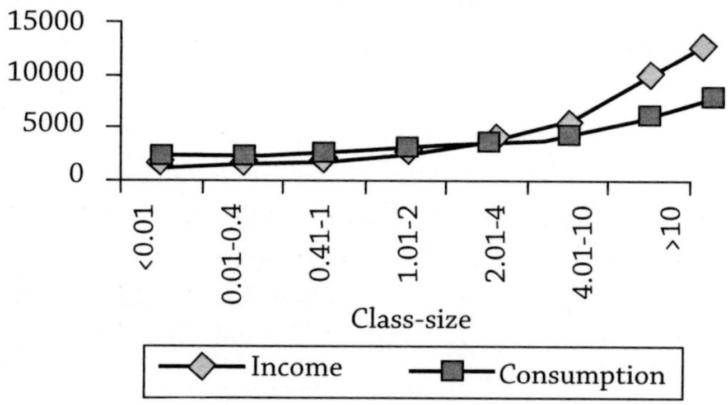

Source: Computed using NSS data 59th Round on Situation Assessment Survey of Farmers 2003 (NSSO, 2005).

NSS Farmers' Survey of 2003 brought out many issues relating to small and marginal farmers. Based on this Survey, NCEUS (2008: 7) says that "some of the general issues that confront marginal-small farmers as agriculturalists are: imperfect markets for inputs/product leading to smaller value realisations; absence of access to credit markets or imperfect credit markets leading to sub-optimal investment decisions or input applications; poor human resource base; smaller access to suitable extension services restricting suitable decisions regarding cultivation practices and technological know-how; poorer access to 'public goods' such as public irrigation, command area development, electricity grids; greater negative externalities from poor quality land and water management, etc."

Credit and indebtedness: Smallholdings need credit for both consumption and investment purposes. Increasing indebtedness is one of the reasons for indebtedness among these farmers in recent years. The overall indebtedness is not higher for small and marginal farmers compared to large farmers. However, the indebtedness for the small & marginal farmers from formal institutional sources is lower than large farmers and the reverse is true in the case of informal sources. The dependence on money lenders is the highest for sub-marginal and marginal farmers. The share of formal source increased with the size of land. At all India level, the share of formal source varies from 22.6 per cent to 58 per cent for small and marginal farmers while it varies from 65 to 68 per cent for medium to large farmers. Dependence of small and marginal farmers on informal sources is high even in states like Andhra Pradesh, Punjab and Tamil Nadu (GoI, 2005).

Impact of climate change: Climate change is a major challenge for millions of people including the poor in India. It would have adverse effects on food security and livelihoods of small farmers in particular. Climate change is expected to have a detrimental impact on the living conditions of farmers, fishers and forest-dependent people who are already vulnerable and food insecure. Rural communities, particularly those living in already fragile environments, face an immediate and ever-growing risk of increased crop failure, loss of livestock, and reduced availability of marine, aquaculture and forest products. In order to have climate change-sensitive and pro-poor policies, there is a need to focus on small farmers. Agriculture adaptation and mitigation could provide benefits for small farmers. The coping strategies would be useful to have long term adaptation strategies. There is a significant potential for small farmers to sequester soil carbon if appropriate policy reforms are implemented. The importance of collective action in climate change adaptation and mitigation is recognised.

Increasing globalisation has added to the problems faced by the smallholding agriculture. The policies of huge subsidies and protection by developed countries have negative effects on smallholding farmers in developing countries. If support is not given to small farms, globalisation may become advantageous for large farms.

Opportunities for Small Farmers

In spite of the above challenges, there are many technological and institutional innovations which can enable marginal and small farmers to raise agricultural productivity and increase incomes through diversification and high value agriculture.

Technological Innovations

It may be noted that agricultural technologies are 'scale neutral' but not 'resource neutral' (Singh *et al.*, 2002). Smallholder-oriented research and extension should give importance to cost reduction without reduction in yields. Therefore, new technological innovations are needed. These include low external input and sustainable agriculture approaches based on ecological principles of farming; organic agriculture based on a similar set of agro-ecological principles but without the use of artificial chemical fertilisers, pesticides or genetically modified organisms; and biotechnology (Thapa and Gaiha, 2011: 18).

The need for adopting the methods of an evergreen revolution has become very urgent now. As Swaminathan (2010) mentions, among other things, there are two major pathways to fostering an evergreen revolution. The first is organic farming. Productive organic farming needs considerable research support, particularly in the areas of soil fertility replenishment and plant protection. The other pathway to an evergreen revolution is green agriculture. In this context, ecologically sound practices like conservation farming, integrated pest management (IPM), integrated nutrient supply and natural resources conservation are promoted. Green agriculture techniques could also include the cultivation of crop varieties bred through use of recombinant DNA technology if they are good in resisting biotic and abiotic stresses or have other attributes like improving nutritive quality (Swaminathan, 2010).

Zero tillage: Cultivation practices such as zero tillage (which involves injecting seeds directly into the soil instead of sowing on ploughed fields) combined with residue management and proper fertiliser use can help to preserve soil moisture, maximise water infiltration, increase carbon storage, minimise nutrient runoff and raise yields. It is expanding rapidly in India. In 2005, in the rice–wheat farming system of the Indo-Gangetic plain, farmers adopted zero tillage on 1.6 million hectares; by 2008, 20–25 per cent of the wheat in two Indian states (Haryana and Punjab) was cultivated using minimum tillage (World Bank, 2010).

Nutrient management: Nitrogen applied in fertilisers, manures, biosolids and other nitrogen sources are not used efficiently by crops. Management strategies to improve the nitrogen use efficiency of crops which reduces fertiliser requirements focus on fertiliser best management practices. A note written for IFPRI by Flynn (2009) says that the best practices should look at application type, application rates, application timing and application placement. For example, balancing application rates of nitrogen with other required nutrients including phosphorus, potassium and sulphur is a major way of improving nitrogen use efficiency. Similarly, appropriate nitrogen application rates are important in order to have effectiveness on yields.

Another way is switching to organic production which can reduce fertiliser use; better use of existing organic sources of nutrients, including animal manure, crop residues, and nitrogen-fixing crops such as legumes. Such organic nitrogen sources may also contribute to raising sequestration of carbon in soils (Flynn, 2009). However, yields have to be maintained with organic farming as compared to cultivation with chemical fertilisers.

Biotechnology: The term biotechnology covers a wide range of scientific techniques and products that can be used in numerous ways to boost and sustain the productivity of crops, livestock, fisheries and forests. Though agricultural biotechnology is used synonymously with genetic modification by general public, there are many techniques in biotechnology apart from genetic modification. The other techniques are: genomics and bioinformatics, marketed-assisted selection, diagnostic procedures, micro propagation, tissue culture, cloning, artificial insemination, embryo transfer and other technologies (Rao and Dev, 2010).

Recently India had two revolutions in technology. One is BT cotton and the other is hybrid maize. Studies on Bt cotton showed that small farmers benefited from the introduction of this technology. A study on four districts of Andhra Pradesh (Warangal, Nalgonda, Guntur, Kurnool) examined, among other things, whether the benefits of Bt Cotton technology are shared by all groups of farmers across social categories and size groups (Rao and Dev, 2010). The green revolution technologies have been utilised by upper strata of farmers and later gradually spread to other strata. But in the case of biotechnological application, the small farmers and SC (scheduled caste) and ST (scheduled tribe) farmers also made use of the technology well since the beginning. The small farmers growing Bt cotton have significantly improved their position compared to the non-Bt growing small farmers. The net income improved by 69 per cent and farm business income improved by 108 per cent. This clearly shows that the small farmers are better off with Bt cotton than without Bt cotton. Same is the case with SCs. Bt cotton led to improving the net income by 59 per cent. The farm business income is higher by three times than non-Bt farmers from SCs. Therefore, it is very clear that the farmers from SCs, who are also generally small farmers, benefited from adopting this technology.

Information technology: Changes in information technology will help in a big way to improve agri-business and incomes of small farmers. Indian private companies and NGOs are global leaders in providing information to farmers, as a spinoff from India's meteoric rise as a world leader in ICTs (information and communication technologies). e-Choupal has expanded access to internet in rural areas. Up to 6,400 internet kiosks were set up between 2000 and 2007 by ITC Limited, one of the largest agricultural exporters. It reaches about 4 million farmers growing a range of crops—soybean, coffee, wheat, rice, pulses or shrimp—in over 40,000 villages. They get free information in their language about local and global market prices, weather forecasts, farming practices and crop insurance. It serves as a purchase centre, cutting marketing costs and allowing farmers to obtain a bigger farm price. The M.S. Swaminathan Research Foundation established Knowledge Centres in Puducherry in 1997. With the support of the Indian Space Research Organisation (ISRO), centres in each village are connected by satellite to a hub at Villianur. The women SHGs (self-help groups) use the centres' computers to manage their business accounts and coordinate their activities, using video links with the other villages.

The declining costs of ICTs are giving small farmers greater access to information. Mobile phone coverage in India is expanding at breakneck speed. Nokia sold several lakhs of new mobile phone handsets, and new subscriptions are averaging 6 million a month, many in rural areas. Computers are now being linked through mobile phone networks to greatly expand the scope of information. By linking communication technologies to market exchanges in commercial centres, even small farmers can overcome the enormous informational asymmetries that limit their bargaining power in traditional supply chains. The revolution in mobile phones is helping the small farmers to get information about crop prices and input prices, and other related information on agriculture.

Institutional Innovations

Smallholding agriculture faces many challenges. But, a number of innovative institutional models are emerging and there are many opportunities for small and marginal farmers in India. Innovations relating to: (a) land and water management, (b) group or cooperative approach for inputs and marketing, and (c) value chains and super markets can enhance productivity, sustainability and incomes of smallholding agriculture.

Institutions for Sustainable Land and Water Management

Development of irrigation and water management are crucial for raising standards of living in rural areas.[2] Major areas of concern in irrigation are: decline in real investment, thin spread of investment, low recovery of costs, decline in water table, wastages and inefficiencies in water use and non-involvement of users. Both investment and efficiency in use of water are needed. Major areas of reforms needed in irrigation are: stepping up and prioritising public investment, raising profitability of groundwater exploitation and augmenting groundwater resources, rational pricing

2. On land and water management, see Vaidyanathan (2006).

of irrigation water and electricity, involvement of user farmers in the management of irrigation systems and making groundwater markets equitable (Rao, 2005). In a recent study, Shah *et al.* (2009) indicate that the impact of the drought of 2009 is expected be less severe than the drought of 2002 due to groundwater recharge in the last few years. Groundwater can be exploited in a big way in Eastern region. Watershed development and water conservation by the community are needed under water management. New watershed guidelines based on Parthasarathy Committee's recommendations were accepted by the Central Cabinet in March 2009. The implementation has to be stepped up in order to obtain benefits in rainfed areas. National Rainfed Area Authority (NRAA) has big responsibility in matters relating to water conservation and watershed development. Assets created under National Rural Employment Guarantee Scheme (NREGS) can help in improving land and water management.

Environmental concerns are among the policy priorities in India; particularly degradation of land and water is alarming. Watershed development under the new guidelines, in general, has an overall positive impact on environment. However, groundwater tables are depleting at an alarming rate. The *de facto* privatisation of groundwater and subsidised power supply are the main culprits. There has been a neglect of minor irrigation sources like tanks. Shortage of drinking water has accentuated and quality of water has declined over time.

An integrated approach is needed for water resources management in the country. An appropriate strategy should integrate institutional approaches with market principles. Since institutional innovation (Water User Associations) is already in place for canal irrigation, it is now time to implement volumetric pricing. There is a need to de-link water rights from land rights in order to ensure equity and sustainability.

Another concern is the land degradation due to excessive use of fertilisers and pesticides. Government has programmemes such as IPM and Integrated Nutrient Management (INM). Keeping in view the ill effects of pesticides and also National Policy on Agriculture, IPM approach has been adopted as a cardinal principle and main plank of plant protection in the country in the overall crop production programmeme. Besides ongoing activities, the thrust area will be pertaining to Pest Risk Analysis (PRA) and post entry quarantine surveillance. This has become essential in the light of the World Trade Organization (WTO) agreement, which will facilitate more and speedier movement of plants, planting materials globally.

Women's collectives: Women's cooperatives, producer women's groups and other forms of group efforts, where they do not already exist, should be promoted to overcome constraints of small and uneconomic land holdings, for the dissemination of agricultural technology and other inputs, as well as for marketing of produce (Agarwal, 2010). There has also been greater emphasis on women's collectives. For example, Deccan Development Society (DDS), an NGO, enables women from landless families to access various government schemes to establish claims on land, through purchase and lease. There are "four critical steps that ensured local food security in an experiment by the DDS in Andhra Pradesh where the *sangams*—women's collectives: (i) improved 6,000 acres of degraded land, (ii) Dalit women took cultivable land on lease, (iii) organised their own public distribution of grains with accent on coarse cereals consumed by 65 per cent of our rural population; built grain banks at village level, and (iv) made systematic collection and preservation of seed varieties" (Krishnaraj, 2006).

Raturi's study (2011) shows that Gujarat and Andhra Pradesh have tried to put in place different institutional environment to make a fundamental change in the institutional arrangement for supporting rural development and agriculture sector. In Gujarat, the state government introduced Krishi Mohatsav. A month long intensive campaign is launched during the month of May each year. "Over 100,000 government officials from the Chief Minister down to staff at the *taluka* level from over 15 departments of the government, and over 1500 scientists, are involved in the programme" (Raturi, 2011). This *mohatsava* serves as an institutional platform at the village level and proved to be an important support for farmers.

An initiative in Andhra Pradesh based on the SHG provides another example of an institutional platform for agriculture. The

Community Managed Sustainable Agriculture (CMSA) programmeme was initiated by the Society for Elimination of Rural Poverty (SERP) in Andhra Pradesh in 2004. The mandate of the programme is to eradicate poverty and to improve livelihoods of the poor. It may also help in nutrition because of improvements in livelihoods. The initiative aims to address the major causes of agriculture distress and helps farmers in adopting sustainable agricultural practices. CMSA has now reached 8033 villages in 503 *mandals* of all 22 districts (Raturi, 2011). It covers about 2.7 million acres and benefit about 1.05 million farmers.

Institutions for Marketing of Smallholdings

For small and marginal farmers, marketing of their products is the main problem apart from credit and extension. There is a silent revolution in institutions regarding non-cereal foods. New production-market linkages in the food supply chain are: spot or open market transactions, agricultural cooperatives and contract farming (Joshi and Gulati, 2003).

One of the most successful producer organisation is the Indian Dairy Cooperative which, in 2005, had a network of more than 100,000 village level dairy cooperatives with 12.3 million members (see Birthal *et al.*, 2008).

Contract farming has a potential to help the small and marginal farmers overcome constraints in accessing inputs, credit, extension and marketing. In recent years, there has been some form of contract arrangements in several agricultural crops such as tomatoes, potatoes, chilies, gherkin, baby corn, rose, onions, cotton, wheat, *basmati* rice, groundnut, flowers, and medicinal plants and is spreading throughout India in states like Andhra Pradesh, Tamil Nadu, Karnataka, Punjab and Maharashtra.

While the pros of contract farming are potentially many, the sponsoring companies may be unreliable, may exploit a monopoly position, and/or have inefficient management and marketing problems that could result in manipulation of quota and non-fulfillment of commitments. Contract farming in India is neither backed up by law nor by an efficient legal system, thereby constrainting its widespread use in the country. The legal system can be improved with legislative measures like the model contract and code of practice, registration of contracts with marketing committees and tribunals for efficient, speedy and corrupt-free dispute resolutions.

There is a need to revamp some of the legal hurdles for agro-processing and Agricultural Produce Market Committee (APMC) Act. Several state governments have already amended their APMC Acts allowing varying degrees of flexibility. However, several states are yet to notify the relevant rules that would make the amendment fully operational. These steps should be speedily completed to provide a boost to promotion of direct marketing, contract farming, and setting up of markets in private and cooperative sectors.

A prominent problem for the small farmers is output price fluctuations. There is a big gap between producer prices and consumer prices. There are different models for marketing collectively by the small and marginal farmers. These are: SHG model, cooperative model, small producer cooperatives and contract farming. Apni Mandi in Punjab, Rytu Bazars in Andhra Pradesh and dairy cooperatives are some of the successful cases in marketing. The real challenge lies in organising the small and marginal farmers for marketing and linking them to high value agriculture. Thus, group approach is needed for getting benefits from marketing.

Super markets and supply chains: Small farmers can benefit from the emerging super markets and value chains. The presence of super markets as retail trade is rapidly expanding in the emerging economies. Reardon and Minten (2011) examine the patterns and dynamics of diffusion of modern food retail in India. They emphasised three surprises in the rise of modern food retail in India. They are:

> (1) that it has occurred since the 1960s with waves of government, coop, and then private retail; (2) that the private retail wave has been extremely fast in particular in its second phase, in the past 6 years, when it grew at 49 per cent per year on average, some 5 times faster than the fast growth being experienced in the GDP; (3) that the rise of private retail chains has been unique or rare in its drivers

(in its great majority by domestic capital, not foreign investment), and "early" (compared with the prior experience in other developing countries) in its penetration of the food markets of the poor, of small cities and even rural areas, of fresh product markets, and its use of diverse formats to help toward the above ends (Reardon and Minten, 2011: 20).

In India, the expansion of modern retailing has the potential to spark investment in marketing efficiency and processing that yields benefits both producers and consumers. In those cases where small producers have been able to integrate into the supply chains, supermarkets have offered enhanced security and considerably higher margins than the traditional clients such as wholesales and groceries. However, there is scope for exploitation in contract farming and super markets if rules are not framed properly.

Policies to Support Small Holders

In the case of smallholding agriculture, Government has to play an important role in improving productivity and incomes of small farmers. Given that 80 per cent of farmers are small and marginal, and, increasingly female, special steps will be needed to improve their effective access to inputs, credit, extension services, and output markets. It is now well recognised that the poor are best empowered if they function as a group rather than as individuals and that this is also the best way to secure economies of scale. Hence for the poor and for women to gain and be effective farmers, we should encourage a 'group approach' (11th Five Year Plan, Vol. 3: 38).

The NCEUS has recommended a special programmeme for marginal and small farmers. The report of NCEUS analyses the status and constraints faced by marginal and small farmers and focuses on the need for a special programme which is aimed at capacity building of these farmers, both the farm and non-farm activities. As the marginal and small farmers suffer from market failures in agriculture in terms of credit, input supplies and marketing of output, access to new technologies etc., NCEUS recommended four measures. These are: (a) special programmes for maginal and small farmers; (b) emphasis on accelerated land and water management; (c) credit for marginal and small farmers; and (d) farmers' debt relief commission.

The Commission strongly advocates that a strategy for marginal and small farmers must focus on group approaches in order to benefit from the economies of scale. A focused approach can be used to incentivise the formation of farmer's groups and apex organisations, and the government and others can facilitate in finding solutions to problems of irrigation, inputs, procurement, markets and risk. The Commission has considered four important models for group approach in the country. These are: cooperatives, producer's companies, farmers' groups such as those in Andhra Pradesh and SEWA (Self Employed Women's Association) farmers' model.

Cooperatives and farmers' groups on the lines of SHGs seem to hold greater promise for expansion. It may be noted that formation of marginal and small farmers' groups on the lines of SHGs has developed under agency structure such as 'Velugu' or Indira Kranti Pradham (IKP) or CMSA in Andhra Pradesh, 'Kudumbashree' in Kerala and SEWA in Gujarat. Such initiatives are being developed in Tamil Nadu, West Bengal, Odisha and Madhya Pradesh as well. As the Commission mentions that the "main lesson of these experiences is that the capacity building and group formation among the poor marginal and small farmers can not be simply seen as an extension of routine departmental activity and as one of the many activities that a programmeme seek to promote" (p.39). These groups under agency approach can be promoted where farmers' cooperatives are not operating.

Rural Non-farm Sector

As mentioned above, the income from small and marginal farms is not enough to take care of daily consumption and they have to borrow to survive. Smallholdings farmers must have some income from rural non-farm activities also. Therefore, promotion of rural non-farm sector is essential for generating incomes for rural population. Poverty cannot be removed with 55 per cent of workers being in the agricultural sector. Ultimately, many of the small and marginal farmers have to be shifted to rural non-farm sector and urban areas.

India currently produces about 50 million tonnes of fruits and 90 million tonnes of vegetables. Only 2 per cent of these fruits and vegetables are processed as against 23 per cent in China, 78 per cent in Phillippines, 83 per cent in Malaysia. Half of those engaged in agriculture are still illiterate and just 5 per cent have completed higher secondary education. Even in 2004-05, around 60 per cent of rural male workers and 85 per cent of rural female workers were either illiterate or educated upto primary level. In other words, lack of education and skills are major constraints. India can learn from China on rural transformation. China experienced a structural transformation in the last three decades. The state's role has been decisive in building up the physical and social infrastructure (including land reforms). India should learn from China on reforms in agricultural growth, rural non-farm employment, public investment and human development. The impact of growth on poverty reduction is quite significant. China started with agricultural reforms, leading to high agricultural growth. The economic and institutional reforms created space for rural non-farm sector (TVEs [Township and Village Enterprises] and others). Diversification towards rural non-form sector in China is one of the important factors responsible for rural poverty reduction (poverty is only 3%).

Rural Infrastructure Development

Regarding protection of agriculture in Organisation for Economic Cooperation and Development (OECD) countries, some suggest that developing countries should also protect their agriculture. However, a better option is to provide more rural and agricultural goods that are undersupplied by the market (Lipton, 2006). It also includes development of rural infrastructure like roads, irrigation, communications, etc. Returns are also high from investments in agricultural R&D (research and development), rural roads and other infrastructure (Hazell, 2011). The rural infrastructure will enable small and marginal farmers to compete with other famers in India as well as in other countries.

References

Agarwal, B. (2010). "Rethinking Agricultural Production Collectives", *Economic and Political Weekly* 45(17).

Birthal, P.S., A.K. Jha, M.M. Tiongco and C. Narrod (2008). "Improving Farm to Market Linkages through Contract Farming: A Case Study of Small Holder Dairying in India", *IFPRI discussion paper* 00814. Washington, D.C.

Birthal, P.S., P.K. Joshi and A.V. Narayanan (2011). "Agricultural Diversification in India: Trends, Contribution to Growth and Small Farmer Participation". ICRISAT. (*mimeo*).

Chand, R., P.A. Lakshmi Prasanna and Aruna Singh (2011). "Farm Size and Productivity: Understanding the Strengths of Smallholders and Improving their Livelihoods", *Economic and Political Weekly* 46(26 and 27).

Flynn, H.C. (2009). "The Role of Nutrient Management in Mitigation", Focus 16, Brief 7. An Agenda for Negotiation in Copenhagen *2020 Vision for Food, Agriculture and the Environment.* Washington, D.C: International Food Policy Research Institute.

Government of India (GoI) (2005). *Indebtedness of Farm Households.* Report no.498. NSSO.

Hazell, Peter (2011). "Five Big Questions about Five Hundred Million Small Farms", Paper presented at the *Conference on New Directions for Smallholder Agriculture.* 24-25 January. Rome: IFAD.

Joshi P.K. and A. Gulati (2003). "From Plate to Plough: Agricultural Diversification in India", Paper presented at the *Dragon and Elephant: A Comparative Study of Economic and Agricultural Reforms in China and India.* New Delhi, India. March 25-26.

Lipton, M. (2006). "Can Small Farmers Survive, Prosper, or be the Key Channel to Cut Mass Poverty", *Journal of Agricultural and Development Economics* 3(1): 58-85.

Krishnaraj, M. (2006). "Food Security, Agrarian Crisis and Rural Livelihoods: Implications for Women", *Economic and Political Weekly*, 30 December.

NCEUS (2008). *A Special Programmeme for Marginal and Small Farmers.* A Report prepared by the National Commission for Enterprises in the Unorganised Sector, New Delhi.

Rao, C.H. Hanumantha (2005). *Agriculture, Food Security, Poverty and Environment.* New Delhi: Oxford University Press.

Rao, N.C. and Dev, S.Mahendra (2010). *Biotechnology in Indian Agriculture: Potential, Performance and Concerns.* New Delhi: Academic Foundation.

Raturi, Rahul (2011). "Implementation Review of Major Centrally Funded Programmemes", Paper presented at the workshop on the *Long Term Future of Indian Agriculture and Rural Poverty Reduction.* New Delhi. 27-29 April.

Reardon , T. and B. Minten (2011). "Surprised by Supermarkets: Diffusion of Modern Food Retail in India", *Journal of Agribusiness in Developing and Emerging Economies* 1(2).

Sarthak, Gaurav and Srijit Mishra (2011). "Size Class and Returns to Cultivation in India: A Cold Case Reopened", *IGIDR Working Paper* No.WP2011-27. Mumbai.

Shah, Tushaar, Ashok Gulati, Hemant P., Ganga Shreedhar, R.C. Jain (2009). "Secret of Gujarat Agrarian Miracle after 2000", *Economic and Political Weekly* 44(52).

Singh, R.B., P. Kumar and T. Headwood (2002). *Smallholder Farmers in India: Food Security and Agricultural Policy*. Bangkok: FAO, Regional Office for Asia and the Pacific.

Swaminathan, M.S. (2010). *From Green to Evergreen Revolution: Indian Agriculture: Performance and Challenges.* New Delhi: Academic Foundation.

of its properties is also gradually lost from the community and *vice versa*. Biodiversity is valuable to communities only till they have knowledge of its properties and know-how to use it. If that knowledge is lost, the biodiversity becomes mere vegetation, not a valuable resource.

What makes agrobiodiversity special is the coordinated way in which rural men and women manage and use different parts of it. They have knowledge of its properties and know many ways to use the resources. Men and women have different kinds of knowledge about the genetic diversity of crops. They may both be involved in selecting crops for cultivation but for different reasons.

Farm men would know more about production issues, agronomic properties and market preferences; so they would have knowledge about features like period of maturity, yield, vulnerability to diseases and pests and for which kind of produce there is market demand. Farm women on the other hand have knowledge about the storage qualities of the grain, its cooking and keeping qualities. So women for instance know which kind of rice keeps longer in storage, which cooks fast or low and after cooking, how long it stays good to eat. Both men and women have knowledge about the digestibility of rice, the varieties that keep you sated and full for a long time and those which are digested fast. This is an important property for farmers and farm labour who eat in the morning before going to work. They want to feel sated for a long period, till they can go home for an early evening meal. The knowledge that rural and indigenous communities have of their bio resources is their greatest asset. Not just crop varieties or animal breeds, communities have the knowledge that enables them to access plants around them for a variety of purposes like food and nutrition, health and veterinary care, toxins for fish bait and hunting, dyes for colouring clothes, gums and resins for assorted uses and so on. Gene campaign has been conducting an awareness game with village children who go to graze cattle. Asked for the names and uses of plants that they could recognise, these children could name up to 200 plants. This knowledge is carried into adulthood and underpins their ability to survive under harsh conditions. This knowledge is of commercial interest to the global community and can be valuable in solving problems and finding easy, affordable solutions to a range of problems. It must therefore be recognised as the intellectual property of such rural and tribal communities.

Table 3.1

Major Crop Species of Indian Origin

Crop Groups	*Crops*
Cereals and millets	Rice (*Oryza sativa)*, little millet (*Panicum sumatrense*), kodo millet (*Paspalum scrobiculatum*)
Grain legumes	Black gram (*Vignamungo*), moth bean (*V. aconitifolia*), pigeon pea (*Cajanus cajan*), horse gram/*kulthi* (*Macrotylma uniflorum*), velvet bean (*Mucuna utilis*)
Fruits	Mango (*Mangifera indica*), banana (*Musa spp.*), *jamun* (*Syzygium cumini*), jackfruit (*Artocarpus heterophyllus*), Citrus group, lime and others, *karonda* (*Carissa congesta*), *khirni* (*Manilkara hexandra*), *phalsa* (*Grewia asiatica*), *bael* (*Aegle marmelos*), wood apple (*Feronia limonia*), *kokam* (*Garcinia indica*)
Vegetables	Eggplant (*Solanum melongena*), ridged gourd and smooth gourd (*Luffaspp.*) round gourd/*tinda* (*Praecitrullus fistulosus*), pointed gourd/*parval* (*Trichosanthes dioica*), *taro/arbi* (*Colocasia esculenta*), yam (*Dioscoreaspp.*), *jimikand* (*Amorphophallus campanulatus*), *kundri* (*Coccinia indica*), cucumber (*Cucumis sativus*), rat tailed radish/*mungra* (*Raphanus caudatus*)
Oilseeds	*Rai, sarson* and *toria* types (*Brassica spp.*)
Fibres	Jute (*Corchorus capsularis*), cotton (*Gossypium arboreum*), sunnhemp (*Crotalaria juncea*)
Medicinal and aromatic plants	*Rauvolfia serpentina, Saussurea lappa*, Indian belladonna (*Atropa acuminata*), Indian barberry (*Berberi saristata*), *Commiphora wightii*
Spices and condiments	Turmeric (*Curcuma domestica*), ginger (*Zingiber officinale*), cardamom (*Elettaria cardamomum*), Bengal/large cardamom (*Amomum aromaticum*), long pepper (*Piper longum*), black pepper (*Piper nigrum*), betel leaf (*Piper betel*), cinnamon (*Cinnamomum spp.*)
Other crops	Sugarcane (*Saccharum officinarum*), bamboos (*Bambusa arundinacea, Dendrocalamus hamiltoni, Sinocalamus giganteus*), *Sesbania sesban*, tea (*Camellia sinensis*)

Source: NBPGR, 2007.

Agrobiodiversity in India

India has been home to considerable diversity in both food and cash crops as well as livestock and poultry. It is one of the major centres of crop diversity mapped by the Russian Scientist Vavilov (see Janick, 2002).

The major crops of Indian origin include all the major food groups of cereals, grain legumes, fruits, vegetables, oilseeds, spices and condiments as well as fibres, medicinal and aromatic plants.

The diversity rich areas in India include the North Eastern states, North Bengal and Sikkim which are rich in the genetic diversity of rice, maize, barley, wheat, buckwheat, *Chenopodium*, *amaranth*, foxtail millet, finger millet, rice bean, winged bean, adzuki bean, *sem*, blackgram, sword bean, soybean, peas, vegetables (*cucurbits* like *Cucurbita, Cucumis, Momordica, Cyclanthera, Luffa, Lagenaria, Benincasa*), fruits (Citrus, *Musa*, pineapple), oilseeds (*Brassica spp.*, *Perilla*, niger, sesame), fibre crops (tree cotton, jute, mesta and *kenaf*), tuberous/rhizomatous types as *taro/yam*, and bamboos.

Orissa and the Chhotanagpur belt of Jharkhand are known for variability in rice, sorghum, finger millet, foxtail millet and proso millet, Dolichos bean, rice bean, chickpea, pigeon pea, horsegram, brinjal, chillies, cucurbit crops, mango, niger, sesame, linseed, *Brassica spp.* and castor. These regions hold rich diversity of rice.

In western India, Rajasthan and Gujarat are home to diversity in pearl millet, sorghum, wheat (drought and salinity types), guar, mothbean, cowpea, blackgram, *mungbean*, *Brassica spp.*, sesame, chilli, cucurbit vegetables, minor vegetables and fruits (*Capparisaphyla, C. deciduasber*), Citrus, forage grasses/legumes and spice crops (coriander, fenugreek, *ajwain*, garlic).

Interesting diversity in wheat, rice, sorghum, small millet, grain legumes, chickpea, pigeon pea, black gram, green gram, cowpea, niger, sesame, *Brassica spp.*, chilli and cucurbit vegetables, Dioscorea, Colocasia, okra, eggplant, chilli, banana, turmeric, ginger, black pepper, cardamom, nutmeg, arecanut is found in Madhya Pradesh and adjoining Maharashtra (NBPGR, 2007).

India's agrobiodiversity is rich and varied, and found in a wide range of ecosystems. Table 3.2 shows the agrobiodiversity hotspots of India.

Genetic Diversity and Food Security

Farmers outside the green revolution zones, especially those in marginal areas, rely on a diversity of crop and livestock types to ensure their food security. This diversity provides choices which help them to cope with a wide range of situations and minimise the risk of loss of farm produce from both crops and livestock. What is referred to as minor or underutilised crops like millets, certain tubers and vegetables are actually of great importance to the livelihoods of rural people and constitute a large percentage of their food. Plants that can thrive in degraded soils and animals that can survive on poor quality fodder are crucial to providing household food and nutrition.

Agrobiodiversity supports food and nutrition in a variety of ways. Farming communities rely on it to increase agriculture productivity, improve food security and boost farm incomes. Agrobiodiversity facilitates agriculture and food production in fragile areas and makes farming systems more sustainable and stable by improving soil health and providing more effective pest and disease control. Farmers having access to genetic diversity are more self-reliant because they can reduce external dependence. Genetic diversity helps to maintain the integrity of local ecosystems and makes available dietary diversity and therefore, better nutritional intake. (Thrupp, 1997).

Genetic diversity is the farmer's biggest insurance policy. It enables him to find solutions for the most diverse kinds of challenges. Having access to a repertoire of crop varieties to choose from, means the farmer will almost always find a variety for a particular situation. If the rains are late, he/she can cultivate a short duration variety of rice which will mature in time before winter sets in. If the monsoons come on time, he/she can cultivate a longer duration variety which may give him more time to pursue some other economic activity. If there is a disease outbreak, the collection of traditional varieties will contain a disease resistant variety that he/she can plant. Traditional

Table 3.2

Agrobiodiversity Hotspots of India

Agrobiodiversity Region	*Districts*
Cold Desert	Western Himalyas covering Ladakh and Kargil. Upper reaches of Lahual-Spiti districts of Himachal Pradesh.
Western Himalayan	Districts of Srinagar, Anantnag, Udhampur, Riasi, Kathua in Jammu & Kashmir, all the districts of Himachal Pradesh except the cold arid region and all the districts of Uttarakhand.
Eastern Himalayan	All the districts of Arunachal Pradesh, Sikkim and Darjeeling district of West Bengal.
Brahmaputra Valley	Districts of Dhubri, Kokrajhar, Bongaigaon, Bareta, Nalbari, Goalpara, Kamrup, Golaghat, Darrang, Morigaon, Nagaon, Sonitpur, Jorhat, Lakhimpur, Sibsagar, Dibrugarh, Dhemaji and Tinsukia.
Khasia-Jaintia-Garo Hills	All the seven districts, i.e., East Garo Hills, West Garo Hills, South Garo Hills, East Khasi Hills, West Khasi Hills, Jaintia Hills and Ri-Bhoi.
North-Eastern Hills	All the districts of Manipur, Mizoram, Nagaland, Tripura and the adjoining Cachar and North Cachar districts of Assam.
Arid Western	Districts of Rajastahan: Sikar, Nagaur, Pali, Hanumangarh, Ganganagar, Jalore, Sirohi, Jodhpur, parts of Jaisalmer and Bikaner, Udaipur, Dungarpur, Churu, and Jhunjhunu.
Malwa Plateau and Central Highlands	Districts of Shadol; Raisen, Bhopal, Sehore, Shajapur, Indore, Ujjain, Mandasaur, RajgarhHoshangabad, Narsinghpur, Jabalpur, Mandla, Umaria.
Kathiawar	Districts of Gujarat: Ahmedabad, Surendranagar, Jamnagar, Rajkot, Porbandar, Junagadh, Amreli, Bhavnagar, Bharuch, Surat, Navsari, Valsad, Banaskantha and Anand.
Bundelkhand	Districts of Jhansi, Banda, Chitrakoot, Hamirpur, Jalaun and Lalitpur in Uttar Pradesh and Damoha, Datia, Panna, Sagar, Tikamagarh and Chattarpur in Madhya Pradesh.
Upper Gangetic Plains	Districts of Hardoi, Sitapur, Barabanki, Lucknow, Unnao, Rae Bareilly, Kanpur, Kannauj of Central Uttar Pradesh and the districts of Maharajganj, Sidharatnagar, Kushinagar, Deoria, SantKabir Nagar, Gorakhpur, Basti of North-Eastern Uttar Pradesh.
Lower Gangetic Plains	Districts of Paschim Champaran, Purbi Champaran, Gopalganj, Siwan, Sitamarhi Muzaffarpur, Saran, Buxar, Bhojpur, Patna, Rohtas, Jahanabad, Vaishali, Samastipur, Darbangha, Madhubani, Sitamarhi, Sheohar in North Bihar.

Gangetic Delta	The Gangetic delta agrobiodiversity region broadly includes the deltaic 24-Parganas districts, but also the districts of Hoogly, Howrah, Nadia, Bardhaman, Birbhum and Murshidabad which flank the river Hoogly. The hotspot areas are the districts of south 24 Parganas, North 24 Parganas, Howrah, Hoogly, Nadia, Bardhaman, Birbhum and Murshidabad.
Chotanagpur	The Chotanagpur region constitutes south and eastern plateau of Jharkhand and contiguous districts in Orissa. Generally referred to as the Chotanagpur Plateau, it comprises all the districts of Jharkhand, Mayurbhanj and Sundargarh districts of Orissa. The hotspot areas are the districts of Singhbhum, Gumla, Ranchi, Lohardaga, Palamau and Hazaribagh and Santhal Pargana in Jharkhand and Mayurbhanj district in Orissa.
Bastar	Districts of Bastar, Bilaspur, Durg, Jashpur, Kabirdham, Kanker, Kirba, Koria, Mahasamund, Kondaigaon, and Rajnangoan.
Koraput	The Koraput agrobiodiversity region forms part of Northern Eastern Ghats in southwestern Orissa and northeastern districts of Andhra Pradesh (Vishakhapatnam, Vijaynagaram, Srikakulam). The hotspot area includes the districts of Malkangiri, Sonabeda, Jeypore, Koraput, Nabrangpur, Kalahandi, Bolangir, Raugada and districts of north eastern Andhra Pradesh, i.e., Srikakulam, Vijaynagaram and Vishakhapatnam.
Southern Eastern Ghats	Districts of Chittoor, Ananthapur, Cuddapah, Kurnool in Andhra Pradesh and Bellary, Raichur and Kolar in Karnataka.
Kaveri	Districts of Chengalput, South Arcot, North Arcot, Thiuvannamalai, Tiruchirapalli, Pudukottai, Thiruarur, Vellore, Kanchipuram, Dharmapuri, Salem, Namakkal, Karur and Dindigal.
Deccan	Districts of Jalna, Hingoli, Parbani, Beed, Nanded, Latur, Osmanabad, Solapur, Sangli, Gondia, Gadchiroli in Maharashtra and the districts of Adilabad, Karimnagar, Warangal and Khammam in Andhra Pradesh and Bidar and Gulbarga in Karnataka.
Konkan	Coastal districts of Thane, Raigad, Ratnagiri, Sindhudurg and part of Sahyadri districts of Pune, Satara and Kolhapur of Maharashtra, all the districts of Goa and Uttar Kannada district of Karnataka.
Malabar	Districts of Kasargod, Kannur, Wayanad, Kozhikode, Malappuram, Palakkad, Thrissur, Idukki, Ernakulam, Alappuzha, Kollam, Kottayam, Pathanamthitta and Thiruvananthapuram in Kerala, Udhagamandalam (Nilgiri) and Kanyakumari districts of Tamil Nadu, and districts of Dakshin Kannada, Kodagu and Udipi in Karnataka.
Islands	Andaman & Nicobar Islands and Lakshadweep.

Note: PPV&FRA *http://plantauthority.gov.in/hotspots.htm*

Source: Protection of Plat Variety and Farmer's Rights Authority.

varieties will also offer options to cope with seasons when there is low rainfall and drought like conditions or too much rainfall and flood like conditions.

Farming communities have faced all kinds of challenges in the past and have wisely conserved those varieties that have helped them overcome those challenges. Therefore, farm men and women across the world have created a vast repertoire of crop varieties with diverse traits. Today, this resource is available to fight new and current challenges to agriculture and therefore to ensure food security.

Having access to a range of crop varieties allows the farmer to minimise the risks to his/her crop production and enables him/her to ride out episodes of biotic and abiotic stress in a more assured manner than if he/she were part of a monoculture crop system. The vulnerability caused by monocultures and genetic uniformity have been highlighted by events of crop failures in the past. The Irish famine in 1846 caused by the potato blight *Phytophthera infestans* which wiped out potato fields planted with just one or two varieties is well known. The US corn crop suffered a 15 per cent reduction in yield and losses of up to US$1 billion in 1970, when a leaf fungus spread rapidly through the genetically uniform crop, causing severe destruction. Other instances of the vulnerability caused from a narrow genetic base are also known; for instance, the outbreak of citrus canker in 1984 in Florida that resulted from reduction in genetic diversity.

How Farmers Perceive Agrobiodiversity

Gene Campaign had conducted a study some years ago in Bihar and Jharkhand, to get a sense of how farmers perceive agrobiodiversity and their views on its conservation. The highlights of the study (Sahai, 2005) were as follows:

- Farmers by and large regretted that traditional varieties are now lost and have been replaced by the HYVs (high yielding varieties).
- Farmers felt that there was an urgent need for local seed banks, offering both traditional seeds and HYVs.

- In irrigated areas where HYVs are cultivated, farmers said that he biggest drawback of traditional varieties was its low yield and that seed is not easily available.
- In rain–fed areas where hardly any HYVs were cultivated, farmers recognised that traditional varieties do better under those conditions. They also complained about the difficulty of accessing seeds of these varieties since neither seed stores nor government agencies provide such seeds.
- Most farmers felt that the loss of traditional varieties is a negative development for agriculture.
- However, a section of younger farmers were not sure whether this loss is a negative development or it has actually been a positive development for the farming community, resulting in the overall development of agriculture.
- Farmers acknowledged that HYVs fare better in terms of yield and marketability but traditional varieties are better in terms of characteristics like amount and quality of straw and resistance to pests and diseases. The traditional varieties were said to be better tasting and were valued for festivals, ceremonies and rituals.
- Most farmers were open to cultivating traditional varieties of crops, at least on a portion of their land. The main impediment to this is lack of seeds.
- Farmers were interested in increasing the cultivation of traditional varieties but wanted incentives to offset the loss of yield compared to HYVs. Some of the desired incentives were assured availability of water, link roads, assured supply of good quality seeds, fertilisers and pesticides, and marketing facilities with price support.

Losing Agrobiodiversity

Diversified food production systems are under threat, and with it the local knowledge and skills especially of women farmers. When agrobiodiversity like cultivated species, varieties and breeds is lost, a wide range of wild and semi–domesticated species that are linked to them also disappear.

Box 3.1

Agrobiodiversity Loss

- Since the 1900s, about 75 per cent of plant genetic diversity has been lost as farmers across the world have abandoned local varieties and land races for genetically uniform, HYVs.
- 30 per cent of livestock breeds are at risk of extinction; six breeds are lost each month.
- Today, 75 per cent of the world's food is generated from only 12 plants and 5 animal species.

Source: Food and Agriculture Organisation (FAO), 1996.

The rapid loss of agrobiodiversity in India is becoming even more evident in recent years. Gene Campaign is currently conducting a study to evaluate the role that rice genetic diversity could play in helping farmers adapt their agriculture to climate change. The study in the Himalayan states of Himachal Pradesh and Uttarakhand and in Haryana, Uttar Pradesh and Bihar in the Indo Gangetic Plains (IGP), has revealed the relatively low value that farmers place on genetic diversity as a coping mechanism or as a problem solving tool when confronted with challenges. Farmers in the IGP consistently rated traditional varieties as 'poor' in participatory varietal trials and were unwilling to even experiment with them as an adaptation strategy.

An alarming 90 per cent of crop varieties are estimated to have been lost from farmers' fields and atleast 50 per cent of animal breeds are practically lost. Natural fishing habitats are over fished and many fish populations have effectively become extinct. Genetic erosion does not stop there. It extends to forest, coasts and wilderness areas.

The causes for genetic erosion and the loss of diversity are many. Research agendas themselves are a cause for genetic erosion. As biodiverse traditional agriculture was replaced by professional agronomy, research goals were set by the Western system which favoured intensification over diversity. This kind of research prioritises only a few well-known crops and species and completely neglects those that are not perceived to have any economic value.

It is only recently that processes like PVS (participatory varietal selection) and PPB (participatory plant breeding) are beginning to be discussed but even now, there is very little research investment in species and varieties of importance to small and landless farmers. Industrial agriculture apart from high-performance crop varieties has also included intensive livestock production, industrial fisheries and aquaculture which had impacted animal and fish genetic diversity.

Other than the National Gene Bank in Delhi, the Government of India (GoI) has not really had a proactive policy for the conservation of genetic resources. Only recently has the National Agrobiodiversity Management Committee been set up but more needs to be done to promote on-farm conservation as well as community-level seed banks that store and make available seeds of locally adapted crop varieties.

On the other hand, there are some government policies which are actively designed to destroy genetic diversity. In the eastern Indian state of Jharkhand, part of the region considered a centre of origin of rice and known for its high level of rice genetic diversity, the state government has a scheme called The Seed Exchange Programmeme. This programmeme asks farmers to bring their traditional varieties of rice for exchange with high yielding varieties. So farmers deposit whichever traditional varieties of rice they have been cultivating and take back an equivalent amount of seed of HYV. There is no programmeme for the conservation of the traditional varieties that are brought in; instead, they are milled and turned into rice, thus destroying large amounts of genetic diversity in a systematic way.

The green revolution and industrial agriculture are widely recognised to be one of the principal causes of the loss of genetic diversity. The promotion of HYVs to the exclusion of almost everything else resulted in farmers cultivating just a few varieties, neglecting the rest over generations. The conservation of genetic resources did not get much more than token attention in national and international agriculture policies. The creation of international gene banks was thought to be enough to conserve genetic diversity. While these banks have to some extent played a role in conserving agrobiodiversity, this has not brought genetic diversity back into cultivation. In addition, the controversial IPR (intellectual property rights) policies of the international gene banks relating to the use of farmer collections stocked with them is cause for concern.

The Green Revolution and biodiversity: The green revolution which is responsible for extensive genetic erosion was in fact a great beneficiary of this diversity. The green revolution became successful because it was able to utilise the genetic diversity in wheat and rice cultivars, to breed new HYVs. Plant breeding for intensification of agriculture aims for widely adaptable varieties that are insensitive to the length of daylight and can therefore be grown anywhere. The Green Revolution varieties were bred for short plant height and high response to chemical fertilisers. The focus on achieving high yield neglected genetic traits for other properties like resistance to pest and disease, so the genetic base of HYVs became very narrow. Other varieties with diverse traits were abandoned in favour of genetically uniform varieties that were selected for high yield.

The increasing population in developing countries has indirectly contributed to the loss of genetic diversity. The pressures of producing more food got translated into intensification with a narrow genetic base to achieve high yields quickly. Higher food output can be achieved in different ways but the conservative thinking of the research establishment has stuck by the Green Revolution model, reluctant to try out more diversified food production systems.

The globalisation of agriculture has resulted in the introduction of exotic species and breeds which have played their part in replacing local species and local diversity. When old varieties are replaced by new and different ones, the genes and gene complexes found in the older, traditional varieties tend to be lost forever.

The industrialisation of the food chain and the control of the food supply has meant that few companies produce and market the food to destinations across the world. The preference is for uniform sized fruit and vegetables that satisfy packaging requirements. So for instance, beans, cucumbers and carrots that are either too short or too long are discarded in favour of uniform size. Thus, only a few species are selected for the cultivation of produce for this uniform and standardised food chain; the others are neglected by farmers and go out of cultivation till the seed also disappears from farm homes and seed stores.

In the case of cereals, wheat varieties are selected only for certain properties; so if the processing industry requires high gluten wheat, that is what farmers will cultivate and supply and other wheat varieties will gradually get lost. In Punjab, the establishment of a potato chip production industry has meant that only the one or two potato varieties suitable for chip production are cultivated by farmers; the rest have been abandoned. Crop systems that produce standardised fruit, cereal and tubers and a few high-performance animal breeds for meat and milk have dramatically reduced genetic diversity from the agriculture sector. This has caused the marginalisation of small scale, biodiverse, agro-ecological food production systems that are far more sustainable in the long run. Faced with global warming, such biodiverse systems are more likely to deliver than the intensification model.

The genetic diversity of cattle in India suffered a serious blow when the livestock improvement programmeme was started. Artificial insemination with high-performance cattle breeds from other (temperate) countries was carried out on a large scale, with the goal of increasing milk yield. As part of the artificial insemination programme, large numbers of bulls of indigenous breeds were either culled or castrated to prevent them from diluting the stock of hybrid cattle that were being produced for high milk output. This resulted in an enormous loss of genetic diversity of indigenous breeds with their properties of resistance to pest and disease, high temperature tolerance, ability to withstand drought and ability to survive on low grade fodder. All these properties are now in high demand, to cope with the conditions created by global warming and climate change.

Research establishments need to rise to the challenge of ensuring adequate food production combined with the sustainability of the farm, the health of the soil and the multiple choices that are made available by biodiversity. They need to move away from the single point fixation with the Green Revolution and industrial agriculture, and widen the basket of choices for the farmer. This can happen if they accept, improve and scale up the many successful models of sustainable food production that exist and that include genetic diversity, community knowledge and a diversified food basket approach.

Conserving Genetic Diversity

Research programmes and government policies must respond urgently to arrest the further loss of genetic diversity and bring in proactive programmemes to restore what is lost. The apparent conflict between productive agriculture and biodiverse production systems must be resolved because it is possible to do so. Increasing the genetic base in agriculture will only increase productivity, not decrease it. The farming community has a natural advantage with biodiverse agriculture because they have sophisticated knowledge of the flora, fauna and soil of their region. This enables them to do their own problem solving and remain viable.

Technology moguls who currently dominate the direction of agricultural policy across the world, hold the view that the genetic diversity of crops have no role to play in ensuring food security. Many who promote GM (genetically modified) crops as the answer to all the world's problems from climate change to biofuels to banishing hunger, refer to traditional crop varieties as unproductive trash that does not need to be conserved. According to them, genetic manipulation will provide all the variability required to breed new varieties of plants and animals and there is no need to maintain collections of low yielding genetic resources. The fact is that the food security of communities and nations cannot be guaranteed without taking recourse from time to time to the repertoire of genes that are contained in the collection of traditional crop varieties and animal breeds.

The collection, characterisation and conservation of agro-biodiversity must receive policy and resource support from government so that the genetic wealth of crop, livestock and fish can be actively maintained. The biased economic incentives that favour high yield alone must be reviewed and biodiversity-rich farming systems must be promoted and incentivised.

The enormous contribution of rural communities to the development, refinement and conservation of large and diverse gene pools must be recognised and rewarded. It's a pity that after much wrangling on international platforms, the concept of Farmers Rights was adopted by FAO but was not enforced. Implementation of Farmers Rights was not made binding (like the IPR in the WTO) and was left to the decisions of individual countries who have largely abdicated responsibility in this regard. India is the only country in the world that has enacted a law granting Farmers Rights (Protection of Plant Variety and Farmers Rights Act 2001).

The use of agrochemicals should be curbed and replaced to the extent possible with biological substitutes that will improve soil micro-flora and therefore, soil health and soil fertility.

Conservation of ecosystems and biodiversity rich areas where wild foods are found should be incorporated into the development programmes from the start, so that there is a mandate to protect them.

Plant and livestock breeding should be done in participatory mode together with farmers in different locations, so that crop varieties and animal breeds that have a broad genetic base, are adapted to local conditions and can be easily accessed by farmers.

In the case of fodder, the focus has been on cattle and little attention is paid to the types of vegetation preferred by small ruminants, animals that marginal and landless farmers tend to keep. Research on this biodiversity will broaden the base of fodder plants and help the keepers of small animals. Research support must also be directed to neglected crops and livestock species which support the livelihoods of communities living in difficult terrains.

An active programme is needed to maintain genetic diversity in field–level community seed banks that are accessible to farmers. Trait evaluation of varieties should be done to identify valuable genes important both for sustainability as well as higher incomes. Such traits in crops and livestock could include pest and disease resistance, better nutritional properties, salt and drought tolerance. In the case of animals, the ability to withstand higher temperatures and lower water availability will be desired traits, more so now, in a warming world.

The PDS (public distribution system) which currently distributes only rice and wheat can be made into an effective mechanism to support genetic diversity. Since procurement is done only from surplus producing states, which are all Green Revolution states, and standards are set for the grain that is procured from there, only grain from HYVs are bought by the government. Traditional rice and wheat varieties are not procured by the Food Corporation of India (FCI) because there is a great deal of diversity in the shape and size of these grains. Instead of buying rice and wheat from only surplus producing states, if the PDS would buy traditional varieties of crops locally from farmers, it would be a great incentive for farmers to continue growing these varieties of rice and wheat and others such as, millets which are both nutritious and climate resilient. Farmers in rain–fed areas are still growing traditional varieties of rice, millets, maize, pulses, oilseeds and vegetables. If there is a good price for these crops, the farmers will not feel the need to shift to HYVs, which get them more assured incomes and the goals of providing food to poor families can also be met.

Ensuring the seed supply of traditional varieties is another way in which their cultivation can be promoted. The formal agricultural system does not offer any support for traditional varieties nor is there any programmeme for the production of these seeds. If farmers lose their farm saved seed, it is very difficult for them to buy these seeds since they are not sold by shops or government outlets.

Gene Campaign's Efforts to Conserve Agrobiodiversity

Recognising the importance of agrobiodiversity, Gene Campaign began some years ago to collect, characterise and conserve the agrobiodiversity of local crops like rice, millets, legumes, vegetables and oilseeds. The focus of the conservation exercise is rice because it is an important staple food and also because India is the 'centre of origin' and the greatest genetic diversity of rice is found here. This is the region where several thousand years ago, rural and tribal communities bred rice from wild grasses and where large numbers of land races and farmers' varieties are found. Gene Campaign decided to focus its conservation efforts in Eastern India for rice where the largest number of genes can be saved for future use and in Uttarakhand where germplasm of the mountain areas is being collected and conserved.

Traditional crop varieties from farmers' fields are collected and the knowledge of the farm family is documented using a structured survey form. At the time of collection, information is recorded about the properties of each variety. This knowledge held by the farming community is extensive and detailed, and documenting it faithfully provides a wealth of information about the genetic properties of crop varieties. It is farmers who reveal whether the variety performs well under drought conditions, is resistant to disease or has a short or long duration to maturity. This valuable information can tell breeders which traits to look for in which varieties.

The seed samples collected from the field are scientifically processed to reduce moisture level and stored in glass jars for medium-term storage and in baskets for short-term storage. The seed collection is conserved in community managed, field level gene-seed banks. These banks are simple rooms, which are moisture and light proof and well aired.

Zero Energy Gene-Seed Banks

The international network of Gene Banks consists of cold gene banks, which are energy intensive as they are maintained at low temperature, for long-term storage of genetic material. The model promoted by Gene Campaign is a labour-intensive, zero energy bank with no energy costs. Both are for *ex situ* conservation of agrobiodiversity. The monthly electricity bill of the cold gene banks runs to several thousands of dollars a month. It is not possible to set up many such gene banks both for reasons of cost and their large carbon footprint. The zero energy gene-seed banks being set up by Gene Campaign have almost no carbon footprint and they are located within the community that administers and uses the bank.

Seed Renewal to Maintain Viability

Multiplication and renewal of the seed samples conserved in the banks is done by a cycle of growing out each sample every year so that the seed retains its viability. The routine growing out of the seed samples exposes the varieties to the prevailing weather and climate conditions, helping them to adjust and adapt. The seed material that is returned to the bank after every grow-out season is adapted to the environment, which includes the climate as well as pests and disease. The material frozen in the cold gene bank does not get a chance to adapt to the local climate and when it is taken out at a time of crisis, it may or may not have the adaptive capacity to provide an efficient crop under the prevailing conditions.

Because Gene Campaign's banks are located in the village, they are owned by the people. Village youth committees supervised by village elders run the banks. The seed in the bank is accessed every season by the farmers who return three times the seed they take, when their harvest comes in. The core collection is multiplied in carefully designed plots in farmers' fields, monitored by trained village youth and Gene Campaign staff. The material that is returned to the bank after renewal is taken from the centre of the field plot to avoid mixing.

In the short–term, the gene-seed banks have begun to serve as a seed source for farmers who can access seed adapted to local conditions. Not all farmers can opt for HYV or hybrid rice cultivation and maintaining a diverse and secure seed source for such resource-poor farmers is important to support their agriculture and local food security. The gene-seed banks provide such locally adapted seed. The field gene-seed bank is also a repository of farmer varieties, which are being registered with the National Plant Variety Authority.

Training Village Youth in Conservation

To give the next generation a stake in conservation, village youth have been trained to collect traditional varieties, process them scientifically and characterise them. They are also trained to multiply the seed samples in plots, harvesting, drying and storing the samples in a carefully segregated fashion. Farmers are trained to maintain careful field protocols and plot designs as trained by the scientists.

Bringing scientific conservation techniques to the field should help to arrest the rapid genetic erosion.

Collabouration with Scientific Institutions

Gene Campaign collaborates with agriculture research institutions, to evaluate the agrobiodiversity in its banks for desirable traits like drought tolerance and disease resistance.

Three hundred twenty five (325) traditional rice varieties from the gene-seed bank collections of Gene Campaign were shared with the Indian Agricultural Research Institute (IARI), New Delhi. The varieties were screened and field tested for resistance to the Bacterial Leaf Blight (BLB) disease over a period of five years. The study shows that eight traditional varieties are resistant to BLB. Two new genes that confer resistance against the rice disease called BLB have been found in the collection of traditional rice varieties from gene-seed banks in Jharkhand. This underscores the crucial importance of conserving traditional crop varieties and the valuable genes that they contain, showing the relevance of such genetic resources to future food security.

It appears that these resistance genes are different to XA 13 and XA 21, which are known to confer resistance to BLB. Farming communities have conserved many genes of importance which need to be characterised and used. Such findings have a great significance for the future of rice breeding and show that traditional crop germ plasm is a valuable repository of genes to which the official research system should pay greater attention than it is doing. Climate change and the accompanying global warming are expected to increase the incidence of crop diseases. Finding genes conferring disease resistance is a sought-after research goal in national and international labouratories. The farming community in developing countries have selected and conserved a range of genetic diversity containing many valuable genes, in traditional crop varieties. Conserving this traditional gene pool is the most efficient and certain means of finding genes to breed new varieties to combat the impact of global warming and climate change on agriculture and food security.

In another study, Gene Campaign has shared 670 traditional rice varieties with the Birsa Agricultural University (BAU), Ranchi, for evaluation for drought tolerance. The studies are ongoing and 14 traditional rice varieties are showing promise for tolerance to drought.

References

Anderson, S. (2003). "Sustaining Livelihoods through Animal Genetic Resources Conservation", in *Conservation and Sustainable use of Agricultural Biodiversity*. Published by CIP-UPWARD in partnership with GTZ, IDRC, IPGRI and SEARICE.

Blench, R. (1997). "Neglected Species, Livelihoods and Biodiversity in Difficult Areas: How should the Public Sector Respond?", *ODI Natural Resource Perspective Paper* 23. London.

Blench, R.M. (2000). "Minor Livestock Species in Africa", in R.M. Blench and K.C. MacDonald (eds.), *The Origin and Development of African Livestock*. London: University College Press.

FAO (1996). Rome Declaration on World Food Security and the World Food Summit Plan of Action, *www.fao.org/docrep/003/w3613e/w3613e00.htm*

————. (1997). "Gender: The Key to Sustainability and Food Security", *SD Dimensions*. May. *www.fao.org/sd/*

————. (2004). *What is food security, Building on Gender, Agrobiodiversity and Local Knowledge.* Rome *http://www.fao.org/sd/LINKS/documents_download/FS4WhatisFoodSecurity.pdf*

Gene Campaign (2001). *Intellectual Property and Indigenous Knowledge: A Case of Unjust Discrimination. http://www.genecampaign.org*

Harlan, J.R. and J.M.J. de Wet (1965). "Some Thoughts about Weeds", *Economic Botany* 19(1): 16-24.

Howard, P. (2003). *Women and Plants, Gender Relations in Biodiversity Management and Conservation.* United Kingdom: ZED Books.

IUCN/DFID. (n.d.). "Biodiversity in Development?", *Biodiversity Brief* No. 6. United Kingdom. *www.iucn.org/themes/wcpa/pubs/pdfs/biodiversity/biodiv_brf_06.pdf*

Janick, J. (2002). *Centre of Origin of Plants.* Lecture 5. Purdue University. *http://www.hort.purdue.edu/newcrop/Hort_306/text/lec05.pdf*

McNeely, J.A. (1995). "How Traditional Agro-ecosystems can Contribute to Conserving Biodiversity", in P. Halladay and D.A. Gilmour (eds.), *Conserving Biodiversity Outside Protected Areas*. Gland and Cambridge: IUCN. pp.20-40. *http://www.iucn.org/about/work/programmemes/forest/?652/Conserving-biodiversity-outside-protected-areas-the-role-of-traditional-agro-ecosystems*

Mekoaur, A. (2002). "A Global Instrument on Agrobiodiversity: The International Treaty on Plant Genetic Resources for Food and Agriculture", *FAO Legal papers online* #24. *www.fao.org/Legal/prs-ol/lpo24.pdf*

Ministry of Law Justice and Company Affairs (n.d.). *The Protection of Plant Varieties and Farmers Rights Act 2001.* Government of India. *http://agricoop.nic.in/PPV&FR%20Act,%202001.pdf*

NBPGR (2007). *Country Report on the State of Plant Genetic Resources for Food and Agriculture in India.* National Bureau of Plant Genetic Resources. January. *www.fao.org/docrep/013/i1500e/nigeria.pdf*

Protection of Plant Varieties & Farmers' Rights Authority (n.d.). *The Agro-biodiversity Hotspots of India. http://plantauthority.gov.in/hotspots.htm*, accessed on 20.08.2013.

Sahai, S. (2010). "Challenges to Genetic Diversity and Implications For Food Security in South Asia", *South Asian Survey* 17(1): 111. A Journal of the Indian Council for South Asian Cooperation. Sage Publication

————. (2011a). *The Agrobiodiversity Commons, Vocabulary of Commons.* Gujarat: Foundation of Ecological Security. pp.417-44.

————. (2011b) *Agrobiodiversity and Food Security.* Farmer's Forum. November-December. pp.57-63. *http://farmersforum.in/agriculture-farming-india/biodiversity/agrobiodiversity-for-food-security/*

Sahai. S., B. Mahanta and W. Ahmed (2005). *Farmer's Perception of Agrobiodiversity; A Study in North India.* Gene Campaign.

Thrupp, L.A. (1997). *Linking Biodiversity and Agriculture: Challenges and Opportunities for Sustainable Food Security.* USA: World Resources Institute.

———. (2003). *The Central Role of Agricultural Biodiversity: Trends and Challenges.* CIP-UPWARD. *http://www.eseap.cipotato.org/UPWARD/Publications/Agrobiodiversity/pages%20020-032%20%28Paper%203%29.pdf*

Warburton, H. and A.M. Martin (1999). *Local People's Knowledge. Best Practice Guideline.* United Kingdom: Socio-Economic Methodologies Programmeme, DFID.

Warren, D.M. (1991). "Using Indigenous Knowledge in Agricultural Development", *World Bank Discussion Paper* No. 127. Washington D.C.: World Bank.

4

M. GOPINATH REDDY AND PRAJNA PARAMITA MISHRA

Livelihoods and Indigenous People

A Case of Mining Project in Odisha

Introduction

Mineral reserves that could be mined profitably were conventionally seen as a valuable part of a country's stock of natural capital along with agricultural land, forests and other natural resources, since countries that could exploit their rich mineral deposits could achieve higher economic growth. However, a different perspective has emerged over the last few decades which takes a more negative view of mining and raises questions as to whether the relationship between mineral extraction and economic development is always universally beneficial (Davis and Tilton, 2005). Mining, it is argued, profoundly impacts local communities in several ways: it affects jobs, migrant workers and land and water resources; it produces air and noise pollution; it also results in the loss of wildlife habitat. Unfortunately, the impact of mining on the livelihoods of the local communities has by and large been neglected. Often, all the benefits accrue to the mining industry and its work force, while the rest of the population in the locality is affected negatively. Local population bears only the costs, so that the distribution of the benefit from the activity is lopsided.

Concept of Livelihoods

What, then, is 'livelihood'? Livelihood is often conceptualised as "incomes in cash and in kind: as well as the social institutions (kin, family, compound, village) gender relations, property rights required to support and sustain a given standard of living" (Ellis, 1998, quoted in Chimhowu and Hulme, 2006). This includes the access to public services like education, health, roads, water, and related infrastructure, and the benefits derived from them. Livelihood approaches involve a conceptual shift from analysing rural people as smallholder farmers to a much broader understanding (Murray, 2002, quoted in Chimhowu and Hulme, 2006). In fact, there are many different ways of defining and analysing livelihood,[1] which differ only in terms of the relative emphasis on different factors rather than any fundamental difference. They all attempt to integrate assets, constraints and human capabilities in a logical and comprehensive manner to analyse the status, form, nature, and condition of livelihoods over space and time (Chimhowu and Hulme, 2006). Among these frameworks, the Sustainable Livelihoods Framework (SLF) has been the most popular, partly because of its robust analytical potential, and also because of its widespread promotion by donor agencies (Chimhowu and Hulme, 2006).

According to SLF, households make a living by using five types of assets/capital: natural (the stock of natural resources and environmental assets), physical (ownership of a house, other consumer goods, access to public goods), human (skills, knowledge, ability to work and good health), social (networks and relationships) and financial (access to credit, savings, other financial assets), in an environment influenced by institutional and structural factors. In this approach, vulnerability is identified as the key factor that households seek to negotiate and mitigate. There are five key features which contribute to the relevance of this framework. First, it views households as making a living in a variety of ways of which farming is just one (Francis, 2001; Murray, 2002). Second, land is just one asset among a group of other assets. Third, it places the interaction of the various capitals within a broader policy environment. Fourth, it allows an investigation into livelihood dynamics in a given geographical and physical context (Murray, 2002). Fifth, it incorporates the important issues of risk and vulnerability.

1. They include the SLF (Carney, 1998; 1999; Scoones, 1998), the Framework for Thinking about Diverse Rural Livelihoods (Ellis, 2000), Capitals and Capabilities Framework (Bebbington, 1999), and the United Nations Development Programme's (UNDP, 1999).

Issues Arising from Review of Literature

Yirenkyi (2008) looked at the socioeconomic impacts and challenges of surface mining by using Gold Fields Ghana Ltd. Tarkwa, Ghana, as a case study. The effects identified are: relocation/resettlement of host communities and its negative effects; disturbance of flora and fauna, disturbance to sacred places, land degradation, noise, air and water pollution. Bury (2005) examined how mining activities are affecting land tenure patterns and livelihoods in the Cajamarca region of Peru. Gold mining activities have contributed to significant shifts in land tenure patterns, land tenure institutions, and land use values throughout the region. Livelihoods are being transformed as household access to economic, human, natural and social resources are rapidly changing in the areas surrounding mining operations. Bury (2004) argued that while access to human capital resources has increased in the past decade, albeit unevenly, access to natural and social capital resources has declined in the Cajamarca gold region of Peru.

Adjei (2007) shows that livelihoods of households in the rural communities in the catchments of the mines in Ghana got threatened by the expansion of concession to the mining companies. The immediate repercussion is taking over farmlands by the miners, which affects livelihoods in its entirety. The study found both positive and negative outcomes to the rural households following the operation of mines in the communities. Kitula (2006) reported the socio-economic and environmental impacts of mining in Geita District, Tanzania. These impacts include: land degradation, damage to water quality, pollution, and harm to livestock and wildlife biodiversity.

Krishnaswamy *et al.* (2006) compared historic data with recent data and found out that mining and associated activities in Kudremukh National Park are the greatest sources of sediment entering the Bhadra River, damaging river ecosystems and disrupting downstream water resources. Sinha *et al.* (2007) studied the problem of local level sustainability of iron ore mining in eastern India. By using household survey data, sustainability of iron ore mining in this region was tested. Substitution of depleting natural capital with other forms of capital can promote long term sustainability of the local economy. This necessitates certain policy interventions to induce the mine operators to reinvest some part of their resource rent in the natural capital of the region.

Maponga and Ruzive (2002) discussed how chromite mining is primarily responsible for environmental problems on the Zimbabwe Great Dyke. McMahon and Remy (2001) investigated the economic, social, cultural, health and environmental impacts of medium and large-scale mining operations on local communities. They compared the developed countries (Canada and Spain) with the developing countries (Latin American countries of Bolivia, Chile and Peru). They concluded that the relationship between mining operations and local communities is undergoing a largely positive evolution. The International Institute for Environment and Development (IIED) and the World Business Council for Sustainable Development (WBCSD), 2002, brought the first in-depth review of the mining sectors from the perspective of sustainable development, undertaken with the support and engagement of mining companies, mining communities, labour, the research community and a broad range of other stakeholders. The World Bank also conducted an independent critique of its activities in the mineral sector (Salim, 2003).

Bebbington *et al.* (2008) addressed how social movement is protesting contemporary forms of mining in Latin America. Taking cases from Peru and Ecuador, their paper argues that the presence and nature of social movements has significant influences both on forms taken by mining industries and on the effects of this extraction on rural livelihoods. Bury (2002) argued that rural development is coproduced by movements, mining companies and other actors, in particular the state.

Kitula (2006) suggested that marked environmental and socioeconomic improvements can be achieved if the government provides technical support to local operators, regulations are improved and illegal mining activity is reduced.

Sweeting and Clark (2000) offered ways in which the mining industry and governments that regulate that industry can minimise the mining sector's negative environmental and social impacts that increase its overall positive contribution to conservation and community development. McMahon and Remy (2001) suggested three major stakeholders (the local community, the mining company and the government [central or state]) to work together to ensure long term sustainable benefits to the local economy.

Maconachie and Binns (2007) explain how diamond mining makes an important contribution to the national economy of Sierra Leone. They argued that if meaningful rural development is to be achieved among desperately poor communities, development strategies must be based on a detailed understanding of the nature of inter-locking livelihoods in the agricultural and mining sectors. Aroca's (2001) study shows that mining is the most important sector of the Chilean II region. The main linkages of the mining sectors are with the three sectors (fishing, utilities [energy], retail and business services) with the highest backward and forward linkages; when these linkages are considered along with mining's levels of production, mining is by far the most important sector.

Khatua and Stanley (2006) look at the lifestyle and livelihoods of affected communities, land use patterns, impact on natural resources and climate change in the context of mining. It focuses on National Aluminium Company Limited (NALCO) and its relationship to resource exploitation. However, the study is based on only secondary data. Patra and Murthy (2006) came with the fact finding reports of NALCO, which show that local tribal communities are complaining about air and dust pollution, noise emissions, unpleasant odor and discharge of effluents without treatment.

Stanley (1996) explains how displacement in NALCO area changed the occupational pattern and led to the division of society into social groups based on class, caste, tribe and sex. It adds to the process of marginalistion. Women's economic status deteriorates as they are forced to stay at home and no longer considered as an economic asset.

Irawan (2005) did a cost-benefit-analysis (CBA) of mining in Indonesia. The study analysed the net social benefits of the mining activity by analysing the environmental costs that have to be borne by the society in order to obtain the benefits of the mining activity. The net present value is estimated at US$ 220.1 million. It compares the benefits with that of forest preservation. Benefits of forest preservation are US$ 12.32 million, but will last for an infinite time, whereas mining will only last for 20 years. Therefore, the study concludes that forest preservation is more desirable than mining. Venkatesan and Wadhwa (2007) did a social CBA of the POSCO (Pohang Iron and Steel Company) steel project in Odisha. They measured the economic internal rate of return (EIRR), which measures the profitability of a project from the perspective of the whole economy rather than the project itself. The sensitivity analysis indicates that EIRR is 16.6 per cent for the base case scenario and 13.9 per cent at the world case scenario, significantly above the hurdle rate of 12 per cent discount rate.

National Institute of Rural Development (NIRD) (Muthayya *et al.*, 1982) conducted a very comprehensive study with the objective of formulating a rehabilitation plan for tribals and other caste groups being displaced from 15 villages around Damonjodi and came with an action plan of development for the region.

Gender and Mining

A significant body of research has been developed in the areas of gender and mining. Case studies around the world have reflected that women role is visible in large scale mining. Another body of research has focused on the role of both women and men in Artisanal and Small scale Mining (ASM) (Lahiri-Dutt 2000). Gender mainstreaming in mining is justified for four reasons (Lahiri-Dutt, 2006):

- Women often are the weakest and poorest in the local community.
- Women are often the most affected by the adverse impacts of mining.
- Women in poor communities are often responsible for household survival.
- The basic right to be heard, enabled and empowered applies equally to women.

Burke (2006) has divided women involved in mining in three different ways. They are: (a) miners—actually involved in the mineral extraction process, either as underground workers in the large mines or in small scale artisanal mines; (b) workers at surface—involved in crushing, sorting or preparation of coal or ore and official staffs as clerks, secretaries, etc.; (c) women as members of the mining community.

Yao (2006) has given a number of reasons why less number of women are employed in the coal mines of China. They are: availability of inexpensive male labour, cultural factors and customs in traditional China where women are regarded as ominous to be present in the mining tunnels. Custom of foot binding also worked against their mobility. Purevjah's (2010) study on Mangolia Mining shows that mining company job advertisement openly expresses a preference for male employees due to general hardness of conditions, which is not suitable for women.

Dreschler (2001) uncovered several factors that are contributing towards female participation in ASM. They are: deterioration of subsistence farming (low prices of agricultural commodities, effects of droughts on farmlands and lack of farmlands), low demand or lack of public and private employment, lack of trading commodities, high inflation rate, high birth rate and extended families. Yakovleva (2007) found out the main drivers of female employment in Ghana is gold mining. They are: need to bring income to households and lack of employment opportunities in the region. Impoverishment of subsistence farmers is another main reason to join mining. Amutabi and Lutta-Mukhebi (2001) found out the causes as pressure on agricultural land, diminished fertility, high cost of agricultural inputs, unpredictable rains and frequent droughts in Western Kenya.

In the Raniganj coal region of India, there are three features of the skewed gender distribution in favour of male labours. They are: male labour migration in search of job opportunities, less economic and social opportunities for women and gender bias in the coal mining industry (Lahiri-Dutt, 2000). Heemskerk (2003) in the gold mines of Surinam shows that women manage mining operations, worked as cooks and cleaned mining camps. Tallichet (1995) in the coal mines of West Virginia shows that women are involved in labouring jobs, which involves mine maintenance.

In artisanal mining as well, though women work in the same miserable condition as men, they are not equally compensated; hence they failed to attain the same decision-making positions as their male counterparts (Labonne, 1996). According to Werthmann (2009),

> What women need in mining camps is practically the same they need in general: the possibility of earning a livelihood without being exploited or harassed, education and health care, and the protection of rights by impartial state authorities.

In many mining camps of Burkina Faso, women form networks or associations that offer assistance in cash or kind when a woman is in need or intervene in cases of conflict with authorities, customers or partners (Werthmann, 2009). There is some evidence of positive impact of mining on women, such as increased access to education and travel, improvement in infrastructure such as roads and transport and thus access to market (Purevjah, 2010).

Study Area and Context

In Odisha and Andhra Pradesh, there is huge discourse going on about the bauxite mining in the Eastern Ghats. Both the states preserve 70 per cent of all India bauxite reserves. In Odisha, bauxite mining had started nearly 25 years back.

Odisha is endowed with a variety of vast mineral deposits and therefore occupies a prominent place in the mineral map of India. Among all the minerals, bauxite is an important one with Odisha having 51 per cent of the deposit. Koraput is the major bauxite bearing district in Odisha and produces 98.82 per cent of the state's total production followed by Rayagada and Sundargarh (Choudhury, 2007). Out of all bauxite areas in Odisha, Panchapatmali deposit of Koraput district bears the largest single deposit in the world. NALCO, a company fully owned by the Government of India (GoI), has developed a mechanised open cast mine in Odisha for annual production of more than 4.5 million tones (Choudhury, 2007). The capacity is being expanded to 6.3 million tonnes per annum.

The NALCO bauxite mine and smelter project called 'the pride of Odisha' by the Government of Odisha (GoO), was incorporated in 1981. NALCO declared a net profit of 608 crore, the highest on record for the first quarter of 2006 and won GoI's Indira Priyadarshini Vrikshamitra Award for its contribution to wasteland development. On the other hand, displacement of *adivasis* and severe pollution of water and air have been documented. NALCO displaced hundreds of tribal families during construction and then polluted downstream. It has turned the tribals from a self-reliant proud community to menial wage earners and landless ecological refugees, within a period of 10 years.

Figure 4.1

Bauxite Reserves in India

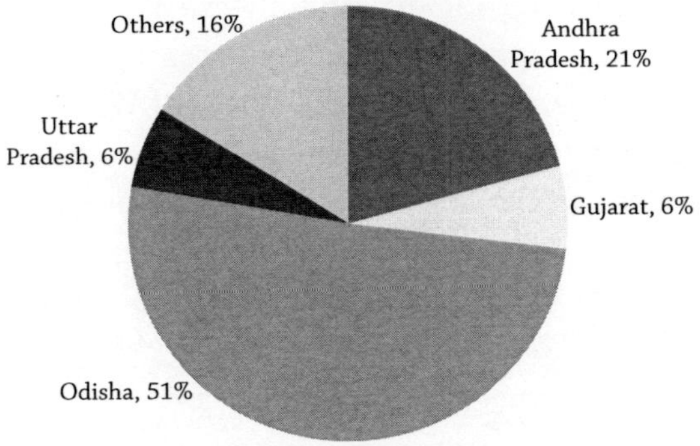

Source: Indian Bureau of Mines (2005).

Objectives of the Study

- To analyse the socio-economic and livelihood impacts and challenges of bauxite mining.
- To assess the environmental affects of the mining project on the region.

Bauxite Mining in South Odisha: A Look at the Past

In the early 1980s, it was clear that the bauxite deposits of South Odisha will be exploited with the help of a western transnational, and the Andhra deposits with the help of a soviet-aided project. NALCO was set up for exploiting the vast bauxite deposits of south Odisha, in collaboration with a French aluminium international company (Srinivasan *et al.*, 1981). There was a public debate on this huge public investment and papers were published in the leading journal, *Economic and Political Weekly* (EPW), raising a number of questions about the ongoing debate (Srinivasan *et al.*, 1981; Subrahmanyam, 1982).

Researchers mentioned that the financial viability and foreign exchange earnings of the project depend on world alumina prices. Further, there are questions regarding the interest rate on the Euro currency loan (Srinivasan *et al.*, 1981). Babani and Srinivasan (1981) also supported the former authors' argument that world alumina prices have never arrived at 15 per cent of the aluminium price; this was against the NALCO assumptions and Subrahmanyam (1982) further supported the argument. There were also questions regarding why this plant was taken up when resources to finance the projects and programmes covered by the Sixth Plan (EPW, 1982) were lacking. However, another review work of EPW (1986) argued that this was a major development in the aluminium industry during the Sixth Plan.

Table 4.1

Displacement Scenario of NALCO

Affected Villages	26	
Affected Families	Tribal	254 (42.55)
	Dalit	56 (9.38)
	Others	287 (48.07)
	Total	597 (100)
Land Acquired (acres)	Mines	427.30 (4.25)
	Township	2638.96 (26.24)
	Plant	6992.50 (69.52)
	Total	10058.76 (100)

Source: Stanley (1996).

In the 1950s, Odisha did not have any industry except a few saw mills and some ice factories near Cuttack (Stanley, 1996). Exploitation of the state's resources started with the building of the Hirakud Dam and the Rourkela Steel Plant in the 1950s. Since the 1970s, resource exploitation increased with more dams and more mining (Stanley, 1996). Stanley gives a clear account of the displacement, compensation and rehabilitation in the NALCO Bauxite Mine and Plant at Damanjodi. According to him, 597 families in 254 villages got displaced, out of which 42.55 per cent were tribal. Out of the total acquired land of 10,058.76 crore, 69.52 per cent was used for the construction of the plant followed by the township.

Stanley (1996) also examined the compensation package given by NALCO. Out of the displaced families, 74 per cent were rehabilitated and 59 per cent received jobs in compensation. Compensation per acre of land was ₹2000 and compensation per tree was ₹100. However, there was no compensation for the common property resources (CPRs).

Table 4.2

Compensation Scenario of NALCO

Families Displaced	597
Families Rehabilitated	441 (73.87)
Jobs Received	352 (58.96)
Compensation per one acre of land (₹)	2000
Compensation per Tree	100
Compensation for CPRs	No

Source: Stanley (1996).

Samal (1996) undertook another study, which covered the NALCO Anugul sector (smelter). He mentioned that the NALCO rehabilitation and resettlement (R&R) policy is regarded as one of the best in India. According to Khatua and Stanley (2006), NALCO paid compensation for *patta* land alone; there was no compensation for CPRs or government and village lands, which are a good source of income for the landless villagers. All these studies encouraged meeting with the displaced people and studying their situations nearly after three decades. With this background, the objective of our study is to compare the situation of the displaced people before and after mining.

A team visited 11 villages and conducted a survey to understand the extent of displacement. All household heads of these villages were interviewed and information from 1,483 households was

Table 4.3

Demographic Features of Affected Villages

Study Zone	*Village*	*Panchayat*	*Block*	*Household Category*				
				SC	*ST*	*OBC*	*OC*	*Total*
Mining Core	Kapsiput	Bhifaarguda	Lakhimpur	1	141	0	0	142
Mining Buffer	Kardiguda	Littiguda	Koraput	0	79	0	0	79
	Putraghati			26	95	79	1	201
Refinery Core	Analabadi	Matalput	Koraput	68	267	144	128	607
	Ambogam	Littiguda		2	131	0	0	133
Refinery Buffer	Mujanga	Mujanga	Dasamanthapur	143	93	0	23	259
	Marchimal	Matalput	Koraput	21	0	15	41	77
ARMP Core	Goudaguda	Charangul	Semiliguda	0	0	0	73	73
	Khoraguda	Podampur	Koraput	4	2	14	13	33
	Champapodar	Mujanga	Dasamanthapur	11	1	9	64	85
ARMP Buffer	Charangaguda	Podampur	Koraput	30	42	0	0	72

Note: ARMP: Ash and Red Mud Pond.

Source: Field Survey (2011).

collected. Demographic features of the villages samples is as follows. In the mining core zone, Kapsiput has 142 households, out of which 141 households belong to the Scheduled Tribe (ST) category. In the mining buffer zone, Kardiguda and Putraghati were two sample villages. Kardiguda has 79 households and all belong to the ST category. Putraghati has 201 households with a mixed population.

In the refinery core zone, Analabadi has 607 households. This is a rehabilitation colony consisting of 11 displaced hamlets of the refinery. It also has a mixed population. The second village in the refinery core zone, Ambogam, consists of 133 households, mostly tribal. This village is almost located in the refinery premises (1.2 km); this village was supposed to be displaced, but NALCO delayed the process and later on gave up the idea. These villagers are the victims of all immediate environmental impacts. In the refinery buffer zone, Mujanga Village has 259 households, dominated by Scheduled Castes (SCs) and STs. Marchimal is another village in this area having 77 households with a mixed population but no tribals.

In the ARMP core zone, Goudaguda is a village with 73 households. All the households belong to the Gouda caste, whose main occupation is livestock rearing. Both Khoraguda and Champapodar are displaced villages in this area. They are now resettled in one place but they still maintain different identities. Khoraguda has 33 households with a mixed population and Champapodar has 85 households dominated by other castes. In the ARMP buffer zone, Charangaguda is a village with 72 households, dominated by SC and ST population. Most of them have lost land because of the railway track constructed by NALCO.

The next section shows the displacement scenario of the affected villagers.

Displacement and Compensation Scenario

In the mining core zone, 51 per cent of the households lost their agricultural land and none of the households received any compensation for this. These villagers were practicing *podu* (shifting cultivation) on the top of the hills and on hill slopes. After getting permission to mine the area, NALCO evicted these villagers and disallowed them from cultivating those patches of land. As these displaced households do not have *patta* for their agricultural lands, they did not receive any compensation for that. In the mining buffer zone, 49 per cent of the households lost their agricultural land to the rehabilitation colony, conveyor belt and another road, which connects the mining area to the refinery site. Almost all the households here received compensation; only two households did not receive compensation because of unclear documentation. The compensation package was ₹1,000 to ₹1,500 per acre for dry land and ₹2,500 to ₹5,000 per acre for wet land.

Table 4.4

Displacement and Compensation Scenario

Study Zone	*Total HHs*	*Affected HHs*	*Assets Lost*		*Compensation Received*	
			Land	*House*	*Land*	*House*
Mining Core	142	72 (50.70)	72	0	0	NA
Mining Buffer	280	138 (49.29)	138	0	136	NA
Refinery Core	740	383 (51.76)	141	361	129	344
Refinery Buffer	336	34 (10.12)	34	0	28	NA
ARMP Core	191	128 (67.02)	86	103	85	103
ARMP Buffer	72	38 (52.78)	38	0	36	NA

Source: Field Survey (2011).

In the refinery core zone, 52 per cent of the households were affected by the refinery. Out of the affected households, 37 per cent (141 households) lost their agricultural land; and of these, 129 households received compensation, while it is still pending for others. The compensation package is the same. On the other hand, 94 per cent of the affected households (361 households) lost their home and homestead area; of these, 344 households received compensation ranging from ₹500 to ₹5,000 depending on the type of home-hut, semi-*pucca*, *pucca*, etc. These households were also settled in the rehabilitation colony and provided with one job (per house) in NALCO.

On the other hand, in the refinery buffer zone, only 10 per cent of the total households got affected. They lost their agricultural land for the refinery, and a part of the red mud pond. Out of the 34 households, 28 received compensation, while it is pending for the others.

In the ARMP core zone, 67 per cent of the households were affected; of these, 67 per cent of the households lost their agricultural land. All the households received compensation except for one. Further, in this area, 80 per cent of the households lost their home and homestead area. The compensation package was the same here.

In the ARMP buffer zone, 53 per cent of the households were affected; of these, 38 households lost their agricultural land and 36 were compensated.

The next section compares the main occupation of the households in the pre and post-displacement scenario.

As a part of the compensation package, NALCO provided jobs to those households that lost their home and homestead area. Therefore, it is interesting to study how the household's main occupation was changed in the post-displacement scenario. It is to be noted here that we have only compared the main occupation of the households in the pre and post-displacement scenario, irrespective of whether or not the household's head was the same person.

In the mining core zone, the main occupation of all households was farming during the pre-displacement period (see Table 4.5). However, in the post-displacement period, 36 per cent were engaged in NALCO as contract/wage employees—they are not permanent employees of the company. NALCO had assigned the contract works to contractors, who in turn recruited the contract/wage labour. Therefore, there was no job security for these people and they received weekly payment. The work in the company has been divided into four categories: high skilled works, skilled works, semi-skilled works and unskilled works. According to the work category, the wage rates are: high skilled worker—₹330 per day; skilled worker—₹280 per day; semi-skilled worker—₹220 per day; and unskilled worker—₹190 per

Table 4.5

Main Occupation of the Households: Pre and Post-Displacement

Main Occupation	*Mining Core Zone*		*Mining Buffer Zone*		*Refinery Core Zone*		*Refinery Buffer Zone*		*ARMP Core Zone*		*ARMP Buffer Zone*	
	Pre	*Post*	*Pre*	*Post*	*Pre*	*Post*	*Pre*	*Post*	*Pre*	*Post*	*Pre*	*Post*
Farmers	118 (100)	75 (63.6)	193 (81.8)	78 (33.1)	665 (94.5)	71 (10.1)	165 (54.8)	100 (33.2)	164 (85.9)	16 (8.4)	38 (52.8)	1 (1.4)
Wage Labourers	0		43 (18.2)		27 (3.8)	207 (29.4)	132 (43.9)	172 (57.1)	22 (11.5)	90 (47.1)	34 (47.2)	65 (90.3)
Others	0			9 (3.8)	12 (1.7)	33 (4.7)	4 (1.3)	19 (6.3)	5 (2.6)	7 (3.7)	0	3 (4.2)
NALCO Contract/ Wage Employee	NA	43 (36.4)		149 (63.1)	NA	98 (13.8)	NA	10 (3.3)	NA	9 (4.7)	NA	3 (4.2)
NALCO Permanent Employees					NA	295 (41.9)	NA		NA	69 (36.1)	NA	
Total	118 (100)	118 (100)	236 (100)	236 (100)	704 (100)	704 (100)	301 (100)	301 (100)	191 (100)	191 (100)	72 (100)	72 (100)

day. In the mining buffer zone, farming was the main occupation (82%) during the pre-displacement period followed by wage labour. However, this percentage was reduced in the post-displacement period and now NALCO contract/wage labour is the main occupation.

In the refinery core zone, farming was the main occupation during the pre-displacement period (94.5%). However, in the post-displacement period, majority of the people are permanent employees of NALCO—this job was the compensation package for the many households that lost their homestead area in this zone. This is followed by wage labour and NALCO contract work. In the refinery buffer zone, during the pre-displacement period, both farming and wage labour were the major occupations. However, post-displacement, wage labour has outweighed farming. Since the extent of displacement was very less here, workers employed in NALCO as contract/wage labour was very less (only 3.3%).

Similarly in the ARMP core zone also, farming was the main occupation during the pre-displacement period. In the post-displacement scenario, it was wage labour and employment in NALCO. Here also, the households lost their homestead land and were provided permanent employment in NALCO. In the ARMP buffer zone, the main occupation was farming and wage labour. However, in the post-displacement period, it was dominantly wage labour. Because of water problem and other environmental impacts, farming is no more a profitable occupation now. As the contractors are exploiting the NALCO contract employees, these people prefer to work as wage labourers rather than as contract employees.

In the tribal and hilly habitations, CPRs play an important role in the subsistence of the livelihoods of the poor and the marginalised. Particularly in these regions, unlike in the plain areas, availability of CPRs to the village communities in terms of basic needs, such as grasing pastures, ponds, streams, and forests for minor forest produce, play an important role in their livelihoods. Access to CPRs is usually free and unrestricted.

Interaction with the affected households in these areas revealed that NALCO does not offer any access to health facilities in terms of issuing health cards and availability of medicines and other facilities.

The attitude of NALCO, a profit-making public sector undertaking (PSU), towards this section of affected people was found to be totally inadequate and unsatisfactory. Further, permanent employment opportunities available to them in the plant were also very limited. Whatever employment was offered was only contractual in nature; moreover, it was offered through contractors and not directly by the company. It was also observed during the survey that once an employed person got married and left the house, the others, especially the elderly, became totally dependent and had no source of regular income. Land-to-land compensation was eminently possible during the early 1980s, but this option was not followed. Unfortunately, the affected households became addicted to certain social evils as a result of the cash compensation.

Many women from areas surrounding the mining activity are working as cleaners for cement works masonry and as helpers. However, they are employed through contractors and not NALCO. Their wage rates are around ₹90 to 120 per day. The women expressed that no adequate transport facilities are provided to reach the mining site. Further, it was observed that people from surrounding villages work in the refinery, and engage in both technical and non-technical sections: people working in the technical sections are technicians, fitters, electricians; while the non-technical people work as maintenance workers, daily wage workers in the boiling section and other works.

It was also found that transport between the refinery and the surrounding villages is a major problem; the men use bicycles or motor cycles for their transport, while the women have to trek long distances-this is very difficult because they have to walk about 9 to 10 km on a *kutcha* road to reach the refinery, and it takes more than one hour of their time. Due to this, they are not able to reach home well in time to spend with their children. They hope that NALCO will provide them with the required transport facilities. Besides the problems enlisted above, there are certain environmental and ecological problems observed in the field. Dust emanating from the conveyor belt carrying bauxite is affecting the agricultural lands and hence their productivity. Unfortunately, there is no mechanism to compensate such losses. Natural resources such as ponds and streams were adversely damaged due to mining and the conveyor belt; hence the water sources got totally diminished.

During the survey, some of the following problems were identified in Goudaguda village: leakage in caustic soda and septic water pipeline led to septic water flows into the agricultural fields; hence soil fertility was affected and crop production decreased. The canal water is contaminated due to caustic mud and septic water. According to the village elders, due to contaminated water affected by caustic mud and septic water, a few livestock died in 1995. For this, the villagers fought against NALCO and received compensation. However, the people are facing health problems such as skin ailments, TB and other health-related issues.

When it comes to other infrastructural facilities, most of the villages are facing water problems. They depend on wells and hand pumps for both drinking and domestic usage. For agriculture they depend on streams, ponds and rainfall. NALCO gets water from the Kerandi River, which is about 8 km away from the refinery. A pipeline is connected to carry water from the river and due to this, some villages lost their agriculture lands. During the survey, the people informed that their request to access water from the pipeline was denied by NALCO, although large quantities of water is wasted due to leakages.

Interactions with associations such as the Peripheral Development Committee (PDC), LDP (Land Displaced Persons) Welfare Association, and LAP (Land Affected Persons) Association show that due to NALCO many people have lost their agriculture lands and houses; but NALCO provided job opportunities only to a selected few, while the rest of them received no benefits. In fact, there was no proper guideline for job recruitment. After job recruitment, NALCO conducted a minimum literacy programme for the displaced people; its duration was for nine months. During this time, some of the displaced people, who got jobs, had died due to health problems and their spouses applied for their husbands' job; but NALCO did not accede to their request. These people are still trying to get jobs with the help of associations.

During the year 1984-85, NALCO started the Peripheral Development Programme—the area which is 10 km from the refinery and mining is considered as a peripheral area. Under this programme, NALCO promised to provide all facilities including health, education, roads, drinking water and infrastructure development (school building, etc.); but did not do so. The presidents of various associations said that as far as their knowledge goes, the peripheral development funds have been diverted to other areas. Further, all association members demand NALCO to provide jobs to all affected people and services to the notified peripheral area. They also insist that local priority should be given for the contract works and contract jobs, and health card access to all the displaced people must be given, irrespective of whether they are directly or indirectly affected.

Mining and its Effects on Common Property Resources

As already mentioned, in tribal and hilly habitations, CPRs play an important role in the subsistence of the livelihoods of the poor and the marginalised. In particular, these regions, unlike in the plain areas, access and availability of CPRs to the village communities in terms of basic needs, such as grasing pastures, ponds, streams and minor forest produce (from forests) plays an important role for their livelihoods. Access to these is usually free and unrestricted, since CPRs are open access resources. However, it may be observed that though various CPRs are available in the sample villages, most of them have been affected by the refinery and ARMP areas. NALCO acquired most of the CPRs such as common lands, streams and grasing land for laying roads, constructing the conveyor belt and building colonies, particularly in the refinery (core) areas. Due to the factory activities, the streams have been logged and forest access to the community is very much restricted. In some villages, the streams and canals are contaminated due to emissions from the plant.

As already mentioned, CPRs significantly enhance the livelihood of the poor in the villages. Mostly their access is open to all sections of the society. It was observed that NALCO acquired village common land in 8 out of the 12 sample villages. Unfortunately no compensation was paid by NALCO to the village communities and the

Table 4.6

Details of the Common Property Resources

Area	*Zone*	*Village*	*Availability of CPRs*	*Impact on CPRs*	*Details*
Mining Area	Core	Kapsiput	Streams, forest and common lands	Yes	Streams are logged, forest is restricted and common land totally acquired
	Buffer	Kardiguda	Streams, forest lands, ponds, etc.	Yes	Streams destroyed, water logged
		Putraghati	Canal, streams, village forest, grazing lands and graveyard	Yes	NALCO occupied all the common land streams and grazing lands for the roads, conveyor belt, and R&R colony
Refinery Area	Core	Analabadi	Canal, streams, village forest, grazing lands and graveyard	Yes	NALCO occupied all the common land streams and grazing lands for the roads, conveyor belt, and R&R colony
		Ambogam	Forest and streams	Yes	NALCO occupied all the common land, streams, and grazing lands for the roads and conveyor belt
	Buffer	Mujanga	Forest, streams, ponds, tamarind trees and other forest products	Yes	Due to red mud pond the CPRs are disturbed
		Marichamal	Canal and forest	Yes	Canal water declined due to water logging
ARMP	Core	Goudaguda	Canal, stream and forest	Yes	Stream and canal are contaminated due to caustic water and septic water
		Khoraguda	Forest	Yes	Restricted
		Champapodar	Forest	Yes	Restricted
	Buffer	Charangaguda	Hill forest and stream	Yes	NALCO acquired some of the land

Source: Field Survey (2011).

Table 4.7(a)

Details of the Common Property Resource Acquisition: Village Common Land

				Village Common Land				
Area	*Zone*	*Village*	*CPR Acquired*	*Acquired*	*Land Possessed (in acres)*	*Land Lost (in acres)*	*Amount Offered*	*Reasons for not Receiving*
Mining	Core	Kapsiput	Yes	Yes	Not Known	Not known	0	Not offered because it is forest land and there is no *patta*
	Buffer	Kardiguda	Yes	Yes	Not known	Not known	0	Not offered because it is forest land and there is no *patta*
		Putraghati	Yes	Yes	4	0	0	Reason not known, but no amount was offered
Refinery	Core	Analabadi	Yes	Yes	0	0	0	Reason not known, but no amount was offered
		Ambogam	Yes	Yes	0	0	0	Reason not known, but no amount was offered
	Buffer	Mujanga	No	–	0	0	0	0
		Marichamal	No	–	0	0	0	0
ARMP	Core	Goudaguda	No	–	0	0	0	0
		Khoraguda	Yes	–	0	0	0	Not offered because it is forest land and there is not *patta*
		Champapodar	Yes	–	0	0	0	Not offered because it is forest land and there is not *patta*
	Buffer	Charangaguda	Yes	–	0	0	0	0

Source: Field Survey (2011).

Table 4.7(b)

Details of the Common Property Resource Acquisition: Village Grazing Land

				Village Grazing Land				
Area	*Zone*	*Village*	*CPR Acquired*	*Acquired*	*Land Possessed (in acres)*	*Land Lost (in acres)*	*Amount Offered*	*Reasons for not Receiving*
Mining	Core	Kapsiput	Yes	Yes	Not known	Not known	0	Not offered because it is forest land and there is no *patta*
	Buffer	Kardiguda	Yes	Yes	Not known	Not known	0	Not offered because it is forest land and there is no *patta*
		Putraghati	Yes	Yes	3	3	0	Reason not known, but no amount was offered
Refinery	Core	Analabadi	Yes	Yes	Not known	Not known	0	Reason not known, but no amount was offered
		Ambogam	Yes	Yes	Not known	Not known	0	Reason not known, but no amount was offered
	Buffer	Mujanga	No	0	0	0	0	0
		Marichamal	No	0	0	0	0	0
ARMP	Core	Goudaguda	No	0	0	0	0	0
		Khoraguda	Yes	Yes	Not known	Not known	0	Not offered because it is forest land and there is not *patta*
		Champapodar	Yes	Yes	Not known	Not known	0	Not offered because it is forest land and there is not *patta*
	Buffer	Charangaguda	Yes	0	0	0	0	0

Source: Field Survey (2011).

Table 4.7(c)

Details of the Common Property Resource Acquisition: Common Forest Land

				Common Forest Land				
Area	*Zone*	*Village*	*CPR Acquired*	*Acquired*	*Land Possessed (in acres)*	*Land Lost (in acres)*	*Amount Offered*	*Reasons for not Receiving*
Mining	Core	Kapsiput	Yes	Yes	Not known	0	0	Not offered because it is forest land and there is no *patta*
	Buffer	Kardiguda	Yes	Yes	Not known	0	0	Not offered because it is forest land and there is no *patta*
		Putraghati	Yes	Yes	300	300	0	Reason not known, but no amount was offered
Refinery	Core	Analabadi	Yes	Yes	Not known	Not known	0	Reason not known, but no amount was offered
		Ambogam	Yes	Yes	Not known	Not known	0	Reason not known, but no amount was offered
	Buffer	Mujanga	No	0	0	0	0	0
		Marichamal	No	0	0	0	0	0
ARMP	Core	Goudaguda	No	0	0	0	0	0
		Khoraguda	Yes	Yes	Not known	Not known	0	Not offered because it is forest land and there is not *patta*
		Champapodar	Yes	Yes	Not known	Not known	0	Not offered because it is forest land and there is not *patta*
	Buffer	Charangaguda	Yes	0	0	0	0	0

Source: Field Survey (2011).

Table 4.8

Source of Drinking Water

		Surface				*Ground Water*						*Impact of Pollution*		
Area	*Zone*	*Canal*	*Streams & Pond*	*Canal & Stream*	*Total*	*Well*	*Well & Water Supply System*	*Leakage Water from NALCO Pipeline*	*Hand Pump*	*Water Supply from Stream*	*Total*	*Not Polluted*	*Polluted*	*Total*
Mining	Core	.	38 (100)	.	38 (100)								38 (100)	38 (100)
	Buffer	.	.	22 (100)	22 (100)				53 (71.6)	21 (28.4)	74 (100)		74 (100)	74 (100)
Refinery	Core	.	20 (100)	.	20 (100)	20 (9.5)	191 (90.5)				211 (100)	175 (82.9)	36 (17.1)	211 (100)
	Buffer	14 (100)	.	.	14 (100)	20 (22.7)	67 (77.3)				88 (100)	18 (20.5)	70 (79.5)	88 (100)
ARMP	Core	.	.	.	.	22 (55.0)	18 (45.0)				40 (100)	18 (45.0)	22 (55.0)	40 (100)
	Buffer	.	.	.	.	.	.	25 (100)			25 (100)	25 (100)		25 (100)

Source: Field Survey (2011).

preceding discussion that the most vulnerable sections, *viz.*, the ST and SC who have lost lands, houses, and other assets could not get back their livelihood status as a result of NALCO's cash compensation policy. Since land scarcity was not there in the 1980s as it is felt now, NALCO should have adopted a land-for-land policy.

With the emergence of the NALCO mining industry, the occupational profile of the households has changed from predominantly farming to NALCO contract/wage employment. Even though permanent employment in NALCO gives good income in terms of assured salaries, the contract/wage employment and the income accrued from it is far from satisfactory. Further, the households have lost self esteem in the process of displacement as majority of them whose main occupation was farming are now working as contract/wage labour.

In the context of NALCO, before mining in this area, the major economic activity of the people was agriculture. At that time, most of the households from all the villages were having agriculture and *podu* lands—they practiced traditional agriculture such as *podu* cultivation, and their secondary occupation was NTFP (non-timber forest products) collection for both self-consumption and sale. Earlier, all the resources including natural water streams, fish ponds, hillocks, grasing lands, common lands and plenty of forest products were available in this area. However, NALCO acquired the agriculture lands, *podu* lands and other forest lands; and due to mining and refinery, most of the households from the surrounding areas lost their agriculture lands and have been restricted from entering into mining and refinery areas. Due to these changes, the people diverted from the agriculture to non-farm business.

In the mining area, due to the mining activity and the conveyor belt, some of the natural streams got destroyed, while some of the streams were diverted into the mining site. Hence, people from the surrounding villages are facing water shortage. Further, due to the mining activity, the stream water is contaminated; and due to the conveyor belt, the people are also suffering from sound pollution. In the refinery and ARMP areas, the surrounding villages are affected by smoke, caustic water and fluids. Hence, the water is contaminated, the agriculture fields' fertility is affected and crop production has been affected. Further, pollution has also affected the livestock. Hence, NALCO has to take some more preventive measures to reduce air, sound and water pollution.

On the whole, the R&R measures by NALCO are found to be piecemeal and ad hoc. The company with its huge profit base could have done much better for these marginalised people. It was observed that the people of the nearby villages still do not have the basic necessities such as drinking water, schooling, medical facilities, etc. The GoO and NALCO should work in unison to improve these areas possessing a rich mineral resource.

References

Adjei, Emmanuel (2007). "Impact of Mining on Livelihoods of Rural Households. A Case Study of Farmers in the Wassa Mining Region, Ghana". M. Phil. Thesis in Development Studies submitted to Department of Geography, Norwegian University of Science and Technology.

Aroca, Patricio (2001). "Impacts and Development in Local Economies based on Mining: The Case of the Chilean II Region", *Resources Policy* 27(2): 119-34.

Amutabi, Maurice and Mary Lutta-Mukhebi (2001). "Gender and Mining in Kenya: The Case of Mukibira Mines in Vihiga District", *JENdA: A Journal of Culture and African Women Studies* 1(2): 1-23.

Babani, Anoop and Kannan Srinivasan (1981). "Orissa Aluminium Complex", *Economic and Political Weekly* 16(52): 2113.

Bebbington, Anthony, Denise Humphreys Bebbington, Jeffrey Bury, Jeannet Lingan, Juan Pablo Munoz and Martin Scurrah (2008). "Mining and Social Movements: Struggles Over Livelihood and Rural Territorial Development in the Andes", *World Development* 36(12): 2888-905.

Bebbington, A. (1999). "Capitals and Capabilities: A framework for analysing peasant viability, Rural Livelihoods and Poverty", *World Development* 27(12): 2021-44.

Burke, G. (2006). "Women Miners: Here, Now and Then", in K. Lahiri-Dutt and M. Macintyre (eds.), *Women Miners in Developing Countries: Pit Women and Others*. Aldershot: Ashgate.

Bury, Jeffrey (2002). "Livelihoods, Mining and Peasant Protests in the Peruvian Andes", *Journal of Latin American Geography* 1(1): 3-19.

Bury, Jeffrey (2004). "Livelihoods in Transition: Transnational Gold Mining Operations and Local Change in Cajamarca", Peru. *The Geographical Journal* 170(1): 78-91.

Bury, Jeffrey (2005). "Mining Mountains: Neoliberalism, Land Tenure, Livelihoods, and the New Peruvian Mining Industry in Cajamarca", *Environment and Planning* 37(2): 221-39.

Carney, D. (1998). "Implementing a Sustainable Livelihoods Approach", in D Carney (ed.) *Sustainable Rural Livelihoods: What Contribution Can We Make?* London: Department for International Development.

———. (1999). *Approaches to Sustainable Livelihoods for the Poor*. London: Overseas Development Institute.

Chimhowu, Admos and David Hulme (2006). "Livelihood Dynamics in Planned and Spontaneous Resettlement in Zimbabwe: Converging and Vulnerable", *World Development* 34(4): 728-50.

Choudhury, Suryanshu (2007). "Bauxite Reserve in Odisha and its Utilisation", *Odisha Review*. December. 28-31.

Davias, Graham A. and John. E. Tilton (2005). "The Resource Curse", *Natural Resources Forum* 29(3): 233-42.

Dreschler, B. (2001). *Small-scale Mining and Sustainable Development Within the SADC Region*. Report Commissioned by the Mining, Minerals and Sustainable Development Project (MMSD) of the International Institute of Environment and Development (IIED). London.

Economic and Political Weekly (1982). "Erosion of Sixth Plan", *Economic and Political Weekly* 17(6): 173-74.

———. (1986). "Shortage or Surplus?", *Economic and Political Weekly* 21(41): 1771.

Ellis, Frank (1998). "Household Strategies and Rural Livelihood Diversification", *Journal of Development Studies* 35(1): 1-38.

Ellis, Frank (2000). *Rural Livelihoods and Diversity in Developing Countries*. Oxford: Oxford University Press.

Francis, E. (2001). *Making a Living, Changing Livelihoods in Rural Africa*. London: Routledge.

Heemskerk, Marieke (2003). "Self-Employment and Poverty Alleviation: Women's Work in Artisanal Gold Mines", *Human Organisation* 62(1): 62-73.

Himansu Sekhar Patra and Aruna Murthy (2012). "Fact Finding Report of NALCO". Based on the visit to the Refinery Plant of NALCO, Damanjodi & Panchapattamali Bauxite Mines. Available at *http://www.freewebs.com/epgodisha/NALCO%20Report[2]-1.pdf* (Accessed 30/1/2012).

IIED and WBCSD (2002). *Breaking New Ground: Mining, Minerals and Sustainable Development*. London and Sterling, VA: Earthscan Publications Ltd.

Irawan, Silvia (2005). "Cost-Benefit Analysis of Mining in Protected Forest: A Case Study of PT Weda Bay Nickel, Central Halmahera, Indonesia". Unpublished Master Thesis. School of Design and Environment. National University of Singapore.

Khatua, Sanjay and William Stanley (2006). "Ecological Debt: A Case Study from Odisha, India", in Athena K. Peralta (eds.), *Ecological Debt: The Peoples of the South are Creditors. Cases from Ecuador, Mozambique, Brazil and India*. Quezon City, Philippines: World Council of Churches, Trioka Press.

Kitula, A.G.N. (2006). "The Environmental and Socio-Economic Impacts of Mining on Local Livelihoods in Tanzania: A Case Study of Geita District", *Journal of Cleaner Production* 14(3&4): 405-14.

Krishnaswamy, Jagdish, Milind Bunyan, Vishal K. Mehta, Niren Jain and K. Ullas Karanth (2006). "Impact of Iron Ore Mining on Suspended Sediment Response in a Tropical Catchment in Kudremukh Western Ghats", *India Forest Ecology and Management:* 187-98.

Labonne, Beatrice (1996). "Artisanal Mining: An Economic Stepping Stone for Women", *Natural Resources Forum* 20(2): 117-22.

Lahiri-Dutt, Kuntala (2000). "Gender Dimension of Mining", *Mining Environmental Management* 8(5):19-21.

———. (2006). "Mainstreaming Gender in the Mines: Results from an Indonesian Colliery", *Development and Practice* 16(2): 215-21.

Maconachie, Roy and Tony Binns (2007). "'Farming Miners' or 'Mining Farmers'? Diamond Mining and Rural Development in Post-Conflict Sierra Leone", *Journal of Rural Studies* 23(3): 367-80.

Maponga, O. and B. Ruzive (2002). "Tribute Chromite Mining and Environmental Management on the Great Dyke of Zimbabwe", *Natural Resources Forum* 26: 113-26.

McMahon, Gary and Remy Felix (2001). *Large Mines and the Community: Socio-economic and Environmental Effects in Latin America, Canada and Spain*. Canada: International Development Research Centre.

Murray, C. (2002). "Livelihoods Research: Transcending Boundaries of Time and Space", *Journal of Southern African Studies* 38(3): 489-510.

Muthayya, B.C., R.N. Tripathy, M.L. Santhanam and O.N. Srivastava (1982). *Displaced Villagers: A Rehabilitation Plan, A Case Study in Nalco Complex at Damanjodi, Koraput District, Odisha*. Hyderabad: NIRD.

Patra, H. and A. Murthy (2006). *Fact Finding Report on NALCO*. Bhubaneshwar: Vasundhara.

Purevjah, Bolormaa (2010). "Artisanal and Small-Scale Mining: Gender and Sustainable Livelihoods in Mongolia", in Kuntala Lahiri Dutt (ed.), *Gendering the Field: Towards Sustainable Livelihoods for Mining Communities.Asia Pacific Environment*. Monograph 6. Canberra: The Australian National University.

Salim, Emil (eds). (2003). "The World Bank Group and Extractive Industries", Vol. 1 of *Striking a Better Balance: Final Report of the Extractive Industries Review*. Washington D.C.: World Bank.

Samal, K.C. (1996). "NALCO-Induced Transformation: Linkage Effects, Displacement, Rehabilitation and Environmental Pollution", *Working Paper* No. 28. Bhubaneswar. Odisha: Nabakrushna Choudhury Centre for Development Studies.

Scoones, I. (1998). "Sustainable Rural Livelihoods: A Framework for Analysis", *Institute of Development Studies Working Paper* 72. Sussex.

Sinha, Suranjan, Rabindra N. Bhattacharya and Rajasree Banerjee (2007). "Surface Iron Ore Mining in Eastern India and Local Level Sustainability", *Resources Policy* 32(1-2): 57-68.

Srinivasan K., V. Vyasulu and S. Rajagopalan (1981). "The Odisha Aluminium Complex: Points Toward a Debate", *Economic and Political Weekly* 16(49): 2005-14.

Stanley W. (1996). "Machkund, Upper Kolab and NALCO Projects in Koraput District, Odisha", *Economic and Political Weekly* 31(24): 1533-38.

Subrahmanyam, K.V. (1982). "Odisha Aluminium Complex", *Economic and Political Weekly* 17(5):168-72.

Sweeting, Amy Rosenfeld and Andrea P. Clark (2000). "Lightening the Lode: A Guide to Responsible Large-scale Mining", *Conservation International Policy Papers.* Washington DC: Conservation International.

Tallichet, Suzanne E. (1995). "Gendered Relations in the Mines and the Division of Labour Underground", *Gender and Society* 9(6): 697-711.

UNDP (1999). *Sustainable Livelihoods.* New York. Available from *http://undp.org/sl/* (Accessed 20 August 2008).

Venkatesan, R. and William; Wadhwa (2007). *Social Cost Benefit Analysis of the POSCO Steel Project in Odisha.* New Delhi: National Council of Applied Economic Research.

Werthmann, Katja (2009). "Working in a Boom-town: Female Perspectives on Gold-mining in Burkina Faso", *Resources Policy* 34(1-2):18-23.

Yirenkyi, Stephen (2008). *Surface Mining and its Socio-Economic Impacts and Challenges.*

Yakovleva, Natalia (2007). "Perspectives on Female Participation in Artisal and Small-scale Mining: A Case Study of Birim North District of Ghana", *Resources Policy* 32:29-41.

Yao Linqing (2006). "Women in the Mining Industry of Contemporary China", in Kuntala Lahiri-Dutt & Martha Macintyre (eds.), *Women Miners in Developing Countries: Pit Women and Others.* England: Ashgate.

5

R.K. MISHRA, PUNAM SINGH AND SHULAGNA SARKAR

Addressing Social Sector Issues in India

A Collaborative Approach to Corporate Social Responsibility

Introduction

India has witnessed several phases of initiatives for implementation of CSR. After dismantling the 'license *raj*,' government introduced much-needed economic reforms in the country, which marked the beginning of the economic liberalisation and the free market economy in India. The major impact of these reforms has been the increased presence of transactional corporations in the country and transformation of Indian businesses into large global enterprises. In spite of the developmental role of government towards the inclusive growth with initiation of various social upliftment schemes, there has been a growing need for the corporate to supplement the efforts of the government. With the changing scenario, an increased focus on the social role of corporates has become the need of hour.

An area which is grabbing significant attention from corporates, researchers and policy makers in India is the area of CSR. The very reason is its inclusion in the Companies Act, 2013. CSR is a concept whereby companies integrate social and environmental concerns in their business operations through continuous stakeholder engagement. The Indian approach to CSR has undergone a tremendous change from philanthropy and charity to mandatory reporting with the enactment of the Companies Act, 2013. CSR has for the first time been recognised in the Company Act. The latest Companies Act, 2013 reflects on the importance of CSR as part of a firm's business strategy. There is a lot of discussion in the Indian corporate sector about the system and structure of implementation of CSR in the perspective of the Companies Act as it is expected that there will be huge amount of money that will flow in the social sector. In the given situation, CSR should act as a channel to facilitate deeper thought and longer term strategies for addressing some of the country's most persistent social, economic and environmental problems. CSR should be able to create an enabling environment by promoting and facilitating far better connect between businesses and communities.

CSR has been explained by numerous researchers and practitioners in their own way and convenience. Yet, the fulcrum of the practice of CSR in organisations extends corporate obligations to include multiple stakeholders such as shareholders, workers, the community, and the natural environment, and the outcomes of policies and programmes directed toward those relationships (Clarkson, 1995; Donaldson and Preston, 1995). Hopkins (1998) has expressed CSR as being concerned with treating the stakeholders of the firm ethically or in a socially responsible manner. Stakeholders exist both within a firm and outside. Consequently, behaving socially and responsibly will increase the human development of stakeholders both within and outside the organisations. CSR is essentially a way of conducting business responsibly. 'Corporate responsibility' is integral to CSR.

The paper aims to discuss the social sector issues in India and it also intends to discuss the collaborative approach through CSR as a tool for inclusive growth. It highlights the role of government, corporate and the civil society in India in initiating structured format for CSR. The paper also discusses few case studies of PPP (Public-Private Partnership or Public-Public Partnership) mode of CSR as well as highlights some of the issues and provides solution in the area of education, health, sanitation and skill development.

The Social Sector Scenario in India

India has chosen the path of mandatory reporting on CSR as it views CSR as a tool for social inclusiveness. The country is facing enormous social problems which are unique and there is a need for a participative approach to solve these national issues. The Government has tried to do its best through the very objectives of the Eleventh Five Year Plan—fast and sustainable inclusive growth. Yet, we see that the nation is trailing in reaching its Millennium Development Goals (MDGs). The scale of the problem is so huge that it requires a collaborative approach from the Government, corporate and society; working as partners to reach the goal of an inclusive society.

Social sector comprises sub-sectors like education, health and medical care, housing and water supply which are very essential for the economic development of any country. Social development paves the way for economic development. Most of the social sector subjects fall within the purview of the states, for which funding is provided through the Centrally Sponsored Schemes (CSS). The Government plays a very significant part in the development of the social sector. Yet, the performance of India in social sector is far behind other developing and developed nations (Table 5.1 and 5.2).

The MDGs set up by the United Nations were adopted by 189 countries in the UN Millennium Summit held in September 2000; India being one of them. The objectives of the goals are to adopt new measures in the fight against poverty, hunger, illiteracy, gender inequality, diseases and environmental degradation. The challenges for the country in achieving the goals have been translated into time bound targets to be achieved by 2015.

Table 5.1

India's MDG Report Card

	2013	*2012*	*2011*	*2010*	*Undergone a Change of*
India MDG Score	6.0	5.5	4.5	4.5	1.5

Source: Global Monitoring Report, 2013: Rural-Urban Dynamics and the Millennium Development Goals. World Bank report.

Table 5.2

Social Indicators: Present Status of India

Parameter	*Data*
Percentage of population below poverty line (2011-12) (Tendulakar Methodology) (Set up by Planning Commission in 2005, the Committee submitted its report in 2009).	21.9
Prevalence of Severe or Moderate Malnutrition in children of 1-5 years (in %) (*http://www.unicef.org/media/files/nutrition_report_2013.pdf*)	38
Infant Mortality Rate (Sample Registration System [SRS] 2012 report) , Maternal & Child Mortality and Total Fertility Rates (*http://censusindia.gov.in/vital_statistics/SRS_Bulletins/MMR_release_070711.pdf*)	42
Maternal Mortality Rate (SRS 2007-2009) (*http://censusindia.gov.in/vital_statistics/SRS_Bulletins/MMR_release_070711.pdf*)	212
Pupil Teacher Ratio: 2013-14 (Higher Secondary) (DISE-2013-14 report, Schools during 2013-14) (*http://dise.in/Downloads/SEMIS-STRC-2013-14/SEMIS-State_Report_Cards_2013-14.pdf*)	41
Literacy Rate (Census 2011)	74.04
Gross Enrolment Ratio (Secondary education) (DISE-2013-14 report, Schools during 2013-14)	76.64
Male Literacy percentage (Census 2011)	82.14
Female Literacy percentage (Census 2011)	65.46
SC Literacy Rate (Census 2011)	66.1
ST Literacy Rate (Census 2011)	59.0
% Availability of drinking water within the premises (Census 2011)	46.6
% of households with no latrine facility (Census 2011)	53.1
Sex Ratio per 1000 male (Census 2011)	943
Child Sex Ratio (Census 2011)	919
Percentage of Schools with Girls Toilets (Census 2011)	91.23

The Companies Act 2013: Scope of CSR in India

The CSR provisions of the Companies Act, 2013 seek to create an enabling environment by promoting and facilitating far better connect between businesses and communities. They aim at facilitating deeper thought and longer term strategies for addressing some of our most persistent social, economic and environmental problems; they will assist in synergising partnerships between corporates, governments, civil society organisations (CSOs), academic institutions and social entrepreneurs. Business resources can be channeled into a diverse array of programmes to address social, economic and environmental problems, and to bring about a sustainable future for all.

The latest Companies Act, 2013 reflects on the importance of CSR as part of a firms' business strategy. Section 135 of the Companies Act deals with CSR and it is for the first time that CSR is included as part of the Companies Act. Section 135 has mandated CSR for all companies operating in India. Schedule VII of the Companies Act lists out the CSR activities. Section 135(5)–CSR expenditure states that the: Board of every company referred to in sub-section (1), shall ensure that the company spends, in every financial year, at least two per cent of the average net profits of the company made during the three immediately preceding financial years, in pursuance of its CSR policy; Provided that the company shall give preference to the local area and areas around it where it operates, for spending the amount earmarked for CSR activities; Provided further that if the company fails to spend such amount, the Board shall, in its report made under clause (o) of sub-section (3) of section 134, specify the reasons for not spending the amount.

The Schedule VII list is framed with an intention that business resources can be channelled into a diverse array of programmes to address social, economic and environmental problems, and to bring about a sustainable future for all.

CSR implementation post Companies Act, 2013: An estimated 7,500 companies fall into this 'Mandatory' CSR-reporting category. CSR activities in the first year would be between ₹12,000 crore and ₹15,000 crore spent on social welfare. Corporates are now required to adopt the 'Project Mode' to execute their CSR programmes.

An activity will qualify as a Project when it includes the following:

- Duration of project.
- Amount allocated to the project.
- Start date/End date.
- Monitoring and documentation.
- Objective evaluation.
- Impact assessment.

Schedule VII

Activities which may be included by companies in their CSR policies relate to:

1. Eradicating hunger, poverty and malnutrition, promoting preventive health care and sanitation and making available safe drinking water.
2. Promoting education, including special education and employment enhancing vocation skills especially among children, women, elderly, and the differently able and livelihood enhancement projects.
3. Promoting gender equality, empowering women, setting up homes and hostels for women and orphans; setting up old age homes, day care centres and such other facilities for senior citizens and measures for reducing inequalities faced by socially and economically backward groups.
4. Ensuring environmental sustainability, ecological balance, protection of flora and fauna, animal welfare, agro forestry, conservation of natural resources and maintaining quality of soil, air and water.
5. Protection of national heritage, art and culture including restoration of buildings and sites of historical importance and works of art; setting up public libraries; promotion and development of traditional arts and handicrafts.
6. Measures for the benefit of armed forces veterans, war widows and their dependents.
7. Training to promote rural sports, nationally recognised sports, Paralympics sports and Olympic sports.
8. Contribution to the Prime Minister's National Relief Fund or any other fund set up by the Central Government for socio-economic development and relief and welfare of the SCs and the STs, other backward classes, minorities and women.
9. Contributions or funds provided to technology incubators located within academic institutions which are approved by the Central Government.
10. Rural development projects.

Social Inclusiveness: Government Initiatives

The progress towards inclusiveness is more difficult to assess, because inclusiveness is a multidimensional concept. Inclusive growth should result in lower incidence of poverty, broad-based and significant improvement in health outcomes, universal access for children to school, increased access to higher education and improved standards of education, including skill development. It should also be reflected in better opportunities for both wage employment and livelihood, and in improvement in provision of basic amenities like water, electricity, roads, sanitation and housing. Particular attention needs to be paid to the needs of the SC/ST and OBC population. Women and children constitute a group which accounts for 70 per cent of the population and deserves special attention in terms of the reach of relevant schemes in many sectors. Minorities and other excluded groups also need special programmes to bring them into the mainstream. To achieve inclusiveness in all these dimensions requires multiple interventions, and success depends not only on introducing new policies and government programmes, but on institutional and attitudinal changes brought about, which take time. The Eleventh Plan gave a special impetus to several programmes aimed at building rural and urban infrastructure, and providing basic services with the objective of increasing inclusiveness and reducing poverty. Some of these programmes were new, while others augmented existing initiatives. Thirteen such flagship programmes are listed in Table 5.3.

Social Sector Gaps: Some Reflections

Education

There are several schemes of Indian government which attempt to provide easy access to education, uplift and improve the education standards in India. Yet, it has been observed that the literacy rate is only 73 per cent as against the fall in population growth rate of 16.16 per cent (2001 Census) to 1.58 per cent (2011 Census). There is a rising scope for corporate to take up CSR initiatives in the area of education. CSR projects may involve both enhancing the process of accessibility to primary, secondary and higher education or may also

Table 5.3

Flagship Development Programmes in India

(Units in Crore)

S. No.	*Programme*	*Ministry/Department*	*2007-08 Actual Expenditure*	*2011-12 BE*	*Total Eleventh Plan*
1	MGNREGA	Rural Development	12,661	40,000	156,301
2	Indira Awas Yojana (IAY)	Rural Development	3,886	10,000	41,486
3	National Social Assistance Programme (NSAP)	Rural Development	3,104	6,158	23,536
4	Pradhan Mantri Gram Sadak Yojana (PMGSY)	Rural Development	6,500	20,000	65,002
5	NRHM	Health & Family Welfare	10,509	18,115	69,214
6	ICDS	Women & Child Development	5,193	10,000	38,980
7	Mid Day Meal (MDM)	School Education & Literacy	5,832	10,380	38,602
8	Sarva Siksha Abhiyan (SSA)	School Education & Literacy	11,477	21,000	77,576
9	JNNURM	Urban Development	5,508	13,700	48,485
10	Accelerated Irrigation Benefit Programme (AIBP) and other water resources programme	Water Resources	5,446	12,650	46,622
11	Rajiv Gandhi Gramin Viduyati Karan Yojana (RGGVY)	Power	3,913	6,000	25,913

contd...

...contd...

12	Rajiv Gandhi Drinking Water Mission (Rural Drinking Water): NRDWP and Total Sanitation Campaign (TSC)	Drinking Water Supply	7,320	11,000	46,722
13	Rashtriya Krishi Vikas Yojana (RKVY)	Agriculture & Cooperation	1,200	7,811	18,550
		Grand Total	81,217	186,539	691,976

Note: MGNREGA: Mahatma Gandhi National Rural Employment Guarantee Act.

NRHM: National Rural Health Mission

ICDS: Integrated Child Development Services.

JNNURM: Jawaharlal Nehru National Urban Renewal Mission.

Source: *Approach to Twelfth Five Year Plan*, Planning Commission, Government of India (GoI).

include establishing educational infrastructure. CSR projects may also include encouraging performers to avail further education through scholarships and funding.

The Right to Education (RTE) Act, which became operational in 2009, has laid a solid foundation on which we need to build. A major achievement is that most children are now in school. The ASER (Annual Status of Education Report) (2011) shows that for the age group 6–14 years in all of rural India, the percentage of children who are not enrolled in school has dropped from 6.6 per cent in 2005 to 3.5 per cent in 2010. The proportion of girls in the age group 11–14 years who were out of school has also declined from 11.2 per cent in 2005 to 5.9 per cent in 2010. As increasing number of children finish elementary school, there will be a need to expand capacity in secondary and higher secondary schools envisaging universalisation of secondary education. The first step to universalisation of secondary education is the universalisation of elementary education. As more and more students are completing their elementary education, there is a need to expand the accessibility of secondary education in the country.

What Needs to be Done?

- Emphasis on both accessibility and enhancing the quality of education in the country.
- Providing training to teachers and trainers for enhancing quality of teaching.
- Developing updated and comprehensive course curriculum.
- Developing effective teaching methodology for primary, secondary and higher education.
- Conducting awareness programmes for adult literacy and promoting girl child and women literacy.
- Extending and improving the quality of the primary school network, as well as scaling up of secondary schools, operating on a hub and spoke arrangement, so that all villages can have adequate access with quality delivery.

Sanitation

Under the TSC, the Government initiated the Nirmal Gram Puraskars (NGPs) which spurred competition to hasten toilet construction, but it does not appear to have ensured sustained use. UNICEF report 2008 covering 162 NGP *Gram Panchayats (GPs)* in six states shows that only 4.0 per cent of GPs were genuinely open defecation free. In 32.0 per cent of the GPs, more than 40.0 per cent of the people are not using the toilets built for them under TSC.

The problem arises because TSC is becoming increasingly state-led and target-driven, and often implemented without any conscious effort to create required awareness at the community level. The Goverment of India (GoI) has restructured the earlier existing rural Sanitation programme and brought about a huge improvement in the quality of life in the rural areas and accelerated sanitation coverage in rural areas. Yet, studies reveal that more than half the population still does not use toilet which is a major cause of bad health. There is a huge scope for organisations to join hands with government to increase accessibility and awareness of sanitation. Expenditure on drinking water and sanitation in rural areas are critical aspects for better health outcomes. This is one area where the corporate sector can help to make a difference through their CSR initiatives.

What Needs to be Done?

- Conducting awareness programmes for building and usage of individual toilets.
- Studying the existing GoI schemes and identifying the implementation difficulties. Suggest sanitation improvement implementation model.
- Special awareness pertaining to women health and hygiene and the need for toilets at home.
- Toilet in schools and especially separate toilet for girls.

Health

The Eleventh Plan had drawn attention to the fact that India's health outcome indicators continue to be weaker than they should be, at our level of development. The Plan had therefore expressed the necessity of allocating additional resources to health and laid down monitorable targets for parameters relating to infant mortality rate (IMR), maternal mortality rate (MMR), institutionalised delivery, extent of full immunisation, etc. Data on these parameters, available for the first three years of the Eleventh Plan, show some improvement. The IMR fell from 57.0 per cent in 2006 to 50.0 per cent in 2009. The percentage of deliveries in institutions increased from 54.0 per cent in 2006 to 73.0 per cent in 2009, while the MMR came down by 32 points to 212 (2007-2009). In the Eleventh Plan, the total public expenditure on health in India by Centre and the states was less than 1.0 per cent of GDP (gross domestic product) and it needs to be increased to 2.0 or 3.0 per cent.

Organisation for Economic Cooperation and Development (OECD) (2011), shares that the total health spending for India in 2011 is only 3.9 per cent of GDP which is the least among OECD countries. The report also finds that the public sector is the main source of health funding in most OECD countries except few. In India, less than one-third (31%) of health spending was funded by public sources in 2011, well below the average of 72 per cent across OECD countries. In 2011, India had only 0.7 physicians per 1000 population, well below the OECD average of 3.2. There was less than 1.0 nurse per 1000 population in India in 2010, much lower than the average of 8.7 in OECD countries. The IMR in India has fallen greatly over the past two decades, almost halving from 81 deaths per 1000 live births in 1990 to 47.2 deaths in 2011. Nonetheless, it remains much higher than the OECD average of 4.1 deaths per 1000 births. Government has taken necessary awareness campaigns and initiatives, yet there is much that the corporate can do to complement the efforts.

What Needs to be Done?

- Access to safe drinking water and acceptable sanitation standards.
- Widespread testing and provision of nutritional supplements for vulnerable sections, particularly adolescent girls, young mothers and children.

- Strengthening the rural health infrastructure, especially Sub-Centres, primary health centres (PHCs) and community health centre (CHS), which includes adequate staffing and ready availability (preferably 24x7) and better mobile linkages (emergency services) to the hospital network.
- Conducting awareness programmes regarding health and hygiene.
- Conduct awareness programmes for health insurance schemes and studying the scope of having more people-friendly health insurance schemes.
- Ageing population health concerns.

Skill Development and Capacity Building

The 66th round National Sample Survey Organisation (NSSO) survey on Employment (2009-10) reveals that: a) the number of young people in education, and therefore, out of the workforce, has increased dramatically causing a drop in the labour participation rate; b) the total number of young working-age (15-24) people who continued in educational institutions doubled from about 30 million in 2004-05 to over 60 million in 2009-10. The survey also shows that between 2004-05 and 2009-10, the overall labour force expanded by only 11.7 million. This was considerably lower than comparable periods earlier, and can be attributed to the much larger retention of youth in education, and also because of lower labour force participation among working-age women. Over the same period, 18 million job opportunities were created on current daily status (CDS) basis. Thus, in absolute terms, unemployment came down by 6.3 million; and the unemployment rate which had increased from 6.06 per cent in 1993-94 to 7.31 per cent in 1999-2000 and further to 8.28 per cent in 2004-05, came down to 6.60 in 2009-10.

Distress migration is another issue of concern which is common in states like Bihar and Odisha. Inspite of having employment generation schemes, not much progress has been made in generating employment and relief to core areas of India. Continuous emphasis on skill development by stalwarts enforces skill development being the key to generating more employment needs to be part of the existing employment generation schemes. A large effort is required where companies as a part of their CSR conduct skill development and capacity building exercises to involve more and more local people for their operations.

What Needs to be Done?

- Imparting degree/diploma in farm technology and veterinary science (2–3 years programme) for rural youth with 10+2 school education.
- Rural youth with 8–10 years of school education can be imparted other kinds of skills that relate to both farm and non-farm based activities such as equipment maintenance and repair.
- Design skill development and capacity building exercises.
- Design a framework for implementation of skill development and capacity building exercises by corporate
- Setting up of more ITIs (Industrial Training Institutes).

Addressing Social Sector Gap: Collaborative Approach to CSR

There are various existing schemes and flagship programmes of government in the area of health, sanitation, education, sustainability, skill development and capacity building (Refer Table 5.3). In spite of numerous efforts by both central and state government for development, a gap is still existing as communicated by the indicators in Figure 5.1. The existing gap in the development of the nation can be dealt using a collaborative approach of government, business and civil society. A collaborative effort from both government and business will pool in a large amount of funds and efforts to channelise easy access of all facilities to all citizens of India. A hand in hand effort will ensure that the CSR vision of the companies will integrate with the vision of the government (Figure 5.1).

The Role of Government, Corporate and Civil Societies

The international prominence of the initiatives for development can be traced to the objectives of MDGs that established businesses as partners of development. However, realising the corporate sectors' constraints in playing the roles as agents of development, the CSR initiatives need to be implemented with the involvement of the civil societies and government agency to assist community development. The role of corporation in assisting the development of the community has also been recognised in objectives of the MDGs that established the position of corporations as partners in development (WBCSD, 2010). However, there are also critics who say that the corporation alone is unable to assist community development through their CSR project (Frynas, 2005; Fox, 2004).

Figure 5.1

Collaborative Approach to CSR

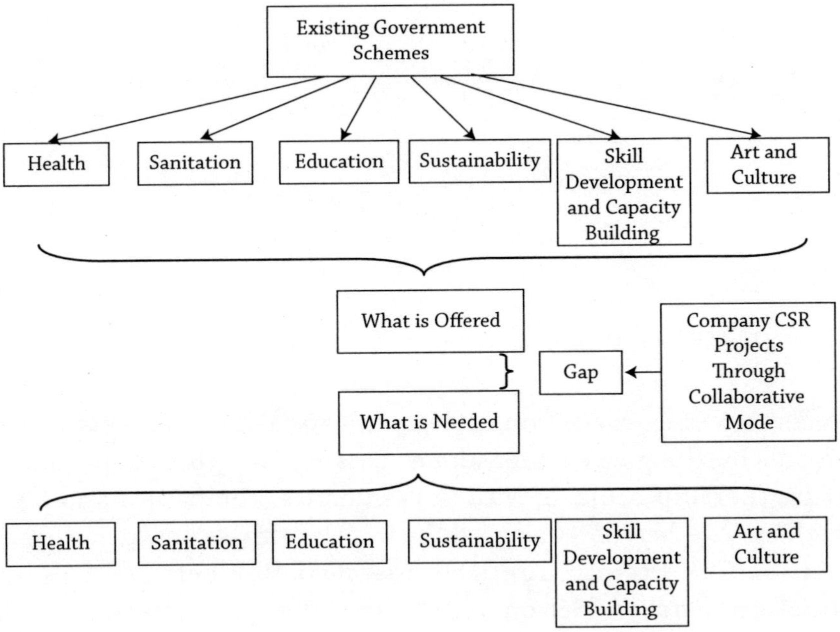

Source: Model Developed by authors.

Figure 5.2

The Role of Government, Corporate and Civil Societies

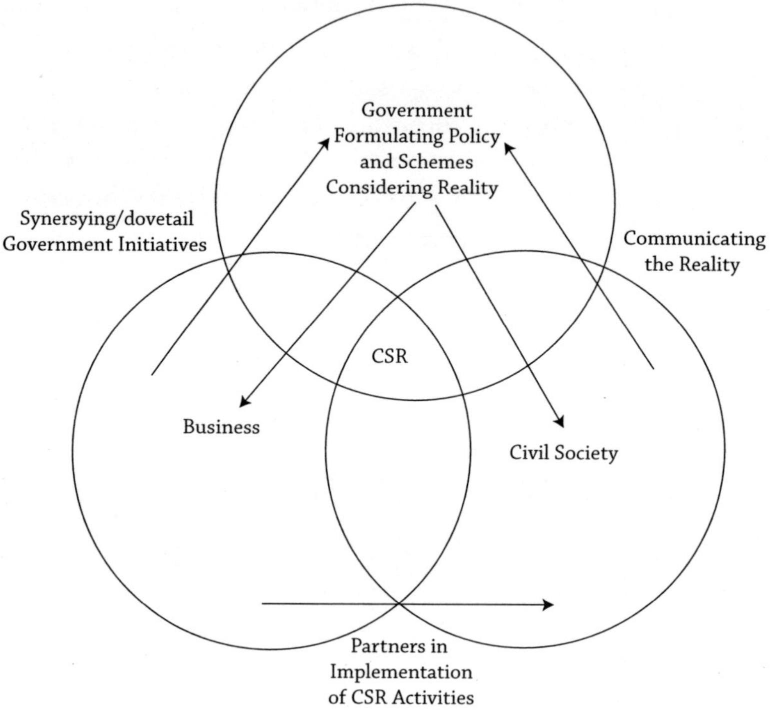

Source: Model Developed by authors.

The crisis at the ground level has made people look for new ways to develop collective action to deal with social demands that cannot be met by the government alone. This has led to the appearance of partnership projects with governments, companies and CSOs working together. CSR has oiled the wheels of these new partnerships and the CSR literature reflects the clear link between CSR and social partnership (Nelson and Zadek, 2000; Gribben *et al.*, 2001; Kjaergaard and Westphalen, 2001). The challenge for governments is to find a way to design and implement public policy that will generate leadership and partnership-based innovation, seeking to maximise the benefits of these innovations by ensuring their systematic acceptance and application among the wider business community.

Role of Government

The two main roles played by the government agency in CSR projects of the corporations are the role of a supporting agency and as leader in the community. These roles have assisted in the implementation of the CSR project with the objectives to develop the community involved. At the macro level discussion, the government sector is expected to play the role as the driver of CSR initiatives by corporations for the benefit of the society (Moon, 2004; Fox *et al.*, 2002).

However at the micro level, the roles are reflected in the implementation strategy which is known among others as public-private partnership (PPP) CSR strategy. The aim of the partnership is to share resources, knowledge and capability between business corporations and the government agency. The government sectors are expected to provide enabling environment to assist and encourage the business corporations to undertake CSR efforts as one of the business strategy in the country. The enabling role played by the government sector would refer to four key roles that are mandating, facilitating, partnering and endorsing (Fox *et al.*, 2002).

The role of government in the development of CSR is centred on its role as mediator, facilitator and partner. The government has a critical role to play in strengthening innovation in ensuring an inclusive growth for which it must enforce on CSR policy formulation based on a reality check.

Role of Corporate

With the prolific number of both public and private sector companies in India, there is a huge fund in flow which needs to be channelised appropriately to reach to the grass–roots level. The role of corporates is to ensure support to the CSOs and also extend an arm to the government for the fulfillment of the vision of developed India.

The corporates are required to envision CSR as a tool for inclusive society and for a sustainable tomorrow. This requires them to formulate a CSR policy in line with their organisational strategy. Corporates need to design CSR projects by understanding the real need of the community and synergise/dovetail the initiatives of the government towards a sustainable inclusive growth. They have to partner with the CSOs to understand the ground realities and with their help develop a successful implementation model with the involvement of the local government.

Role of Civil Society

The term CSOs may be wider in scope and include an array of organisations, including NGOs (non-governmental orgnisations) and not-for-profit organisations. Among others, CSOs include trade unions, religious institutions, academic institutions, ethnic tribal groups as well as different charitable organisations and foundations. Civil society has a crucial role to play in strengthening of local institutions and in bringing innovation into government programmes. The government must strongly encourage partnerships with civil society including not only NGOs, but also academic institutions, professional associations and universities. The precise institutional arrangements could vary, depending on the requirement and context, but the need for such partnership needs to be emphasised in the design of programmes. The relationships could be either in-sourcing or out-sourcing, so that the synergy of the government and civil society can truly be harnessed.

The role of CSO includes awakening of all stakeholders. CSOs have played a critical role in pushing for CSR globally. Campaigning groups have been key drivers of inter-governmental negotiations, ranging from the regulation of hazardous wastes to a global ban on child labour and the elimination of slavery. The CSOs are also expected to be implementers of CSR initiatives of companies in different spheres, particularly related to community issues. CSOs have a critical role in influencing public policy and opinion, and corporate CSR decisions through advocacy, networking, lobbying and public campaigns, thereby shaping and delivering CSR programmes. The grass–roots CSOs usually are required to have deep knowledge about communities and their needs to enable stakeholder engagement and dialogues.

The major factors that CSOs should consider while selecting a company for partnership in a project-based model through a collaborative approach are:

- *Clearly Defined Objectives:* CSOs should pay careful attention to what corporations want to achieve during their initial discussions with them. The corporations' and NGOs' objectives should be well defined; a clear agreement on desired outcomes, their measurement and impact on concerned stakeholders should be established.
- *Long-term Commitment:* CSOs should partner with organisations which have a long-term focus and realise that the benefits from the partnership will accrue over a long period of time, and they should be able to look beyond the immediate gains of a proposed campaign.
- *Mutual Understanding:* CSOs should partner with an organisation which can understand its objectives and goals. Mutual understanding can lead to building realistic expectations and a fair degree of trust.

Case Reflections on CSR through PPP (Public–Public Partnership/Public-Private Partnership) Mode

Azim Premji Foundation (APF)—Partnership with Sarva Shikha Abhiyan (SSA), Karnataka: This project is under implementation in Karnataka in one 135 schools. APF has developed e-learning material (education software) on CDs in different languages including English, Kannada, Hindi and Telugu. The foundation is using solar panels for running of computers in areas without electricity. Rooms and computer hardware have been made available through SSA funds. The Foundation has a computer facilitation scheme, namely, 'Young India Fellow', for innovative use of the computer facilities after/before schools hours for payment of wages to the facilitator.

EDUCOMP—Assam: Educomp has launched an e-learning project for SSA Assam in 500 schools on BOOT (Build, Own, Operate, and Transfer) basis. Computer-aided learning systems through BOOT provides for an integrated package of hardware, customised software and training of teachers. E-learning material has been developed in three different local languages of Assam to meet the requirement of different mediums of instructions in the state.

Case of Rajiv Gandhi Institute of Petroleum Technology (RGIPT): Bharat Petroleum has been associated as one of the founding members along with The Ministry of Petroleum and Natural Gas (MoP & NG), GoI to set up the RGIPT deemed university through an act of Parliament. RGIPT is co-promoted as an energy domain-specific institute by six leading oil public sector units (ONGC, IOCL, OIL, GAIL, BPCL and HPCL) in association with the Oil Industry Development Board (OIDB). The prime objective of the institute is to provide world class education, training and research to roll out efficient human resources to meet the growing requirements of the petroleum and energy sector.

Case of Gandhi Gramin LPG Vitrak Yojana: GAIL is supporting integrated livelihood programmes in villages especially for small and marginal farmers. GAIL along with other oil PSUs is contributing towards provision of liquefied petroleum gas (LPG) connections to below poverty line (BPL) families under Rajiv Gandhi Gramin LPG Vitrak Yojana. This collaborative combined effort of the oil PSUs has made a large impact on the upliftment of weaker sections of the society.

Case of Hindustan PreFab Ltd.: Cloudburst at Leh, India (August, 2010) had caused severe casualties in terms of life and property. Thousands of people were left homeless and basic infrastructure was destroyed. Ten (10) Central Public Sector Enterprises (CPSEs) in India as part of social responsibility took the initiative of relief work at the drastic weather conditions of sub-zero temperature between -10°C to-25°C at Leh. As construction in such environment is not easy, they undertook a PPP model with Hindustan Prefab Ltd. (HPL) to make the constructions possible. HPL qualifies as a specialised agency under Clause 3.3.xi of guidelines on CSR for CPSEs for carrying out CSR projects on behalf of other CPSEs. 170 one-room expandable prefab houses at Solar Colony, Choglamsar, Leh (J&K), have been successfully completed in a record time of 41 days and handed over to the beneficiaries through District Administration, Leh (HPL, CSR Case Study, 2011). Many more such infrastructures like hospital, houses and schools were constructed in record time.

Conclusion

CSR has gained prominence globally and has been discussed as one of the tools for the corporate sector to contribute to the process of developing the community. Discussion about corporates' responsibility to societal cause has grabbed more attention in the context of the Companies Act, 2013, which has made CSR mandatory for the Indian corporate. It cannot be denied that in spite of numerous initiatives of the government, there is a huge gap between what is being done and what needs to be done? In the backdrop of the Companies Act, 2013, CSR in a collaborative form can make a significant impact on addressing the social sector issues in India. This calls for a collaborative approach to CSR through PPP mode. The objectives of this collaborative approach are to share resources, knowledge and capability between business corporations, the government and civil society organisations. The CSR projects that are principally initiated by the business sectors have to be encouraged to be implemented with the involvement of the government to ensure that there is no duplication of initiatives and the initiatives of the corporate complements the effort of the government. The collaborative approach to CSR thus seeks to create an enabling environment by promoting and facilitating far better connect between businesses, government, civil societies and communities by channelising business resources into a diverse array of programmes to address social, economic and environmental problems, and to bring about a sustainable future for all.

References

ASER (2011). *Annual Status of Education Report (Rural) 2010.* Mumbai: Pratham Resource Centre. Retrieved on October 15, 2013 from *http://www.pratham.org/aser08/ASER_2010_report.pdf*

Clarkson, M.B. (1995). "A Stakeholder Framework for Analyzing and Evaluating Corporate Social Responsibility", *Academy of Management Review* 20: 92-117.

Census of India (2011). *Provisional Population Totals: Paper 1 of 2011.* New Delhi: The Registrar General & Census Commissioner, Ministry of Home Affairs, Government of India. Retrieved November 2 , 2012 from *http://censusindia.gov.in/2011-prov-results/prov_results_paper1_india.html*

Donaldson, T. and L.E. Preston (1995). "The Stakeholder Theory of the Corporation: Concepts, Evidence and Implications", *Academy of Management Review* 20(1): 65-91.

Ethical Corporation (n.d.). *UK Ethical Corporation Survey 2009.* Available at: *www.ethicalcorp.com/csr* [Accessed on 23 February 2011]

Fox, T. (2004). "Corporate Social Responsibility and Development: In quest of an Agenda", *Development* 47(3): 29-36. *http://dx.doi.org/10.1057/palgrave.development.*1100064

Fox, T., H. Ward and B. Howard (2002). *Public Sector Roles in Strengthening Corporate Social Responsibility: A Baseline Study.* Washington, DC: World Bank.

Frynas, J. (2005). "The False Developmental Promise of Corporate Social Responsibility: Evidence from Multinational Oil Companies", *International Affairs* 81(3): 581-598. *http://dx.doi.org/10.1111/j.1468-2346.2005.00470.x*

Gribben, C., K. Pinnington and A. Wilson (2001). *Governments as Partners: The Role of the Central Government in Developing New Social Partnerships.* Copenhagen: The Copenhagen Centre.

Hopkins, M. (1998). *A Planetary Bargain: CSR Comes of Age.* Basingstoke: Macmillan.

Hindustan Prefab Ltd. (2011). *CSR Case Study, 2011.* Retrieved on 10 November 2013. *http://www.iica.in/images/2_Sh_Jaiveer_Srivastava_%28Hindustan_Prefab_Ltd%29.pdf*

Kjaergaard, C. and S. Westphalen (2001). *From Collective Bargaining to Social Partnerships: New Roles of the Social Partners in Europe.* Copenhagen: The Copenhagen Centre.

Moon, J. (2004). "Government as a Driver of Corporate Social Responsibility", *ICCSR Research Paper Seriess* (20): 6-7.

Nelson, J. and S. Zadek (2000). *Partnership Alchemy: New Social Partnerships in Europe.* Copenhagen: The Copenhagen Centre.

National Sample Survey Office (NSSO) (n.d.). *Employment and Unemployment Situation in India, 2009-10.* NSS Report No. 537(66/10/1). 66th Round Survey. July 2009-June 2010.

OECD (2011). *Health at a Glance 2011: OECD Indicators.* OECD Publishing. *http:// dx.doi.org/10.1787/health_glance-2011-en*

Planning Commisison (2011.) *Faster, Sustainable and More Inclusive Growth: An Approach to 12th Five Year Plan (2012-17).* New Delhi: Government of India. Retrieved on August 4, 2013 from *http://planningcommission.gov.in/plans/planrel/12appdrft/appraoch_12plan.pdf*

UNICEF (2008) *Impact Assessment of Nirmal Gram Puraskar Awarded Panchayats.* Preapared for UNICEF by TARU. Retrieved on 1 November 2013 from *http://www.indiawaterportal.org/sites/indiawaterportal.org/files/Impact%20Assessment%20of%20Nirmal%20Gram%20Puraskar%20awarded%20panchayats_TARU_2008.pdf*

World Business Council for Sustainable Development (WBCSD). (2010). *Accelerating Progress towards the Millenium Development Goals Through Inclusive Business.* Retrieved October 29, 2012 from *http://www.wbcsd.org*

6

BINOY GOSWAMI

Impact of Social Sector Expenditures by Government on Health and Educational Attainments

An Investigation Across Indian States

Introduction

It is well accepted that private activities guided by market signals are often inadequate for making widespread and equal provision of certain services like basic education and primary health care (Dreze and Saran, 1995). Hence, public provisioning of basic health care and education is an imperative for ensuring mass access to these major ingredients of human development. Governmental effort in these areas consists of two broad dimensions: (a) allocation of fiscal resources, and (b) effective deployment of the allocated resources for ensuring that intended services are actually delivered. Keeping this in mind, the present paper attempts to analyse the trends and patterns of expenditures of the governments (Central and state combined and the expenditures of the state governments separately) in social sector in general and health and education in particular, and their outcome in terms of the health and educational attainments of the states. Accordingly the following issues have been formulated as the specific objectives of the paper.

- To analyse the trends and composition of social sector expenditures[1] by governments (Central and state combined and the states separately).
- To profile the health and educational attainments of the states.

- To explore the correspondence of the health and educational attainments of the states with the efforts that they have put in in terms of social sector expenditures.
- To test if there is any tendency of convergence in health and educational advancements across states of the country.

The paper has been organised into seven sections. Section 2 elaborates on data and methodology. Section 3 analyses the trends and patterns of social sector expenditures in India. Health and educational attainments of the states have been presented in Section 4. Section 5 explores the correspondence of the health and educational attainments of the states with the efforts that they have put in in terms of expenditures in health and education. Section 6 tests if there is convergence in health and educational advancements across states of India. Section 7 ends with a few concluding remarks and discusses the implications of the findings of the paper for policy.

Data and Methodology

Source of Data

The paper is based solely on secondary data. While *Indian Public Finance Statistics* published by Ministry of Finance (MoF), Government of India (GoI) presents data on combined social sector expenditures of the central and state governments, information on social sector expenditures of various states has been collected from *Study of State Finances* published by the Reserve Bank of India (RBI). Data relating to various indicators of health and educational attainments for different states of India have been gathered from various issues of the Census reports, Sample Registration System (SRS), Office of the Registrar General, Ministry of Home Affairs and website of the Ministry of Human Resource Development and Ministry of Health and Family Welfare.

Methodology

The first objective has been fulfilled by analysing data on social sector expenditures. The analysis of the expenditures in the social sector has been done at two levels. First, an analysis of the combined expenditures (Central and state governments together) in the social sector in general and in health and education in particular has been carried out. Secondly, trends in expenditures by the states on health and education over the period of time have been analysed.

In order to fulfill the second objective, data on health and educational attainments of the states have been analysed at two points in time depending on the availability of data. This allows us to compare the performance of the states in terms of the attainments in health and education over the period of time. While literacy rate, gross enrolment ratio (GER) and retention rate are considered as indicators of educational attainment, infant survival rate and life expectancy at birth have been used as indicators of attainment in health. Further, a composite index of the aforementioned indicators has been constructed separately for education and health at two points in time. While constructing the composite index, sub-indices for each of the indicators have been constructed at the first stage by following the formula: actual value–minimum value/maximum value–minimum value. The final value of the composite index has been obtained by taking geometric mean of the sub-indices.

The third objective has been fulfilled by examining the correspondence of the improvement in the indicators of educational and health attainments during the decade of 2001-2011 with per capital expenditures on education and health by the states during the same decade.

The fourth objective requires examining Beta (β) convergence among the states of India in terms of the indicators of educational and health attainment. Beta (β) convergence shows decrease in dispersion of the ith values of a variable over time. The standard process to verify β convergence is to run the following regression (Young *et al.*, 2004):

$$\text{Log}\,(Y_{it}/Y_{i',\,t-1}) = a - \beta \log\,(Y_{i',\,t-1}) + u_{it}$$

Where Y_{it} is the ith values of the variable at time period t and $Y_{i',\,t-1}$ is ith values of the variable at time period t–1. A negative value of β implies a negative correlation between the growth in the variable and the initial value of the variable. Thus, a significant and negative value of β would suggest convergence among the ith observations over time.

In terms of the shares in the social sector expenditure in India, education, health and rural development receive the highest importance (Table 6.2). The expenditure on education as a percentage of GDP after a marginal fall from 2.96 per cent in 1990-91 to 2.66 percent in 2005-06, increased to 3.26 per cent in 2011-12. Though the expenditure on education as a percentage of GDP has shown improvement in recent time, we are however, still at a halfway distance given the goal post of an outlay of 6.0 per cent of GDP on education as aspired by the United Progressive Government's (UPA-I) in the common minimum programme. On the other hand, within the social sector, the share of education declined from 44.08 per cent of the total social sector expenditure in 1990-91 to 39.80 per cent in 2011-12. Again, while expenditure on health as percentage of GDP has remained marginally above 1.0 per cent during the period 1990-91 to 2011-12, the share of health in the total social sector expenditure, however, has been declining steadily. The expenditure on rural development as a percentage of GDP increased from 0.88 per cent to 1.15 per cent during the period 1990-91 to 2009-10 and then declined marginally to 1.11 per cent in 2011-12. The increase in the expenditure on rural development may substantially be attributed to the augmentation in the outlay earmarked for the Mahatma Gandhi National Rural Employment Guarantee Act (MGNREGA). In terms of the share of expenditure on rural development in total social sector expenditure, there have not been much of variations during the period 1990-91 to 2011-12. On the other hand, the expenditure on 'other items'[2] as a percentage of GDP increased from 1.61 per cent in 1990-91 to 2.65 per cent in 2009-10 and then slipped to 2.49 per cent. The share of the other items in total social sector expenditure increased from 23.85 per cent in 1990-91 to 32.90 per cent in 2009-10 and then declined to 30.58 per cent in 2011-12.

Trends in Social Sector Expenditures in General and in Education and Health in Particular at the State Level

Table 6.3 shows the efforts put in the social sector by the states relative to the sizes of their budgets. Among the general category states, economically backward states like Bihar, Madhya Pradesh,

Table 6.3

State-wise Social Sector Expenditure as Percentage to GSDP

State	*1980-85*	*1985-90*	*1990-95*	*1995-2000*	*2000-05*	*2005-10*
Andhra Pradesh (AP)	6.8	8.9	7.1	7.1	6.8	7.9
Bihar	6.1	8.1	8.9	9.5	10.4	13.6
Chhattisgarh	–	–	–	–	7.5	11.2
Goa	–	8.7	9.9	7.3	7.5	7.2
Gujarat	5.3	7.1	6.0	5.7	6.5	5.1
Haryana	4.4	5.5	4.9	5.1	4.5	4.9
Jharkhand	–	–	–	–	10.9	11.9
Karnataka	5.4	7.8	7.3	6.8	6.5	7.4
Kerala	7.6	9.2	7.9	7.8	6.7	5.8
Madhya Pradesh (MP)	5.5	7.9	7.4	7.5	7.5	9.3
Maharashtra	4.9	6.6	5.7	5.3	5.6	5.8
Odisha	7.2	8.5	9.2	9.2	8.0	8.4
Punjab	4.8	5.7	4.7	4.3	4.3	4.4
Rajasthan	6.5	8.7	7.9	7.8	8.6	9.3
Tamil Nadu (TN)	6.4	7.8	7.8	6.7	6.4	6.7
Uttar Pradesh (UP)	4.8	6.5	6.7	6.1	6.4	9.0
West Bengal (WB)	5.6	6.3	6.4	5.9	5.4	5.7
Arunachal Pradesh (ArP)	–	23.6	23.2	23.7	21.8	26.5
Assam	6.5	8.9	8.8	8.4	8.1	10.1
Himachal Pradesh (HP)	11.4	15.1	13.2	13.3	11.1	11.7
Jammu & Kashmir (J&K)	8.8	12.8	15.2	14.1	12.3	16.0
Manipur	17.4	21.1	17.7	18.6	16.2	20.4
Meghalaya	14.0	15.7	15.1	13.9	12.8	15.1
Mizoram	–	30.3	33.4	30.9	27.5	30.3
Nagaland	24.1	29.0	20.5	17.6	13.2	14.7
Sikkim	17.5	27.3	25.3	28.9	27.8	30.4
Tripura	11.2	19.0	19.1	17.8	14.4	30.5
Uttarakhand	–	–	–	–	8.0	10.6

Note: "–" denotes data not available.

Source: *Statistics of School Education, 2011*, Ministry of Human Resource Development, Government of India.

Rajasthan and Uttar Pradesh have been increasingly stepping up their efforts in the social sector as opposed to the relatively richer states like Gujarat, Punjab, Haryana and Goa. The efforts made by these states in terms of devoting the shares of budgets to the social sector have been rather unimpressive relative to the backward states during the period 1980-1985 to 2005-2010. Two other states which have devoted relatively smaller share of GSDP (gross state domestic product) to the social sector are West Bengal and Maharashtra. Again, though the efforts of the states like Andhra Pradesh, Odisha and Karnataka in the social sector have been comparatively higher, they had spent more on social sector during the period 1985-1995 than they are spending now. Among the special category states, except for Assam and Himachal Pradesh, rest of the states has been devoting larger shares of their budgets to the social sector relative to the general category states.

While Table 6.3 gives an impression about the trends in expenditure made by the states in the social sector relative to the sizes of their budgets, it may not reflect the real scenario for the following two reasons. Firstly, the size of the economy/budget of a state may be small and secondly, a higher share of GSDP devoted to the social sector need not necessarily mean a higher level of per capita expenditure if the population size of the state is large. Table 6.4 which shows the state-wise trend in per capita social sector expenditure establishes this point. Although Bihar, Madhya Pradesh and Uttar Pradesh have devoted larger shares of their budgets to the social sector, their efforts in terms of per capita expenditure in the sector have been relatively very less during the period 1980-1985 to 2005-2010.

Among the general category states, per capita social sector expenditure in Goa and Maharashtra have been relatively higher. A few other states which have spent relatively higher amount in per capita terms in the social sector are Andhra Pradesh, Tamil Nadu, Karnataka and Haryana. Kerala is one state where per capita social sector expenditure has been low. However, Kerala's case is a unique one and cannot be compared to other states. Kerala's records in terms of the indicators of human development exceeded those of the other

Table 6.4

State-wise Trend in Per Capita Social Sector Expenditure

State	*1980-1985*	*1985-1990*	*1990-1995*	*1995-2000*	*2000-2005*	*2005-2010*
General Category						
AP	145	308	516	988	1,516	3,155
Bihar	115	258	455	663	761	1,597
Chhattisgarh	–	–	–	–	1,207	3,396
Goa	–	770	1,612	2,745	4,555	7,933
Gujarat	170	364	595	1,115	1,756	2,773
Haryana	156	330	561	1,029	1,473	3,257
Jharkhand	–	–	–	–	1,283	2,756
Karnataka	124	304	565	1,029	1,504	3,081
Kerala	185	367	627	1,301	1,835	2,821
MP	141	330	606	1,038	777	1,252
Maharashtra	161	361	648	1,142	2,537	5,219
Odisha	128	248	459	870	1,134	2,348
Punjab	178	369	568	947	1,429	2,348
Rajasthan	133	290	529	953	1,427	2,472
TN	152	335	668	1,156	1,687	3,219
UP	92	205	373	579	778	1,685
WB	142	258	437	785	1,129	2,066
Mean	**144.43**	**339.8**	**614.6**	**1,089**	**1,576**	**3,022**
Special Category						
ArP	–	1,034	1,857	3,141	4,356	8,294
Assam	134	306	524	802	1,294	2,503
HP	287	636	1,069	2,184	3,374	5,838
J&K	251	558	998	1,575	2,380	4,557
Manipur	341	713	1,015	1,941	2,699	4,965
Meghalaya	298	591	1,059	1,691	2,597	4,689
Mizoram	–	1,435	2,668	4,416	6,369	9,812
Nagaland	574	1,243	1,673	2,251	2,906	4,943
Sikkim	397	1,231	1,869	3,989	6,489	12,526
Tripura	242	671	1,065	1,942	2,996	4,451
Uttarakhand	–	–	–	–	1,745	3,969
Mean	**315.5**	**842**	**1,380**	**2,393**	**3,382**	**6,050**
CV*	**0.554**	**0.650**	**0.635**	**.634**	**.670**	**0.625**

Note: i) *: Coefficient of variations for all states; ii) "–" denotes data not available.

Source: RBI, *Study of State Finances*.

Indian states way back in the 1950s and 1960s (Veron, 2001). This impressive performance of Kerala was possible through appropriate state intervention during the earlier time when the state had spent more in the social sector. Hence, Kerala may not have to spend more now in the social sector since it has the advantage of the higher base level effect. Again, Gujarat, Punjab, West Bengal, Rajasthan, Odisha are the states which have spent less than the average per capita social sector expenditure of the general category states. Among the special category states, except for Assam, all the remaining states have spent higher level of social sector expenditure in per capita terms as compared to the general category states. Within the special category states, Sikkim, Arunachal Pradesh and Mizoram have been spending more in the social sector in per capita terms relative to the other states in the category. Notwithstanding the state-specific reasons, the higher level of average social sector expenditure by the special category states as compared to that of the general category states may to a large extent be attributed to the hilly terrains of the special category states. Due to their peculiar topography, the population density is sparse in the special category states and hence the cost of providing social sector services to the masses in these states is higher (Goswami and Bezbaruah, 2011). It is clear from Table 6.4 that the per capita social sector expenditures in all the states in the general and special categories have increased over time. However, variation in the per capita social sector expenditures among the states has been very high and it has remained higher since 1980.

Tables 6.5 and 6.6 show state-wise expenditure on education and health as a percentage of the total social sector expenditures and GSDP respectively. Among the general category states, Bihar, Jharkhand, Odisha, Rajasthan and Uttar Pradesh had spent more than 3 per cent of their GSDP on education at all the four points of time under consideration during 2000-01 to 2011-12. In fact, in 2011-12, Bihar, Chhattisgarh and Jharkhand had spent around 5 per cent of GSDP on education. Again, except in 2006, West Bengal, Madhya Pradesh and Goa had also devoted more than 3 per cent of GSDP to education over the same period. The efforts of the remaining states in the general category, however, had been far from being impressive.

Table 6.5

State-wise Expenditure on Education as Percentage to Social Sector Expenditures and GSDP

	As % of Social Sector Expenditure				*As % of GSDP*			
State	*2000-01*	*2005-06*	*2009-10*	*2011-12*	*2000-01*	*2005-06*	*2009-10*	*2011-12*
General Category								
AP	37.36	36.04	28.09	35.09	2.86	2.34	1.93	2.80
Bihar	54.23	51.04	43.30	39.71	7.65	5.87	4.73	4.92
Chhattisgarh	25.94	30.32	28.78	36.33	1.13	2.85	3.91	5.38
Goa	45.08	39.81	43.38	45.98	3.95	2.81	3.10	3.91
Gujarat	38.20	39.25	35.94	41.71	4.01	2.09	2.26	–
Haryana	39.46	41.88	39.76	40.19	2.50	2.03	2.65	2.56
Jharkhand	–	34.42	34.84	36.80	–	3.97	4.18	5.23
Karnataka	46.21	41.92	35.09	39.44	3.62	2.80	2.88	3.15
Kerala	50.13	46.63	50.00	50.43	4.12	2.92	2.92	3.26
MP	38.53	31.38	36.93	38.44	3.88	2.70	3.23	–
Maharashtra	60.93	44.48	47.39	47.16	4.29	2.49	2.74	–
Odisha	43.21	42.98	44.39	39.03	4.58	3.15	3.93	3.89
Punjab	47.83	57.07	53.74	48.90	2.74	2.41	2.14	2.89
Rajasthan	45.52	42.89	42.89	41.19	4.52	3.74	3.99	–
TN	45.69	36.86	37.72	37.86	3.37	2.30	2.61	2.80
UP	50.76	45.10	35.38	43.18	3.81	3.51	3.65	4.79
WB	47.50	48.58	43.49	43.99	3.45	2.65	3.26	3.40
Special Category								
ArP	23.79	32.57	36.20	33.09	4.57	7.01	9.83	8.95
Assam	63.28	56.52	44.69	51.52	5.77	4.80	4.96	6.95
HP	46.07	43.12	46.57	52.08	6.52	5.09	6.02	6.40
J&K	42.53	31.10	36.93	44.97	6.06	4.96	6.58	8.29
Manipur	62.15	45.03	36.62	37.29	9.94	8.24	7.58	9.53
Meghalaya	40.89	40.58	40.44	43.70	6.60	4.84	4.88	7.08
Mizoram	41.33	40.24	35.90	42.90	13.45	10.88	11.00	–
Nagaland	43.26	40.56	43.63	43.96	8.08	5.31	5.34	7.38
Sikkim	52.01	44.64	43.06	33.06	15.82	12.87	10.49	–
Tripura	45.95	45.00	42.74	40.38	8.09	5.58	6.56	6.56
Uttarakhand	67.19	47.38	53.43	43.03	1.83	4.89	5.20	4.36

Note: "–" denotes data not available.

Source: Computed from basic data taken from *State Finances : A Study of Budgets*, RBI.

Within the general category, while Uttar Pradesh, Punjab, Jharkhand, Haryana and Chhattisgarh had stepped up expenditure on education out of their budgets during the period 2000-01 to 2011-12, the remaining states showed a declining trend over the same period. On the other hand, in terms of share of education in total social sector expenditure, except for Chhattisgarh and Madhya Pradesh in 2006, all the states within the general category had devoted above 35 per cent of total social sector expenditure to education during 2000-01 and 2011-12. Bihar, Goa, Haryana, Odisha and Rajasthan had earmarked around 40 per cent of social sector expenditure for education. Kerala, Maharashtra, Punjab and West Bengal had spent around or above 45 per cent of social sector expenditure on education. The remaining states had spent relatively less. Again, all the special category states had spent higher percentage of their budgets on education as compared to the general category states. Except Uttarakhand in 2000-01, all the states in this category had spent more than 4 per cent of their GSDP on education. Sikkim, Mizoram, Manipur and Arunachal Pradesh had consistently devoted higher shares of GSDP to education as compared to other states within the special category. On the other hand, as a percentage of social sector expenditure, Assam, Himachal Pradesh, Meghalaya, Nagaland, Tripura and Uttarakhand had allocated above 40 per cent for education over the period 2000-01 to 2011-12. Arunachal Pradesh was the only state which spent relatively very less in this regard. While Assam, Manipur, Sikkim, Tripura and Uttarakhand had shown a declining trend in terms of the allocation of social sector expenditure for education, the remaining states within the special category had shown an increasing trend.

Table 6.6 shows trends in expenditures on health across states in India as a percentage of social sector expenditures and GSDP. All the states, except Chhattisgarh, Haryana, Maharashtra, Tamil Nadu and Uttar Pradesh, spent more than 1 per cent of GSDP. However, in the subsequent time, the efforts on health by all the states but Bihar, Goa, Jharkhand, Uttar Pradesh and Chhattisgarh in the general category declined to less than 1 per cent of GSDP. In fact, states like Haryana, Maharashtra, Punjab and Tamil Nadu had always devoted less than 1 per cent of GSDP to health over the period 2000-01 to 2011-12.

Table 6.6

State-wise Expenditure on Health as Percentage to Social Sector Expenditures and GSDP

State	*As % of Social Sector Expenditure*				*As % of GSDP*			
	2000-01	*2005-06*	*2009-10*	*2011-12*	*2000-01*	*2005-06*	*2009-10*	*2011-12*
General Category								
AP	13.20	11.04	10.96	10.53	1.01	0.72	0.75	0.84
Bihar	13.50	11.72	8.37	9.57	1.90	1.35	0.91	1.18
Chhattisgarh	8.12	7.69	6.83	8.22	0.35	0.72	0.93	1.22
Goa	16.67	15.86	16.31	16.07	1.46	1.12	1.17	1.37
Gujarat	9.55	9.66	9.90	11.14	1.00	0.51	0.62	–
Haryana	8.92	9.69	8.29	8.23	0.56	0.47	0.55	0.52
Jharkhand	–	15.03	9.95	9.96	–	1.74	1.19	1.42
Karnataka	13.32	9.88	9.02	9.92	1.04	0.66	0.74	0.79
Kerala	13.28	13.20	14.29	14.61	1.09	0.83	0.83	0.94
MP	12.06	10.46	9.38	10.12	1.21	0.90	0.82	–
Maharashtra	10.66	9.07	8.19	9.00	0.75	0.51	0.47	–
Odisha	11.41	8.77	9.27	8.08	1.21	0.64	0.82	0.80
Punjab	16.30	17.17	14.10	13.79	0.94	0.73	0.56	0.81
Rajasthan	12.59	10.97	10.84	12.13	1.25	0.96	1.01	–
TN	12.44	11.38	11.91	10.44	0.92	0.71	0.82	0.77
UP	12.08	15.13	12.82	11.17	0.91	1.18	1.32	1.24
West Bengal	15.56	13.83	11.79	10.20	1.13	0.75	0.88	0.79
Special Category								
ArP	18.59	10.20	12.46	13.09	3.57	2.19	3.38	3.54
Assam	11.66	9.24	15.53	11.29	1.06	0.78	1.72	1.52
HP	15.18	14.07	13.71	13.57	2.15	1.66	1.77	1.67
J&K	18.77	15.05	16.99	18.46	2.67	2.40	3.03	3.40
Manipur	14.77	8.77	13.54	18.81	2.36	1.60	2.80	4.81
Meghalaya	13.79	14.40	16.39	14.40	2.23	1.72	1.98	2.33
Mizoram	13.78	10.51	17.11	11.48	4.48	2.84	5.24	–
Nagaland	16.30	15.03	15.06	15.02	3.04	1.97	1.84	2.52
Sikkim	13.55	12.02	12.15	12.84	4.12	3.47	2.96	–
Tripura	9.52	13.82	12.66	13.62	1.68	1.71	1.94	2.21
Uttarakhand	9.69	12.67	9.22	11.11	0.26	1.31	0.90	1.13

Note: "–" denotes data not available.

Source: Computed from basic data taken from *State Finances : A Study of Budgets*, RBI.

On the other hand, as percentage of social sector expenditure, Andhra Pradesh, Goa, Kerala, Punjab, Rajasthan, Tamil Nadu, Uttar Pradesh and West Bengal had allocated more than 10 per cent of the total social sector expenditure for health. It has been observed that except for the states of Chhattisgarh, Gujarat and Kerala, remaining states in the general category had registered a declining trend in the share of health in social sector expenditure over the period 2000-01 to 2011-12. On the other hand, all the special category states (Uttarakhand is an exception) had spent more on health in terms of percentages of their GSDP as compared to the general category states. Among the special category states, Sikkim, Mizoram, Manipur, Jammu & Kashmir and Arunachal Pradesh had spent comparatively more. Again, expenditure on health as a percentage of social sector expenditure in the special category states had been more than 10 per cent except for some points in time in case of some states. Nagaland, Jammu & Kashmir and Meghalaya had continuously spent more on health as a percentage of social sector expenditure relative to the other states in the special category over the period 2000-01 to 2011-12.

Educational and Health Attainments of the Indian States

This section presents the educational and health attainments of the states in India over the period 2001 to 2011. While Table 6.7 shows the achievement of the states in education, Table 6.8 presents health attainments of the states. In terms of literacy rate, all the states improved their performance over the period under consideration. However, scope of further improvement exists for all the states and especially the states of Andhra Pradesh, Arunachal Pradesh, Assam, Bihar, Karnataka, Madhya Pradesh, Rajasthan, Uttar Pradesh and Jammu & Kashmir should work harder in this respect. On the other hand, in case of gross enrolment ratio (GER), except for Assam and Nagaland, GER in all the states increased over the period 2001 to 2011. Bihar, Goa and Uttar Pradesh are the states where the improvement in GER had been spectacular. However, a higher value of GER above 100 need not necessarily mean a better performance. GER above 100 shows either entry of over aged students into a specific class or repetition of classes by the students. Hence, higher values of GER in the north-eastern states are a cause of concern. While improvement in GER is a welcome development, this however, is just the first step. Retaining the enrolled students in the school is the major challenge in which most of the states seem to have a lot to work. Though the retention rate improved in all states except in Assam during the period 2001 to 2011, it was still very low. In states like Meghalaya, the retention rate in the classes I-X was only 22.6 per cent in 2011. Goa, Haryana, Himachal Pradesh, Tamil Nadu and Punjab are the states where the retention rate improved substantially over the period 2001 to 2011.

Again, in terms of the composite index of the indicators of educational attainment, except for Kerala and Himachal Pradesh retaining their first and second position respectively in both 2001 and 2011, the positions of rest of the states changed over the period 2001 to 2011. While the fall in the positions of Assam and Maharashtra had been drastic, improvement in the positions of Arunachal Pradesh, Madhya Pradesh and Uttar Pradesh had been noteworthy.

In so far as attainment in health is concerned, all the states but Mizoram and Meghalaya, recorded improvement in infant survival rate over the period 2001 to 2011 (Table 6.8). In case of life expectancy at birth, the figures of all the states (for which they are available) had improved over the period under consideration. However, there is considerable scope of improvement in both the dimensions for all the states. On the other hand, in terms of the composite index of health attainment, while Kerala retained its first position in both the points in time, the positions of rest of the states had changed.

The indicators of educational and health attainment as shown in Tables 6.7 and 6.8 show the overall performance or achievement of the states in those dimensions over the period 2001 to 2011. However, attainment of all the groups or sections of the population in a state may not be uniform. It may not be uniform across the locations in a state. In other words, some groups of population or some regions may lag behind the rest. This point is

Table 6.7

State-wise Indicators and Composite Index of Educational Attainment

	Indicators							
	Literacy Rate		GER		Retention Rate		Rank of the States as per the CI of Educational Attainment	
States	2001	2011	2001	2011	2001	2011	2001	2011
AP	66.64	75.60	81.87	92.00	29.88	53.80	14	16
ArP	54.34	66.95	100.35	152.00	22.83	38.30	21	14
Assam	63.25	73.18	99.54	84.00	24.39	22.60	16	25
Bihar	47.00	63.82	61.35	102.90	18.70	37.80	25	22
Goa	82.01	87.40	67.99	101.00	57.79	71.90	4	6
Gujarat	69.14	79.31	103.26	107.20	27.78	42.10	13	17
Haryana	67.91	76.64	73.13	90.50	63.49	81.10	5	8
HP	76.48	83.78	91.40	111.00	68.20	84.00	2	2
J&K	55.52	68.74	83.01	104.20	51.06	56.40	10	13
Karnataka	60.47	67.66	98.41	99.30	38.35	56.70	11	15
Kerala	90.86	93.91	91.03	96.20	80.85	-	1	1
MP	63.74	70.63	91.80	122.60	22.12	48.90	19	11
Maharashtra	76.88	82.91	101.05	100.00	47.72	61.80	3	10
Manipur	69.93	79.85	89.60	155.00	46.10	54.70	8	3
Meghalaya	62.56	75.48	95.47	153.60	16.56	22.60	24	20
Mizoram	88.80	91.58	96.28	150.70	28.87	46.30	9	5
Nagaland	66.59	80.11	92.07	85.40	35.06	24.90	12	24
Odisha	63.08	73.45	90.54	104.80	24.95	36.00	18	19
Punjab	69.65	76.68	73.75	103.10	60.33	69.50	6	9
Rajasthan	60.41	67.06	99.06	99.30	24.64	31.50	17	23
Sikkim	68.81	82.20	113.26	123.80	14.67	30.10	22	18
TN	73.45	80.33	95.01	112.00	41.60	74.10	7	4
Tripura	73.19	87.75	91.74	115.40	23.08	41.60	15	12
UP	56.27	69.72	54.91	109.50	36.57	76.00	23	7
WB	68.64	77.08	86.00	90.10	21.48	35.80	20	21

Notes: i) GER is for the classes I-VIII; ii) Retention Rate (RR) is the opposite of dropout rate, i.e., RR=100–dropout rate. The RR has been shown for the classes I-X; iii) CI=composite index[3], refer to Appendix Table A-6.1 for the values of the composite index; iv) "–" denotes data not available.

Source: Literacy rate has been sourced from Census, 2011; the source for GER and dropout rate (i.e., retention rate) is the Ministry of Human Resource Development, Government of India.

Table 6.8

State-wise Indicators and Composite Index of Attainment in Health

States	*Infant Survival Rate*		*Life Expectancy at Birth*		*Rank of the States as per the Values of the CI of Attainment in Health*	
	2001	*2011*	*2004*	*2006-10*	CI_1	CI_2
AP	934	957	64.4	67.4	9	18
ArP	956	968	-	69.9	-	9
Assam	922	945	58.9	62.2	14	25
Bihar	933	956	61.6	66.9	11	20
Goa	964	989	-	69.5	-	4
Gujarat	936	959	64.1	69	10	16
Haryana	931	956	66.2	68.8	6	17
HP	936	962	67	71.5	4	2
J&K	955	959	-	65.9	-	21
Karnataka	942	965	65.3	68.8	7	15
Kerala	984	988	74	74.5	1	1
MP	903	941	58	62.9	16	24
Maharashtra	951	975	67.2	69.5	3	11
Manipur	975	989	-	69.9	-	3
Meghalaya	948	948	-	70	-	14
Mizoram	977	966	-	70	-	10
Nagaland	-	979	-	69.9	-	5
Odisha	902	943	59.6	63.5	15	23
Punjab	946	970	69.4	70	2	7
Rajasthan	917	948	62	67.6	12	19
Sikkim	948	974	-	69.8	-	6
TN	947	978	66.2	69.1	5	12
Tripura	951	971	-	69.9	-	8
UP	915	943	60	64.2	13	22
WB	947	968	64.9	69.5	8	13

Notes: i) Infant Survival Rate (ISR)=1000–Infant Mortality Rate (IMR); ii) CI_1 corresponds to the ISR of 2001 and life expectancy at birth in 2004 and CI_2 corresponds to the ISR of 2011 and projected life expectancy at birth during 2006-2010. Refer to Appendix Table A-6.2 for the values of the composite index; iii) "–" denotes data not available.

Source: The source for IMR is the SRS, Office of the Registrar General, India, Ministry of Home Affairs; the literacy rate for 2004 and the projected literacy rate during 2006-2010 have been sourced from the *Compendium of India's Fertility and Mortality Indicators*, based on SRS and the Register General India. *Report of the Technical Group on Population Projections 2006-10*, Ministry of Health and Family Welfare, Government of India respectively.

explored in Figures 6.1 to 6.5. While Figures 6.1 and 6.2 reflect the gender gap in the indicators of attainment, Figures 6.3 and 6.4 represent the caste dimension of the problem. On the other hand, Figure 6.5 shows the rural-urban divide in the IMRs prevailing in the states. Figure 6.1 shows that except for in Arunachal Pradesh, Meghalaya and Tripura, the IMRs for female are higher than those for males in all the remaining states under consideration in 2011. Again, Figure 6.2 shows that the literacy rates for female are lower than those for male in 2011 in all the states under consideration. Thus, it becomes clear from Figures 6.1 and 6.2 that women are at a disadvantageous position when it comes to the attainments in education and health. On the other hand, Figure 6.3 shows that except for in a few states, the retention rates of students belonging to SC and ST in classes I-X are lower as compared to the overall retention rates in the same class in the remaining states. A similar scenario may be seen in Figure 6.4 which shows that the literacy rates of SC and ST in 2001 are lower as compared to the overall literacy rates in the all but a few states.

The Gender Dimension

Figure 6.1

Gender Gap in Infant Mortality Rate Across States in 2011

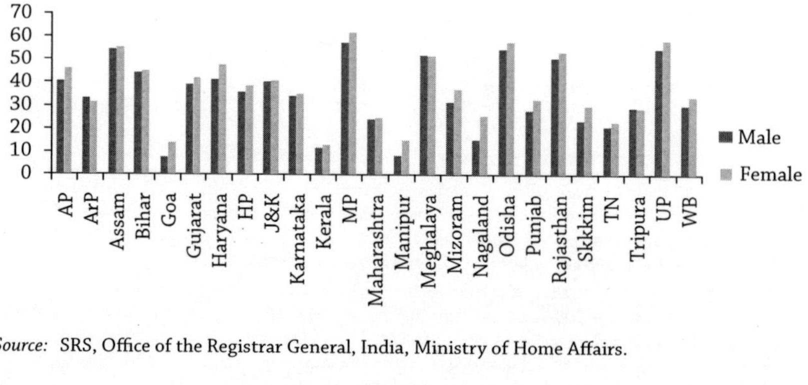

Source: SRS, Office of the Registrar General, India, Ministry of Home Affairs.

Figure 6.2

Gender Gap in Literacy Rate Across States, 2011

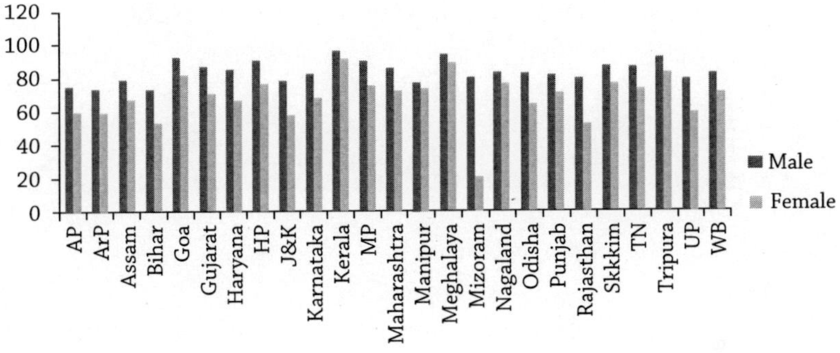

Source: Census of India, 2011.

The Caste Dimension

Figure 6.3

Caste-wise Retention Rate in Classes I-X Across States in 2010-11

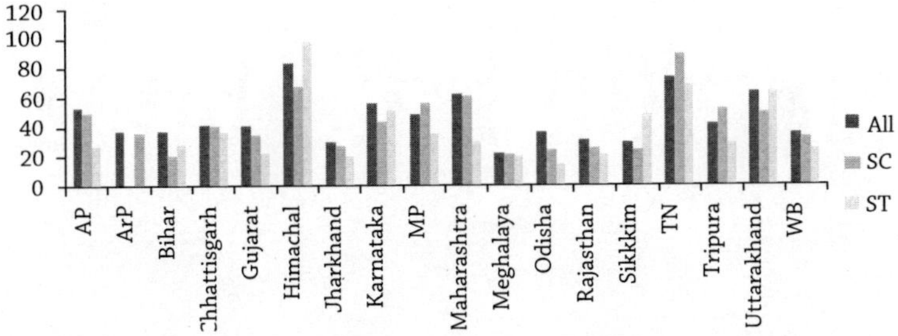

Source: SES 2010-11, Ministry of Human Resource Development, Government of India

Statistics of School Education

Figure 6.4

Caste-wise Literacy Rates Across States in India, 2001

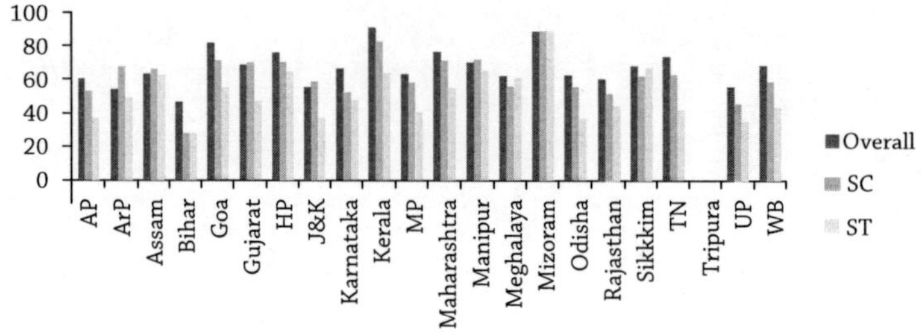

Source: Census of India, 2001 and Department of Secondary and Higher Education, Ministry of Human Resource Development, Government of India.

The Rural-Urban Divide

Figure 6.5

Rural-Urban Gap in Infant Mortality Rate in 2009 Across States of India

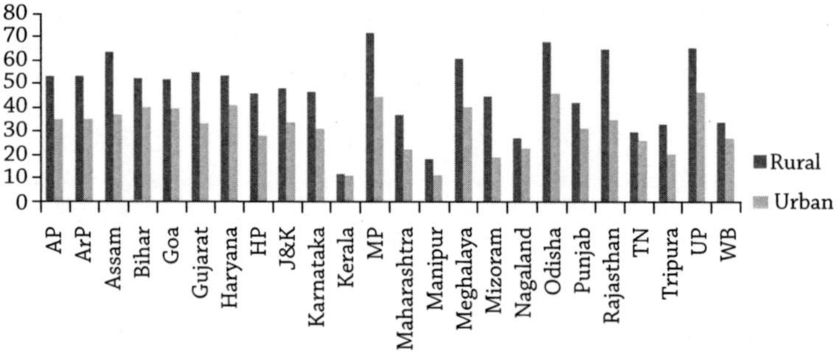

Source: SRS, Office of the Registrar General, India, Ministry of Home Affairs.

Adding the Sources of Disadvantages

Figure 6.5 is representative of the glaring rural-urban divide in the attainment in the social sector. In all the states under consideration, the infant mortality in the rural area is higher than that in the urban area. Only in Goa and Kerala, the rural-urban divide is not very striking. Thus, another source of disadvantage in so far as attainment in the social sector is concerned is space; people living in the rural area are at a relatively disadvantageous position. Thus it transpires from Figures 6.1 to 6.5 that gender, caste and space are the sources of disadvantage in so far as attainment in the social sector is concerned. Now, if these sources of disadvantages are added, the result will be even precarious which is shown in Table 6.9. The literacy rates of the rural women belonging to SC and ST are much lower than the overall literacy rates in the states under consideration. It implies that for certain sections of the population, the attainments in education and health are poor as compared to the overall educational and health attainments of the states.

Table 6.9

Overall Literacy Rate and Literacy Rates of Rural Female SC and ST

State/UTs	*Overall*	*SC*	*ST*
AP	60.47	39.79	24.48
Assam	63.25	54.94	51.04
Bihar	47	14.13	13.3
Goa	82.01	60.34	31.43
Gujarat	69.14	51.17	34.6
HP	76.48	59.44	52.5
J&K	55.52	45.26	23.88
Karnataka	66.64	35.56	33.32
Kerala	90.86	76.39	57.28
MP	63.74	39.44	27.24
Maharashtra	76.88	54.71	39.88
Manipur	70.53	61.38	57.58
Meghalaya	62.56	40.55	53.97
Mizoram	88.8	100	77.71
Odisha	63.08	38.76	22.07
Rajasthan	60.41	31.18	25.22
TN	73.45	48.79	29.48
UP	56.27	28.33	18.34
WB	68.64	44.46	27.88

Source: Census of India, 2001 and Department of Secondary and Higher Education, Ministry of Human Resource Development, Government of India.

Correspondence of Decadal Per Capita Expenditure in Education and Health with Attainments in Outcome Indicators

This section examines the correspondence of social sector expenditures made by the states and their achievements in education and health. The present exercise has been done by using scatter diagram (Figure 6.6). The figure shows the correspondence of decadal per capita expenditure[4] on education and improvement in literacy rates across states in India over the period 2001 to 2011. It is clear from Figure 6.6 that the improvement in the literacy rates in Uttar Pradesh and Bihar had been higher given their relatively lower level of decadal per capita expenditure on education. These two states might have deployed the expenditures effectively which helped the states to improve substantially from a very low level of literacy rate in 2001. However, the general impression that one may have from Figure 6.6 is that the relation between the decadal per capita expenditure on education and improvement in the literacy rate is that of an inverted U type. This implies that the contribution of the incremental expenditure towards improvement in the literacy rate would be more in those states where the literacy rate is lower and relatively less in the states which have already achieved higher level of literacy rate. This is because further improvement after reaching a higher level is difficult. The case of Himachal Pradesh requires an explanation which shows lower level of improvement at a higher level of expenditure. The literacy rate in this state was already relatively higher in 2001. Hence, further improvement by a large margin might not have been accomplished. Besides, the state being a hilly state may require relatively higher level of per capita expenditure for providing the social services.

Figure 6.6

Correspondence of Decadal Per Capita Expenditure on Education and Improvement in the Literacy Rate Across States During 2001-2011

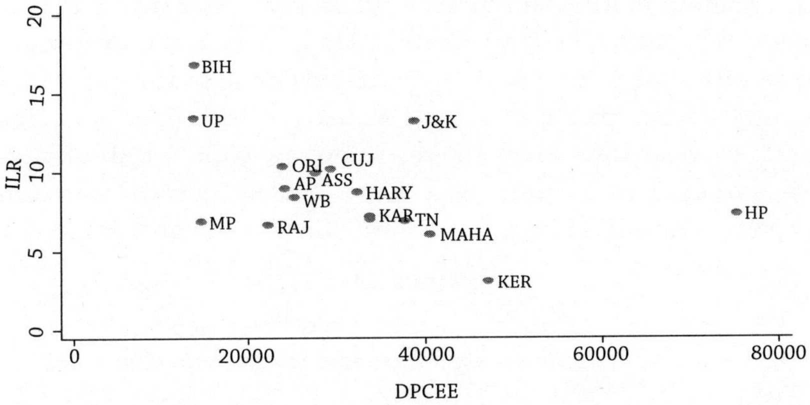

Notes: ILR: Improvement in the Literacy Rate; DPCEE: Decadal Per Capita Expenditure on Education.

Figure 6.7 shows that as in case of the improvement in the literacy rate, the improvement in the retention rate in the relatively backward states like Bihar, Uttar Pradesh and Madhya Pradesh had been spectacular given the lower level of decadal per capita expenditure on education in these states. However, even after such spectacular improvement, the retention rates in Bihar and Madhya Pradesh are still very low and the states have to work harder to improve further. The case of Himachal Pradesh is the same as in the previous instance. Assam's case is a peculiar one showing rather negative improvement at a level of expenditure at which the retention rate in some other states had improved reasonably. Assam's case requires further exploration at the ground level. However, one reason for this lackluster performance in Assam may be that the deployment of expenditure might not be effective. The expenditures by the government may not reach the people for whom they are intended to. Besides other state-specific socio-economic factors may also be responsible for the decrease in the retention rate which requires ground level investigation. Notwithstanding the importance of the state-specific socio-economic factors, the issue of effective deployment of expenditure or governance, however, requires some attention. Except for Kerala, Haryana and Punjab, some other states like Rajasthan, Odisha, West Bengal, J&K and Gujarat had very low retention rates in 2001. These states however, could not improve as much in terms of retention rate over the period 2001 to 2011 as Bihar, Madhya Pradesh and Uttar Pradesh even after spending higher amount relative to the later three states in per capita terms during the decade. This indicates that the deployment of the expenditure may not be very effective in those states. On the other hand, Tamil Nadu is the only state where the retention rate improved substantially corresponding to a relatively higher level of decadal per capita expenditure on education indicating an effective use of the money.

Figure 6.7

Correspondence of Decadal Per Capita Expenditure on Education and Improvement in the Retention Rate Across States During 2001-2011

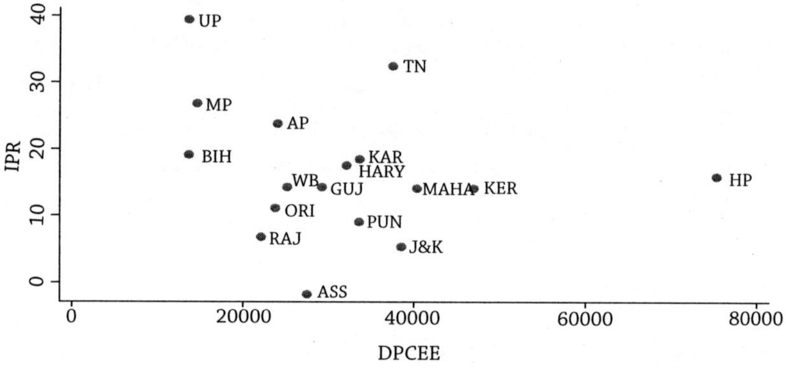

Figure 6.8 shows the correspondence of decadal per capita expenditure on health and improvement in the infant survival rate over the period 2001 to 2011 across states. It shows that the relatively backward states like Bihar, Uttar Pradesh, Rajasthan, Odisha and Madhya Pradesh had performed better given a comparatively lower level of expenditures. The infant survival rates in these states were lower in 2001. In Kerala, the improvement in the infant survival rate was lower even after spending a relatively higher level of decadal per capita expenditure on health. This is because the infant survival rate was already higher in Kerala. The case of J&K requires a mention. The improvement in the infant survival rate had not been noteworthy although the state had spent a relatively higher level of expenditure.

Figure 6.8

Correspondence of Decadal Per Capita Expenditure on Health and Improvement in the Infant Survival Rate Across States During 2001-2011

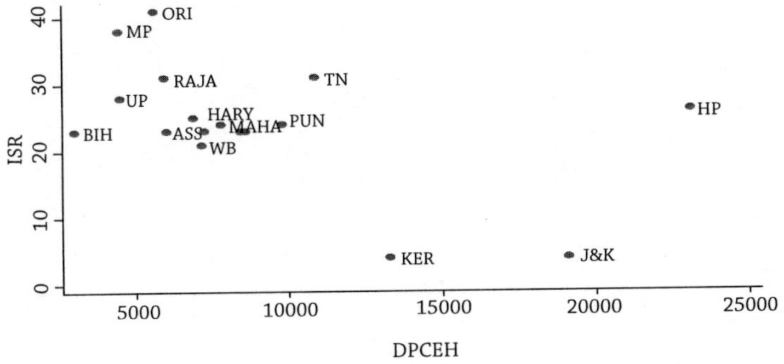

Notes: IISR: Improvement in the Infant Survival Rate, DPCEH: Decadal Per Capita Expenditure on Health.

Figure 6.9 also shows that the improvement in the life expectancy at birth had been more in the relatively backward states of Bihar, Madhya Pradesh, Uttar Pradesh, Rajasthan, West Bengal and Odisha at a relatively lower level of expenditure. Kerala and Punjab, although had spent relatively more, the life expectancy at birth could not be improved much probably because it was already higher in these states.

Thus, the following issues transpire from the above discussion. Firstly, a comparison of the Figures 6.6 and 6.7 with Figures 6.8 and 6.9 reveals that all the states had spent relatively less on health as compared to education in per capita terms during the decade 2001-2011. Thus, there is a scope of augmenting the allocation of money on health. Secondly, mere higher allocation of resources does not automatically pay off; money has to be deployed effectively. In other words, governance in the delivery of social services needs to be improved. Thirdly, it transpires from Figures 6.6 to 6.9 that the marginal returns from expenditures in the relatively backward states are higher. This makes a strong case for increasing the allocation of expenditures in social sector in these states so that these states improve faster and catch up with the rest of the states.

Figure 6.9

Correspondence of Decadal Per Capita Expenditure on Health and Improvement in the Life Expectancy at Birth Across States During 2001-2011

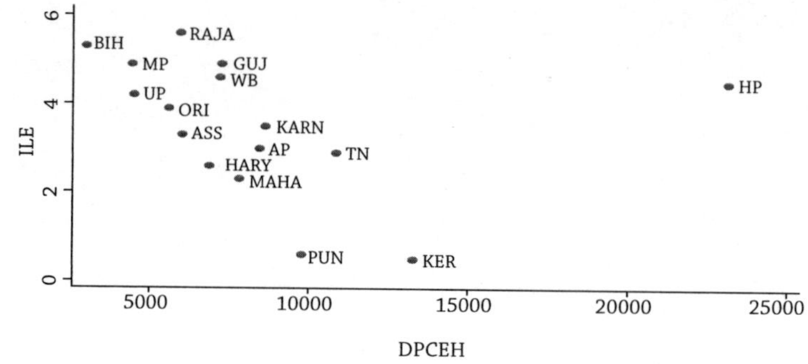

Convergence Across States in Terms of Attainment in Educational and Health Indicators

The results of regression analysis for testing the convergence among the states in terms of the indicators of attainments in education and health have been presented in Table 6.10. Since the data used in the regression analysis are cross-section data, the test for checking the presence of heteroskedasticity has been performed before estimating the equations. The heteroskedasticity consistent robust standard error has been estimated wherever the problem is present.

The results presented in Table 6.10 show strong evidence of convergence among the states in terms of all the five indicators of attainments in education and health. In all five regression models, the independent variables have negative and significant coefficients implying convergence among the states. While, in case of the regression model for testing convergence in retention rate the coefficient of the independent variable is significant at 5 per cent level of significance, in the remaining cases the coefficients of the independent variables are significant at 1 per cent level of significance. Thus, it may be concluded that the relatively backward states are fast catching up with the already better performing states. In other words, improvement in the indicators of educational and health attainments in the backward states have been relatively faster and substantial.

Table 6.10

Results of Regression Analysis for Testing Convergence Among the States in Terms of the Indicators of Educational and Health Attainments

	Results of Convergence Test in Literacy Rate
Variables/Constant	Estimates of the coefficient
LNLR_2001	- 0.36** (0.05)
Constant	1.63** (0.19)
R^2	0.72
	Results of Convergence Test in GER
LNGER_2001	- 0.76** (0.22)
Constant	3.61** (0.96)
R^2	0.35
	Results of Convergence Test in RR
LNRR_2001	- 0.28* (0.10)
Constant	1.34** (0.37)
R^2	0.24
	Results of Convergence Test in Infant Survival Rate
LNISR_2001	- 0.43** [0.08]
Constant	3.00 ** [0.55]
R^2	0.60
	Results of Convergence Test in Life Expectancy at Birth
LNLE_2001	- 0.29 ** (0.07)
Constant	1.25 ** (0.28)
R^2	0.60

Note: ** and * indicate significant at 1 per cent and 5 per cent level of significance respectively.
The independent variables in all the five regression models are the log of the values of the relevant indicators in 2001.
Figures within ( ) and [ ] are the standard errors and the heteroskedasticity consistent robust standard error.

Conclusion with Implications for Policy

The present paper has attempted to analyse the trends and patterns of expenditures of the governments in the social sector in general and health and education in particular, and their outcome in terms of the health and educational attainments of the states. It has been found that the combined social sector expenditures as a percentage of public expenditures and GDP have gone up in recent time. Within the social sector education, health and rural development have continued to receive the majority shares of expenditures. At the state level, except for a few states, most of the states have shown a declining trend in their budget allocations for education and health over the period 2000-01 to 2011-12. Besides, the allocation of expenditures for health has been substantially less as compared to that for education in all the states. Hence, there is a scope for improving the allocation of expenditures for health.

All the states, but one or two in certain dimensions, have improved their records in terms of the indicators of educational and health attainments. However, there exists ample scope for further improvement in all regards in many of the states. Again, the attainments in education and health have not been uniform across castes, gender and space within the states. Thus, certain sections of the population have lagged behind the rest.

It has been found that the correspondence of decadal per capita expenditures on education and health with the attainments in these areas is stronger in the relatively backward states. In other words, the marginal returns from expenditures in the relatively backward states are higher. Hence, the relatively backward states could improve faster and catch up with the rest of the states. This is the reason as to why there is a strong tendency of convergence among the Indian states in all the indicators of educational and health attainments. Thus, it is strongly advocated that the allocation of expenditures in social sector in these states is further stepped up so that these states improve faster and thereby the overall performance of India gets improved. Even within the states, more expenditure should be deployed for improving the conditions of those sections of population, namely women, people belonging to SC and ST and people living in rural areas, which are lagging behind. However, mere increase in the allocation needs not necessarily improve the performance of the states or the conditions of the people at disadvantageous positions. The increased allocation should be utilised effectively. In other words, governance in the delivery of the social services should be streamlined. Ahluwalia's (2010) elucidation even for a relatively developed state like Punjab corroborates this point. However, it is hoped that governance in the delivery of social services will improve in time to come. As Goswami and Bezbaruah (2011) have put it: "With a shift in focus of our social sector policy from a 'government providing approach' to an 'entitlement-based approach' manifested for example in the NREGA and Right to Education Act, it is expected that the delivery mechanism of public services would improve." Strengthening of grass-roots level institutions and application of technology may improve the delivery mechanism significantly.

Notes

1. Expenditures in social sectors include money spent on 'social and community services' and 'rural development' (Dev and Mooij, 2002). Again, social and community services comprise of: (a) education, art and culture, (b) scientific services and research, (c) medical, public heath, water supply and sanitation, (d) family welfare, (e) housing, (f) urban development, (g) broadcasting, (h) labour and employment, (i) relief on account of natural calamities (plan expenditure), (j) social security and welfare (plan expenditure), and (k) others. Expenditures on rural development come under economic services which basically relate to anti-poverty programmes. Both plan and non-plan expenditures incurred on these items have been considered in our study. Expenditure on food subsidy has not been considered as a component of social sector expenditure in our study as it is difficult to identify as to which part of food subsidy goes to the poor and which component benefits the producers of food grain (Mooij and Dev, 2004).
2. Other items include housing, urban development, welfare of Schedule Tribes (STs), Schedule Castes (SCs) and other backward classes (OBCs), labour and labour welfare, social security and welfare, nutrition and relief on account of natural calamities.
3. The maximum and minim values considered for constructing the sub-indices included in the composite index are shown as follows:

Indicators	*Maximum value*	*Minimum value*
Literacy rate	100	0
Gross enrolment ratio (GER)	113. 26 in 2001 and 155 in 2011 (the maximum values of GER among the states)	0
Retention rate	100	0
Infant survival rate	1000	0
Life expectancy at birth	82.3 (as per the new methodology for constructing Human Development Index [HDI])	20

4. This exercise has been done keeping in mind that expenditure incurred today will not produce result immediately. Hence, the expenditures incurred on education and health during the entire decade has been considered. The decadal expenditure on education and health incurred by a state is divided by the average of the sizes of population below the age of 14 in 2001 and 2011 in the state in order to find out the decadal per capita expenditure on education and health. The population below the age of 14 years has been considered because all the indicators of educational and health attainment under consideration correspond to the age group of 0-14.

References

Ahluwalia, Isher Judge (2010). "Social Sector Development: A Perspective from Punjab", in Shankar Acharya and Rakesh Mohan (eds.), *India's Economy: Performance and Challenges.* Oxford University Press. pp.285-327.

Dev S. Mahendra and Jos Mooij (2002). "Social Sector Expenditures in the 1990s: Analysis of Central and State Budgets", *Economic and Political Weekly* 37(9): 853-66.

Dreze, Jean and Mrinalini Saran (1995). "Primary Education and Economic Development in China and India: Overview and Two Case Studies", in K. Basu, P. Pattanaik and K. Suzumura (eds.) *Choice, Welfare and Development*. New Delhi: Oxford University Press. pp.182-241.

Goswami, Binoy and Madhurja Prasad Bezbaruah (2011). "Social Sector Expenditures and their Impact on Human Development: The Indian Experience", *Indian Journal of Human Development* 5(2): 365-85.

Mooij, Jos and S. Mahendra Dev (2004). "Social Sector Priorities: An Analysis of Budgets and Expenditures in India in the 1990s", *Development Policy Review* 22(1): 97-120.

Veron, Rene (2001). "The New Kerala Model: Lessons for Sustainable Development", *World Development* 29(4): 601-17.

Young, Andrew T., Matthew J. Higgins and Daniel Levy (2004). *Sigma-Convergence versus Beta-Convergence: Evidence from U.S. County-Level Data.* Available at *http://www.biu.ac.il/soc/ec/wp/6-03/6-03.pdf Accessed on 5/9/2011*

APPENDICES

Table A-6.1

State-wise Values of the Composite Index of Educational Attainment

	Values of the Composite Index	
States	*2001*	*2011*
Andhra Pradesh	0.524	0.623
Arunachal Pradesh	0.479	0.631
Assam	0.514	0.448
Bihar	0.362	0.543
Goa	0.658	0.743
Gujarat	0.559	0.614
Haryana	0.653	0.713
Himachal Pradesh	0.749	0.796
J&K	0.592	0.639
Karnataka	0.586	0.626
Kerala	0.839	0.806
Madhya Pradesh	0.689	0.649
Maharashtra	0.634	0.691
Manipur	0.444	0.756
Meghalaya	0.602	0.553
Mizoram	0.485	0.744
Nagaland	0.575	0.479
Odisha	0.501	0.563
Punjab	0.649	0.708
Rajasthan	0.507	0.513
Sikkim	0.466	0.582
Tamil Nadu	0.635	0.755
Tripura	0.515	0.648
Uttar Pradesh	0.464	0.721
West Bengal	0.482	0.543

Table A-6.2

State-wise Values of the Composite Index of Attainment in Health

	Values of the Composite Index	
States	CI_1	CI_2
Andhra Pradesh	0.816	0.853
Arunachal Pradesh	-	0.881
Assam	0.759	0.800
Bihar	0.789	0.848
Goa	-	0.886
Gujarat	0.814	0.868
Haryana	0.831	0.865
Himachal Pradesh	0.840	0.892
J&K	-	0.841
Karnataka	0.828	0.869
Kerala	0.924	0.930
Madhya Pradesh	0.742	0.805
Maharashtra	0.849	0.880
Manipur	-	0.890
Meghalaya	-	0.872
Mizoram	-	0.881
Nagaland	-	0.886
Odisha	0.757	0.811
Punjab	0.866	0.882
Rajasthan	0.786	0.851
Sikkim	-	0.882
Tamil Nadu	0.838	0.878
Tripura	-	0.882
Uttar Pradesh	0.766	0.818
West Bengal	0.826	0.877

7

N.J. KURIAN

Equitable and Inclusive Health Care in India

More than six decades of planned development and about seven decades after the Bhore Committee Report,[1] India remains one of the unhealthiest countries in the World. While India accounts for about 16 per cent of the World population, its share of infant mortality and maternal mortality are more than 30 per cent each. Life expectancy at 65 is almost 15 years less than that of developed countries. Half of the Indian women and children are malnourished. Indeed, India's position in the global health scenario is not at all commendable. Latest comparable international data indicate that health indicators of India are behind those of all our neighbours except Pakistan.

Unimpressive overall achievements are not the only problem with the Indian health sector; important issues of health inequity are also there. Four types of disparities/imbalances exist in the country. They are: (i) disparities between regions (IMR [infant mortality rate] in Madhya Pradesh is five times that in Kerala), (ii) Disparity between urban and rural areas (IMR in rural areas is double that in urban areas), (iii) Imbalance between social classes (IMR of SCs [scheduled castes] is 40 per cent higher than that of Others), (iv) Imbalance between genders (except in a few states like Kerala and Mizoram, in most of the states' IMR is significantly higher among girls compared to boys).

There exists serious mismatch between the declared objective of universal health care through public system and public expenditure based on government budget support. Public expenditure of

1. This committee, known as the Health Survey and Development Committee, was appointed in 1943 under the chairmanship of Sir Joseph Bhore. The committee submitted its report in 1946.

1 per cent of GDP on health care in India is one of the lowest among all countries of the world. About 80 per cent of the total health expenditure of 5 per cent of GDP is accounted for by the private sector. Since insurance-paid or employer-paid health care plays only a minor role, most of the private expenditure is borne by the households themselves. Indeed, National Sample Survey Organisation (NSSO) surveys have indicated that one of the major reasons for continuing high level of poverty in the country is the burden of expenditure on health care. Some recent studies have indicated that a sizable section of the poor do not seek medical care in the event of illness on account of lack of paying capacity.

According to the division of responsibilities between the Union and the states in our Constitution, the major responsibility for provision of health care falls on the states. Even after the recent significant step up in Central expenditure through the National Rural Health Mission (NRHM), the states account for about 70 per cent of the total public expenditure on health in our country.

The NRHM is Government of India's flagship programme to provide accessible, affordable and accountable quality health services to the poorest households in the remotest rural areas. It was initiated in 2005 as a seven year Mission with substantial external assistance. As per the mandate of the aid-givers, the NRHM was being reviewed and concurrently evaluated on an annual basis. A Common Review Mission (CRM) undertakes appraisal of the public health system through field visits by a team of public health scholars and practitioners, senior academics and government officials, members of civil society and development partners. It reflects on the implementation of NRHM strategies and policies, and identifies midcourse corrections which may be needed. It also encourages sharing of experiences across the states and across different sections involved in planning and implementation.

The report of the third CRM, the latest available CRM report, is a documentation of the progress of the NRHM in a sample of 17 states. It also identifies the areas that require strengthening of the health systems to meet NRHM goals. Some of the notable findings are: (a) NRHM has succeeded in increasing the share of institutional deliveries across the states, (b) the fresh funds flow under the Mission enabled most of the fund-starved states to improve the infrastructure facilities somewhat, (c) the experience with Accredited Social Health Activist (ASHA) is mixed, (d) on the whole the gap between high performing and low performing states has come down in terms of major health indicators.

The major Millennium Development Goals (MDGs) of India for health sector are reducing MMR (maternal mortality ratio) from 254 to 100 and IMR from 55 to 28 by 2015. However, the latest data available from the Sample Registration Survey (SRS) Bulletin and the information available from CRM reports clearly indicate that India is unlikely to achieve its MDGs.

As a lead up to formulation of Twelfth Five Year Plan Health Policy, the Planning Commission set up a High Level Expert Group (HLEG) with Dr K. Srinath Reddy as chairman. This group was tasked with the formulation of a plan for Universal Health Care (UHC). Five crucial recommendations of HLEG are:

(1) Raise public expenditure on health from the current level of 1.2 per cent of GDP to at least 2.5 per cent by the end of the Twelfth Plan and to at least 3.0 per cent of GDP.
(2) Ensure availability of essential medicines by increasing public spending on drug procurement.
(3) Use of general taxation as the main source of health financing.
(4) Not to involve insurance companies or other private companies in the provision of basic health care.
(5) Reorient health spending significantly on primary health care.

HLEG defined UHC as ensuring equitable access for all citizens, resident in any part of the country, regardless of income level, social status, gender, caste or religion, to affordable, accountable, appropriate health services of assured quality (promotive, preventive, curative and rehabilitative) as well as public health services addressing the wider determinants of health delivered to individuals and populations, with the Government being the guarantor and

significant. Despite the huge public spending, most Americans pay for access to health care via private health insurance plans. These plans offer favourable prices to the wealthy and the young but exclude the poor, the old and the sick. Nearly a sixth of Americans are without any health care protection. The new system under the Obama care: (1) will cover more and cost less, (2) provide basic health care to all, (3) subsidise the poor, (4) will not discriminate against the poor and the sick, (5) the expansion will be financed by tax on the very wealthy and their health plans and (6) it will subject insurance plans to more stringent government regulations. A state run insurance plan is offered as an alternative to private plans.

The Obama care is bitterly opposed by the potential losers *viz.*, the insurance companies, the pharma companies and the very rich for obvious reasons. The medical profession is also not too happy about the Obama care as the fabulous incomes earned by the doctors are also likely to come down under the new set up. Indeed, the very large and fast growing health care industry in the USA is being controlled and exploited by an unholy alliance of these three powerful groups at the cost of the public and the government. The main gainers from the scheme will be the currently excluded *viz.*, the unemployed, the poor, the sick, the old and the other marginalised in the US society.

After the above somewhat detailed discussion of the US health care system, we shall now turn to the Indian system for a closer examination. The problems connected with our health system continue to be politically insignificant and publically invisible. For elections to Union Parliament or the State Assemblies, health care has not been an important campaign platform. Perhaps the only exception was the 2004 Lok Sabha election when the UPA manifesto promised to raise public expenditure on health from less than 1 per cent to 2-3 per cent of GDP. There is little public debate in the country about health care as it is inexpensive to the Indian state. There has been a steady decline in the share of public expenditure in the country. Now the state accounts for less than one-fourth of the total. According to the latest available UN statistics, India is at the bottom of the pile in terms of public share of the GDP spent on health care.

A little bit of digression about the development of India's health care system may be appropriate at this stage. Parallel to the William Beveridge Committee in Britain India, had the Joseph Bhore Committee which came up with somewhat similar recommendations. The result of acceptance of major recommendations of the Committee was the setting up of nationwide health care machinery with reasonable norms in terms of coverage, personnel and institutional linkages. One of the priority recommendations lost on the way was the role of 'Basic Doctors'. An admired aspect of NHS of Britain is that it is relatively inexpensive—below Organisation of Economic Co-operation and Development (OECD) average expenditure. The major factor which contributed to cost-efficiency of NHS is the presence of the general practitioners (GPs) who act as gate keepers to expensive hospital treatment and specialist care. Similar is the case in Scandinavian countries where primary care physicians serve the same purpose. In general most of the European countries and Canada have GPs or primary physicians (PPs) who act as gate keepers for expensive care.

When one looks at the development of Indian health care sector with hindsight one thing is quite clear—doing away with the Licentiates of Medical Practice (LMPs) without an alternate arrangement for producing adequate number of medical practitioners to serve in the rural areas of our country as primary doctors or basic doctors was a big mistake. Whatever was the logic behind that deviation from the Bhore Committee recommendation, the country is still suffering for it. After more than 60 years of planned and unplanned development, the country has failed to provide qualified medical practitioners in its vast countryside. Still talk is on for producing rural doctors on the basis of a shorter medical education programme. However, this is unlikely to work out as rural people are sufficiently empowered to demand parity with urbanites in this respect. The stipulation that newly qualified MBBSs should practice in rural areas for a minimum period before admission to postgraduate programmes has never been taken seriously by the authorities or the medical community. In the meanwhile, majority of the poor in rural areas and urban slums depend on unqualified medical practitioners or the so-called 'quacks' for their health care.

In the initial scheme of things there was one primary health centre (PHC) at the community development block level for a population of 80,000 to 100,000 with two doctors and the needed support staff. Below the PHC level, there was a Sub-Centre for every 5,000 population which was manned by an auxiliary nurse midwife (ANM) supported by a male health worker. Though the Bhore Committee norms were much more generous in terms of coverage and personnel, even the above norms were not fulfilled in many states. The key health person at the village level *viz.,* ANM was never posted in very many villages of the backward states. Same was the case with the male health workers. The main reasons for this non-conformance were inadequate finances and trained personnel. Thus, the two personnel who were to provide the primary health care at the village level and refer the serious cases needing attention of doctors to the PHCs were absent in many villages.

Coming to the PHCs the two doctors who were supposed to be there were not there more often than not. Reasons were several. First of all there were overall shortages of doctors. More importantly even if available and posted to PHCs the doctors did not want to serve in remote areas where there was no electricity, potable water and proper accommodation. It was unrealistic to expect young doctors trained in city medical colleges with all amenities and equipment to go to remote areas unless they were highly motivated to serve the rural poor unmindful of the living conditions. Out of the two doctors at the PHC one was expected to be a female doctor mainly to take care of women's health. However, only rarely lady doctors were posted.

Above the PHCs there were referral hospitals at the *Taluka*/District level in the original scheme. Highly specialised care was expected to be provided at the medical colleges, almost all of which were in the government sector at that time.

Private sector health care providers were always there, playing an important role especially in areas where government outreach was minimal. However, most of them were not-for-profit hospitals and dispensaries run by charitable trusts and religious organisations. Of course, in several parts of the country practitioners of indigenous medicines *viz.*, Ayurveda, Siddha and Unani as well as Homeopathy were filling the gap in the availability of medical care. Besides, hundreds of thousands of 'quacks' have been practicing their kind of medicine which is often a combination of modern medicine and one or more of the indigenous medicines or homeopathy.

From the early 1970s, the central funding for the health sector was stepped up. But the major thrust of central funding was population control through family planning. The salaries of two key functionaries *viz.*, ANMs at the sub-centres and the female doctor at the PHCs as well as the cost of all family planning material and incentives for all concerned came from the central funds. Normally all funding to the states for development activities is time-bound. After the end of a Five Year Plan, the central funding will stop and continuation of the scheme will become the committed liability of the state governments. Central assistance for family planning is one of the rare exceptions where the committed expenditure is treated as plan expenditure and borne by the Centre, plan after plan. A number of states, however, could not benefit much out of this arrangement. For example, in states like Bihar and Odisha there were no ANMs to be posted at PHC sub-centres as there were no ANM training schools in these states.

Family Planning Programme suffered a major setback in the Hindi belt of the country on account of the excesses during the Emergency period in the mid-1970s. The recovery took at least one decade. In the meanwhile the Programme was repackaged and renamed with a more humane and compassionate sounding name: Family Welfare Programme. As part of the reform of the programme, targeting in a narrow sense was done away with. However, some of the erroneous assumptions behind the policy planning remains unresolved. There is enough evidence to show that acceptance of small family norm is significantly positively related to the level of education of the couple, especially that of the mother and negatively related to the level of infant mortality. Therefore investment in human development to increase female literacy and to reduce IMR may be a better policy option rather than current incentive-based approach. A third option advocated by some and practiced in some states is based on disincentives like denial of welfare rights to the third child or denial of democratic rights like holding elected position in *panchayats*, etc. are out right violations of human rights and democratic rights.

In the late 1970s, the Alma Atta Declaration of 'Health for All' by the turn of the century by the World Health Organization (WHO) was a landmark event for the health policy makers across the World. In India the immediate result was a revisit of the existing health policy and a new National Health Policy was brought out in 1982. The salient feature of this policy was to strengthen the health infrastructure in the country across the board. New norms were introduced for the establishment of PHCs and referral hospitals. A PHC was to be provided for every 30,000 population and in every block one of the PHC was to be upgraded to a 25 bedded referral hospital known as Community Health Centre (CHC). These CHCs were to be provided with specialist services and surgical facilities. Central funding to the states for building the needed infrastructure was stepped up. Similarly, additional Central funds were provided to the states to train and employ additional medical and paramedical personnel.

The net result of the above policy thrust was an earnest attempt on the part of several states to strengthen the basic health care infrastructure in the 1980s. However, the progress was quite uneven across the country. On the whole, those states which had already better health infrastructure and which were in a better fiscal position to absorb the Central funds by providing the matching contribution did very well. On the other hand, backward states with backward health infrastructure and shortage of resources did poorly. The net result was a widening of the health facilities between the more developed and less developed states. With the economic reforms in the wake of the fiscal crisis in the early 1990s, there was a severe compression of central funding for social sector and in particular to the health sector. Most of the states also resorted to reduced spending on health services to reduce their fiscal deficit. Almost all the infrastructure development works were stopped. For reducing revenue expenditure and improving revenue deficit, the states typically reduced the budget on drugs and other essential supplies. To reduce the salary bill of the employees the standard practice was not to fill up the posts of retiring staff, however, crucial they may be for the efficient functioning of the system. This neglect of the health care sector continued for a decade and a half till the NRHM was initiated in 2005. Even after the initiation of NRHM, the downward trend in health expenditure has not been reversed in some of the states.

In the meanwhile there has been a great spurt in the private health care sector. Many new initiatives have come up in the private sector, especially in the 'for profit' sub-sector of the private sector. Several corporates entered the field and established world-class hospitals in the metros and even in tier II cities. Significant private investment took place in diagnostic facilities, and medical equipments, fully utilising the tax concessions allowed for such investments. For manning such hospitals and facilities, a very large number of doctors and trained paramedics were drawn from the government sector by offering incentivised remuneration. This fast growth in high quality medical facilities has, no doubt, qualitatively and quantitatively improved the availability of tertiary health care facilities in the cities. Obviously the cost of such health care is quite high. Vast majority of the ordinary citizens are priced out of such facilities. Only the rich and those who are covered by costly insurance can afford their services.

Encouraging private sector 'for-profit' health care facilities and discouraging public sector health care facilities appear to be part of the public policy since the inception of economic reforms in our country. Instead of continuing the efforts to strengthen the public health care machinery initiated in the early 1980s under the National Health Policy, a totally different policy approach was followed since the inception of the economic reform processes. The crux of this policy approach is that private sector will have a dominant role even in the provision of basic health care. The alibi for this is the fiscal constraint and the perceived inefficiency of public sector provisioning of health care. A global survey of health care systems clearly indicates that none of the successful systems is based on market-led primary health care. The only significant example is the US system which is considered a 'failed system' as noted earlier.

Unlike in the US, the vast majority of the workers in India are self-employed. The insurance companies are only cherry-picking by offering insurance cover to well-heeled private sector employees and the very rich. The government's attempt at salvaging the situation by floating an insurance scheme for the poor by sharing the premium payment between the Centre and the states is neither here nor there. This is on account of the facts that the amount of coverage is too small and that the vast majority of the poor remain uncovered under the Scheme even after almost a decade of its starting. More importantly, in the absence of any hospital worth its name within a distance of say 100 kilometres from a remote village, how can a poor villager make use of the benefit of this insurance in an emergency situation. Moreover, the insurance covers only the cost of hospitalisation whereas the major share of health expenditure for the poor is on account of outpatient care.

NRHM is a sort of afterthought to counter the negative effects of the neo-liberal market-based approach to the health sector. As the CRM reports indicate, this programme is only a partial success. More importantly its achievements have been least impressive in regions where improvements are most needed. Another major limitation of NRHM is that it is too narrowly focused on maternal and child health at the cost of other important aspects of health care. After dilly-dallying for years the government finally decided early this year to launch the National Urban Health Mission (NUHM), the counterpart of NRHM. Unfortunately, the neo-liberals in the government had their way and as a result the programme is going to be implemented in the PPP (public-private partership) mode.

As noted at the beginning of this chapter, as a lead up to the formulation of the Twelfth Plan Health Policy, a HLEG was set up by the Planning Commission, Government of India, to formulate a plan for Universal Health Care. Its most important recommendation was 'Not to involve insurance companies or other private agencies in the provision of basic health care'. However, it is a sad fact that the spirit of this recommendation is missing from the Health Chapter of the Twelfth Plan document. The Plan Document covertly and overtly pushes a PPP model even for primary health care. This was done even after the Ministry of Health and the experts in the field expressed strong reservations about this approach.

Having discussed the overall developments in the health care sector so far, we shall now devote the rest of this chapter for highlighting a few specific issues which have important bearing on the future of this sector.

Health Care Financing

As noted earlier the total expenditure on health care in this country is around 5 per cent of the GDP. This figure is comparable to those of most countries at our stage of development. Indeed, some countries like China and Sri Lanka spent less than 5 per cent of their respective GDPs on health care but have achieved significantly higher levels of health indicators than India. The important issue is the division between public and private sectors. There is hardly any country other than India where Government accounts for just about 20 per cent of the total. If we want to improve our key human development/health indicators like life expectancy, infant mortality, maternal mortality etc., there is no way other than increasing the share of public expenditure significantly. The private sector is concerned only about curative health care where they can make their money. Preventive and promotive health care is hardly cared for by the private sector because of the 'public goods' nature of their outcomes. Again, basic health needs of the poor including their curative care are not adequately met by the private sector. As noted earlier, the HLEG for the Twelfth Plan had recommended that these requirements have to be necessarily met from general taxation. A dedicated health cess, as in the case of education, may be the ideal source of financing.

Regional Imbalances

An important concern is the striking regional differences in health attainments and health expenditure across the states. The National Commission on Macroeconomics and Health in its report submitted in 2005 has estimated the additional funds requirements in different states for providing basic health services and associated supportive services like drinking water, sanitation and nutritional requirements. They clearly indicate that the requirements of backward states are vastly higher than that of states which have achieved higher levels of health indicators. Since health services are principally the responsibility of the state governments, the backward states will find it extremely difficult to raise additional funds for meeting this requirement. The 12th Finance Commission had recommended some level of grants to backward states for filling their health sector deficits. Though the grants were not significant compared to the needs it was a good beginning. However, unfortunately the 13th Finance Commission did not think it necessary to repeat it. It is hoped that the 14th Finance Commission which is in the works currently will revisit this important issue.

Medical and Para-medical Personnel

It is well-known that there is a huge gap in India between the need and availability of not only doctors but also of nurses, ANMs and other paramedical personnel. This gap arises partly due to migration of our doctors and nurses to developed countries which offer much higher remuneration. But the main reason for this huge deficit is our poor manpower planning for the health sector. As far as the shortage of doctors is concerned this is partly the creation of the policy makers, especially the allopathic doctors in the Indian Medical Council, Ministry of Health and the Planning Commission. Doctors wanted to ensure that there was shortage so that their market value remained high. The same sentiment ensured that medical education remained costly so that not many medical colleges are established either in the public sector or the private sector. Of late there is a flooding of new medical colleges, mostly in the private sector. But there are two problems with them; they are mostly located in states which have better doctor-population ratio and they are too expensive so that their output-doctors will not be available for serving ordinary people. Since the inception of the modern medical education in India, a fairly high percentage of those passing out have been migrating to developed countries, especially to the UK and the US, so much so that today doctors of Indian origin constitute the largest single contingent after the native born British and Americans in their respective countries. Most of them were the beneficiaries of the highly subsidised medical education in this country. The cost of this brain drain may run into billions of rupees to the Indian exchequer.

Nurses and other paramedical personnel are equally important for effectively running a health care system. Somehow our planners and policy makers failed in training them in adequate numbers. Since training of such personnel is relatively inexpensive, even if trained persons leave the country for better opportunities the social costs are minimal. Indeed, job opportunities for our trained paramedics are likely to increase in the coming decades in view of the increasingly aging population in the developed countries and the increasing need for geriatric care for which physical presence of the care-giver is essential and as such cannot be outsourced to BPOs.

Drug Quality and Pricing

For the very poor who have to shell out a share of their own meager income to buy health care, one of the most burdensome component is the cost of medicines. Often the MRP of branded medicines can be prohibitively expensive. It is well known that there is some kind of unholy alliance between the medical profession and the drug industry which is frequently updated through the visits of medical representatives to the doctors. More often, the relatively inexpensive generic medicines are quite sufficient to treat the illness. Another problem with drugs is their quality. Often the drug stores sell to the unsuspecting patients or their representatives' spurious medicines or outdated medicines which may do more harm than good. This has to be tackled by effective regulatory machinery and inspection mechanism. The former problem of prohibitive drug prices has been effectively solved by the state government of Tamil Nadu through centralised procurement and distribution of essential generic medicines. Apparently the price to be paid is a fraction of the market price and quality is ensured. Several states are in the process of adopting the Tamil Nadu lead.

Social Determinants of Health

It is well recognised that determinants of health are not purely medical. Social and economic factors are equally important. The poor health of people of lower social strata is due to social exclusion, and the steep social gradient is due to the unequal distribution of power, income, goods and services. Caste is inextricably linked to and a proxy for social status in India. The restricted access of those from lower castes to clean water, sanitation, nutrition, housing, education, health care, and employment is due to a toxic combination of poor social policies and programmes, unfair economic arrangement and bad politics. The structural determinants of daily life contribute to the social determinants of health and fuel inequalities between social groups.

Poverty and social exclusion have a multiplicative effect on the social determinants of health, with those at higher risk for diseases also having a higher probability of being excluded from health care facilities and services. The findings of the Commission on Social Determinants of Health (WHO, 2008) are that countries at all levels of income, health and illness follow a social gradient: the lower the socio-economic position, the worse the health indicators. The Commission recommended three principles for action: 1) improving the conditions of daily life; 2) tackling the iniquitous distribution of power, money and resources; and 3) raising the public awareness of issues, measuring the problems and evaluating the actions. Of the three, the second one is most difficult to tackle as is being faced by the present US administration in its efforts to reform the health sector of that country.

Some of the public policy interventions suggested are:

- Providing supplemental nutrition and psychological stimulation to improve the physical and mental growth of underprivileged and stunted children.
- Provision of primary and secondary education and accessible health care universally regardless of the ability to pay.
- Managing urban development with the provision of affordable housing, clean water and sanitation in addition to addressing rural land tenure and livelihoods.

- Provision of fair and continuous employment and a universal public distribution system.
- Establishment and strengthening of universal social protection schemes.
- Continuing the ongoing affirmative action in education and health care for the underprivileged.
- Strengthening the mid-day meal scheme, the Sarva Shiksha Abhiyan, the Right to Education Act, the Food Security Act, and NRHM.
- Taking measures for strengthening gender equity.
- Social and political inclusion of the poor and the marginalised in policy making.

There is an inextricable link between health and human rights. The WHO has strongly argued for rights-based approach to health to overcome the persistence of discrimination and human rights violation in the health sector. Without adequate health/health care, dignified life is impossible. Life with dignity can be ensured only if health care is a fundamental right protected by the Constitution. An amendment to the Constitution to add an Article 21-B enshrining basic health care as a fundamental right is urgently called for.

References

Banerjee, Abhijit, Angus Deaton and Esther Duflo (2004). "Health Care Delivery in Rural Rajasthan", *Economic and Political Weekly* 39(9).

Government of India (1981). *Sixth Five Year Plan, 1980-1985.* New Delhi: Planning Commission.

———. (1985). *Seventh Five Year Plan, 1985-1990.* New Delhi: Planning Commission.

———. (1992). *Eight Five Year Plan, 1992-1997.* New Delhi: Planning Commission.

———. (1997). *Ninth Five Year Plan, 1997-2002.* New Delhi: Planning Commission.

———. (2000). *Mid-term Appraisal of the Ninth Five Year Plan.* New Delhi: Planning Commission.

———. (2001). *National Human Development Report.* New Delhi: Planning Commission.

———. (2002). *Tenth Five Year Plan, 2002-2007.* New Delhi: Planning Commission.

———. (2005). *Mid-term Appraisals of the Tenth Five Year Plan.* New Delhi: Planning Commission.

———.(2007). *Eleventh Five Year Plan, 2007-2012.* New Delhi: Planning Commission.

———.(2007a). *A Comparative Analysis across the NSSO 42nd, 52nd and 60th Rounds.* Ministry of Health and Family Welfare in Collaboration with WHO Country Office for India.

———. (2009a). *Health Accounts of India.* National Health Accounts Cell, Ministry of Health and Family Welfare.

———. (2009b). *Third Common Review Mission Report.* New Delhi: Ministry of Health and Family Welfare.

———.(2010). *Mid-term Appraisal of the Eleventh Five Year Plan.* New Delhi: Planning Commission.

———. (2011a). *National Human Development Report*. New Delhi: Institute of Applied Manpower Research.

———. (2011b). *High Level Expert Group (HLEG) Report.* Planning Commission, New Delhi.

———. (2012). *Twelfth Five Year Plan, 2012-2017*. New Delhi: Planning Commission.

———. (2013). *Economic Survey, 2012-13.* New Delhi: Ministry of Finance.

———. (various dates). *Sample Registration System Bulletin* (various issues). New Delhi: Census Commissioner and Registrar General of India.

International Institute of Population Sciences (n.d.). *National Family Health Survey-III (2005-06).* Mumbai.

Kurian, N.J. (2010a). "Issues of Health and Equity in India", *India Social Development Report 2010.* OUP and Council for Social Development.

———. (2010b). "Financing Health Care in India", *The Hindu*, January 16.

Shariff, Abusaleh (1999). *India–Human Development Report: A profile of Indian States in the 1990s.* New Delhi: Oxford University Press.

Sinha, Amarjeet (2010). "Crafting a Credible Public System for Health and Nutrition for All", Theme Paper presented at the *International Consultation on Human Development in India.* Organised by Institute of Human Development at New Delhi during February 5-6.

UNDP (2011). *Human Development Report*. New Delhi: Oxford University Press.

WHO (2008). *The Final Report of the Commission on Social Determinants of Health.* Switzerland: WHO Press, World Health Organization.

8

S. GALAB AND P. PRUDHVIKAR REDDY

Patterns and Determinants of Transition in Stunting Among Younger Children in Andhra Pradesh

An Analysis Based on Longitudinal Data

Introduction

A brief review of some of the important studies on the patterns and determinants of nutrition has unfolded many concerns. The prevalence of child malnutrition in India is among the highest in the world. Levels of malnutrition among children below three years remain unacceptably high. In 2005-06, 46 per cent of children below three years of age were underweight, 38 per cent were stunted and 19 per cent were wasted. Progress in reducing undernourishment among children over the past seven years—between 1998-99 (corresponding to NFHS-2) and 2005-06 (corresponding to NFHS[1]-3)—has been poor (Shiva Kumar, 2007). Improvements in nutritional status have not kept pace with the reduction in poverty (Radhakrishna and Ravi, 2004). Further, the reductions lagged far behind that achieved by other countries with similar economic growth rates. Malnutrition got concentrated in a few geographical locations and among specific social groups. At the all-India level, the high levels of child malnutrition can be explained in part by the limited access to and reach of health services, and the poor feeding habits largely responsible for the onset of malnutrition in the early stages of a child's life. The incidence of child malnutrition is particularly high among poor households where

1. NFHS: National Family Health Survey.

Figure 8.1

Conceptual Framework Understanding Causes of Malnutrition

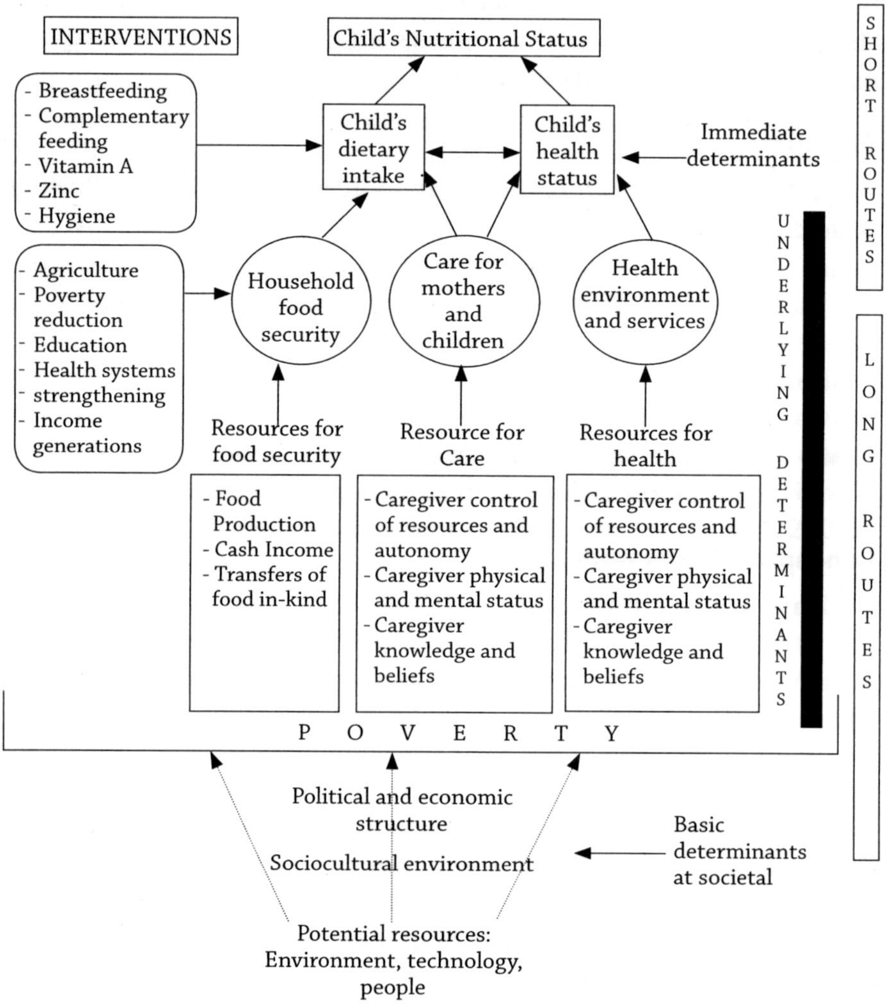

Sources: Ruel, 2008; Engle *et al.*, 1999.

are three main underlying causes, *viz.*, inadequate access to food and or/poor use of available food; inadequate child care practices; and poor water and sanitation and inadequate health services. These underlying causes interact with each other. The other household characteristics considered are the age of the mother and height of the mother. These represent biological production function. They are in turn influenced by root causes that reach down deep into the political, economic, cultural and religious systems and institutional structures that govern society. They control the amount and use of potential human, economic and organisational resources available at the household level; and determine the status and autonomy of women; and the degree of social justice in society (Pridmore and Hill, 2009). In order to capture the status and autonomy of the women, education and working status of mother, the awareness of mothers regarding reservation for women, Dalits and tribes in the local governance structures participation in public domain (community institutions and participation in decision-making at household level (private domain) are to be considered. All the characteristics are considered as household level factors. These are specified by Hi in the theoretical model presented in the next section. In order to account for the community factors that may also include structural factors at cutting edge level, sentinel site dummies are introduced into theoretical model as indicated in the next section. These dummies are indicated by Ki in the model.

Theoretical Framework

Studies of determinants of children's nutritional status can be located in the economic models of household behaviour, which have their roots in both the model of household production and in the farm household model. The idea in both sets of model is that the household allocates time and goods to produce commodities, some of which are sold on the market, and some of which are consumed at home and for some, no market exists at all. According to this, the households face preferences that can be characterised by the utility function U which depends on consumption of a vector of commodities, X, and a vector of leisure, L:

$$U=u(X,L) \quad (1)$$

The production function for the consumption goods depends on a vector of household input supplies. The household chooses the optimal consumption bundle, given this production function and a budget constraint, which states that at given market prices and wages, total consumption including the value of time spent in leisure activities cannot exceed full income. This household model can be modified to include human capital outcomes by relaxing the assumption of perfect substitutability between home produced and market goods. This is due to the fact that most human capital outcomes cannot be purchased in the market and the household production framework also lends itself to the integration of biological, demographic and economic considerations.

Child nutrition can be thought of as being generated by a biological production function (age of mother, height of mother, gender of children, birth order of children and age of children) in which a number of input allocations such as nutrient intake and general care result from household decisions. Households therefore choose to maximise child nutrition, given the resources and information constraints they face. In order to model child nutrition, equation (1) can be modified to include supply of child growth (*N*), by assuming that good nutritional status is desirable in its own right and that households make consumption decisions. Equation (1) can therefore be adapted to obtain:

$$U=u(X,L,N) \quad (2)$$

The corresponding budget constraint can also be tailored to include inputs into a child health production function and the resulting constrained utility function solved for the optimal quantities of child nutrition supplied to the market. The reduced form nutritional production function allows us to estimate the following equation for each child:

$$Ni = N(C_i, H_j, K_l, U_k) \quad (3)$$

Where Ci are child characteristics, such as age, sex, and the relation to the parents; H_j are household characteristics, such as household demographics, parental education levels, household resources, and the availability of sanitation and sewerage facilities; K_l

are community characteristics, such as the accessibility and quality of health services and relative food prices; and U_k is a random error term that represents the unobservable individual, family, and community characteristics that affect the child's nutritional outcomes and is assumed to be uncorrelated with the x variables (for details refer Strauss and Thomas, 1995; Behrman and Deolalikar, 1988; Kabubo *et al.*, 2009).

Empirical Model Specification

There was a stream of theoretical literature on child development in economics that treats childhood as a single period. The implicit assumption of this approach is that inputs into the production of skills at different stages of childhood are perfect substitutes. There is evidence that treats childhood as multiple periods. In order to account for a large body of this evidence, it is important to build a model of skill formation with multiple stages of childhood, where inputs at different stages are complements and where there is self-productivity of investment (higher skills leading to higher skill accumulation) but also can model 'critical periods'. Shortfalls in skill investments at critical stages of development might lead to permanent reductions in the skill accumulation growth path (Cunha and Heckman, 2007). It has been documented that the children who experience malnutrition during the first two years of childhood continue to suffer from malnutrition. Hence, the investment in nutrition during the first two years of early childhood is highly critical period in childhood development. Hence, we follow the basic approach of Cunha and Heckman in the specification of the model. Therefore, the nutritional status of the children who have grown five year old in round 2 from one year old in round 1 can be specified as follows:

$$N_t = F_t\,(N_{t-1}, I_t) \qquad (4)$$

N_t is the nutritional status at the five year old children, N_{t-1} is the nutrition status of the same children when they were one year old, and I_t is the investment made between the two rounds. We are interested in analysing the investment behaviour of the household on nutrition during the childhood of one year to five year old. Hence, we include the variables that reflect investment on nutrition in the round 1 rather than the nutritional status in round 1 in our model. Therefore, in our model specification, we explain child nutrition/malnutrition (N_{it}) for child *i* at the age of five year with the investments from the earlier round when the child was one year old as well as the investment made in the second round when the child was five year old and investment made between the periods. The investment made in the earlier round is captured through a vector of variables (Xi_{t-1}) that reflect the investment in the earlier period. Similarly, the investment made up to the age of five year old from the earlier period is captured through a vector of variables (X_{it}) that reflect the investment there on. The model can thus be specified as follows:

$$Y_{it} = aX_{it} + bX_{it-1} + U_{it} \quad (5)$$

Y_{it} is the Z score of HAZ (height for age) of i_{th} child in t_{th} period. The X_{it} and X_{it-1} relate to the investments of children and household characteristics in the t and t-1 periods.

$U_{it} = U_i + H_h + E_{it}$,

Where U_i is the effect of unobserved characteristics of the children.

H_h is the effect of unobserved characteristics of the households.

E_{it} is the effect of observed and unobserved characteristics of the sentinel sites dummies.

We control the observed and unobserved effect of the communities by including the sentinel sites dummies in the model (5). Model (5) can then be specified as follows:

$$Y_{it} = aX_{it} + bX_{it-1} + \sum_{j=1}^{20} C_j d_j + \epsilon_{it} \quad (6)$$

d_j is the dummy of the j_{th} sentinel site; C_j refers to coefficient of dummy variable d_j and ϵ_{it} is the error term.

Then the other question is whether the government programmes, like NREGS and school feeding programme have contributed to the decline in the stunting of the children. The programme dummies are included in the above model to capture this. The final model is then as follows:

$$Y_{it} = aX_{it} + bX_{it-1} + \sum C_j d_j + \sum K_l d_l + \sum_{it} \quad (7)$$

This model has been estimated by ordinary least squares (OLS) method to identify determinants of round 2 HAZ. The determinants of the persistent stunting of child i is identified through the estimation of model (7) by replicating the z score of HAZ where Y_i takes value 1 if the child i is stunted in both the rounds and 0 if the child i was not stunted in both the rounds. The determinants of what moves a child i from being stunted through the estimation of model (7) by replacing the z score of HAZ by Y_i takes value 1 if the child i was stunted in round 1 but not so in round 2 and 0 if the child i is stunted in both the rounds. Similarly, the determinants of what moves a child i into being stunted through the estimation of model (7) by replacing the z score of HAZ by Y_i takes value 1 if the child i was stunted in round 2 but not so in round 1 and 0 if the child i is not stunted in both the rounds. All these models are estimated by probit regression (for the details on the similar methodology for the probit models see Himaz, 2009).

Database

This paper draws data from a unique panel survey of 2014 children, their communities and households conducted in 2002 and 2006 of the Young Lives project coordinated by the University of Oxford. The survey was carried out across 20 sentinel sites in the three regions of Andhra Pradesh. The children were aged one to one and half year age in 2002 (Round 1) and four and half to five and half at Round 2 (for details refer Galab *et al.*, 2008). The details of the data used from the Young Lives project in the analysis are as follows:

The children of younger cohort have been grouped into two categories, *viz.*, normal and stunted children on the basis of the z-scores in the second round. The children are further classified on the basis of z-scores in the first and in the second round into four categories namely, children who are normal in both the rounds; stunted in both the rounds (persistently stunted); stunted in the first round and normal in the second round (moving out); and normal in the first round and stunted in the second round (moving in).

According to the conceptual framework for understanding the determinants of nutrition of children, immediate factors that influence nutrition of children are diet consumed by the children and health status of the children. These factors themselves are interdependent. A child with inadequate dietary intake is more susceptible to disease. In turn, disease depresses appetite and inhibits the absorption of nutrients in food components for a child's energy. Dietary intake must be adequate in quantity and in quality, and nutrients must be consumed in appropriate combinations for the human body to be able to absorb them. We don't have the data on the quantity of the diet consumed by the children. But, we have the data on the different food items consumed by children in last 24 hours preceding the day of survey from the mothers in the round 2. As the combination of dietary intake is equally important, a diet diversity score has been worked on the basis of the items consumed by the children. We do have data on the status of health of the children in both the rounds. We have assumed that the health status in round 1 will have influence on the health status in round 2. We have data on the incidence of ill-health of the children in the last 24 hours proceeding the day of survey and also on the long term ill-health problems collected from mothers in round 1. A score of ill health has been constructed on the basis of the incidence of ill-health in the last 24 hours. Thus the data from both the rounds have been used to capture the immediate factors that influence the nutritional status of the children. The less diverse diet and high ill-health status of the children increase the malnutrition of the children. The descriptive data has unfolded that the stunted children consume less diversified diet and are more likely to suffer from illness than the non-stunted children (Table 8.2).

We have also tried to construct variable from both the rounds of survey to capture the underlying factors that influence the nutritional status. Household food security is one of the underlying factors. In this regard we have data collected in the round 2. We have asked the mother of the children whether the household has experienced food insecurity in the last 24 months. This information helped us to capture the experience of food insecurity by the households. The other indicator that also enables us to capture the adequacy/inadequacy of resources is per capita per month consumer expenditure (food and non-food) of the households. This also helps us to examine the relationship between household poverty and child nutrition. The children of the households who have less per capita income and who experience food insecurity are more likely to suffer from malnutrition. It is evident from the descriptive data that households of stunted children are more probable to be food insecure, have fewer resources (per capita expenditure) at their disposal to spend on the children than the households of non-stunted children (Table 8.2).

Another set of underlying factors are related to care for mothers and children. In other words, factors related to safe motherhood and childhood practices. The safe motherhood practices include antenatal care and safe deliveries for the mother and safe childhood practices include immunisation, feeding and caring practices. These practices are assessed against the World Health Organization (WHO) contemplations. The mothers were asked in the round 1 data collection whether they have had their first antenatal care checkup within three months of pregnancy, whether they have had their delivery in the hospitals, whether they have had their children vaccinated during one year in the round 1 and whether they have had their children vaccinated when the children have grown five year old in the round 2, how many months they have breastfed their children of one year old, and whether they have introduced supplementary nutrition when the children were 6 months old. The responses to these questions form our database to formulate safe motherhood and safe childhood practices. The positive response to these questions effect positively the nutritional status of children. The pooling of data from both the rounds enabled us to construct a near complete picture of safe motherhood and childhood practices effectively. Households of stunted children are less probable to practice safe motherhood (timely antenatal care, institutional delivery) and safe childhood practices (received complete cycle of immunisation, breastfeeding, timely introduction of supplementary food) (Table 8.2).

Health environment at the home front is another dimension of underlying factors which influence the nutritional status of the children. Access to safe drinking water and sanitation facilities ensures a healthy environment at home front. The data from both the rounds helped us to capture the healthy environment that influences positively the nutritional status of children. Households of stunted children are less expected to have the access to safe drinking water and toilet facilities than the households of non-stunted children (Table 8.2).

Women are more likely to allocate resources at the margin to the interests of their children than men (Galab and Reddy, 2010). The lower the autonomy and control over resources relative to men's, the less able they are to do so. In short, lower status relative to men restricts women's capacity to act in their own and their children's best interests. The social network of women (the number of groups in which the women has memberships), the awareness levels of women, participation of women in household decision-making relating to livelihoods, educational status of women and working status of women have been assessed to capture the status of women from the available data of the two rounds. The higher the score on these dimensions of women empowerment, the better the status of the child nutrition. Similarly, the caste affiliation of the households in the hierarchal social structure of the society also has influence on the nutritional status. The nutritional status of children belonging to scheduled castes (SCs) and scheduled tribes (STs) is at low level than the children belonging to other communities (Thorat and Sadana, 2009).

Around 33 per cent of younger children, 5 year olds were stunted in round 2 in Andhra Pradesh. Across the caste groups, the percentage of children stunted was found to be the highest among STs (41), followed by SCs and backward castes (around 38) and other castes (24). The percentage of stunted children was higher in rural areas (40) than in urban areas (21). It was higher boys (38) than girls (32). Among the wealth groups, it was the highest among 1st quartile (49), followed by the 2nd and 3rd quartiles (around 36) and the 4th quartile (21) (Table 8.1).

The percentage of children who had moved into stunting (normal in round 1 but stunted in round 2) was 20 for backward castes and around 15 for all the other caste groups. Similarly, the percentage of children who moved out of being stunted (stunted in round 1 but became normal) was 14 for STs; 10 per cent for SCs; 8 per cent for backward castes and 6 per cent for other castes. Among the rural and urban areas, the urban areas were in advantage situation with regard to the mobility in stunting. Similarly girls were better placed compared to the boys; and the poor were in disadvantage position among the wealth groups (Table 8.1 and Figure 8.1).

So far we have constructed the factors relating to the socio-economics of the households that influence the child's nutritional status. We do have data collected from both the rounds to construct variables for capturing the character of inputs of the biological production of the households, which includes age of the mother (in years), height of mother (in cms, capturing partly genetic factors as well as the mothers accumulated investments in health that have an impact on child health, especially prenatal), age of the child (in months), gender of the child, and birth order of the child. Mothers with lower age and lower height produce shorter children (children of malnutrition). Children of higher birth order, and relatively older children from boys are found to be children of malnutrition (Rozana, 2009).

Mothers of stunted children are less educated and have not participated in household decision-making, are working mothers (including working in NREGS[2]), are younger mothers, are shorter than the mothers of non-stunted children. The stunted children are of higher birth order, female and children belonging to social groups of STs and backward classes compared to the non-stunted children. The stunted children are less likely to access formal schooling than the non-stunted children (Table 8.2).

The persistently stunted children eat less diversified diet and are more likely to suffer from long term health problem than the children who move into being stunted. Households of persistently stunted

2. NREGS: National Rural Employment Guarantee Programme.

Figure 8.2

Pattern of Mobility in Stunting According to Different Category of Households

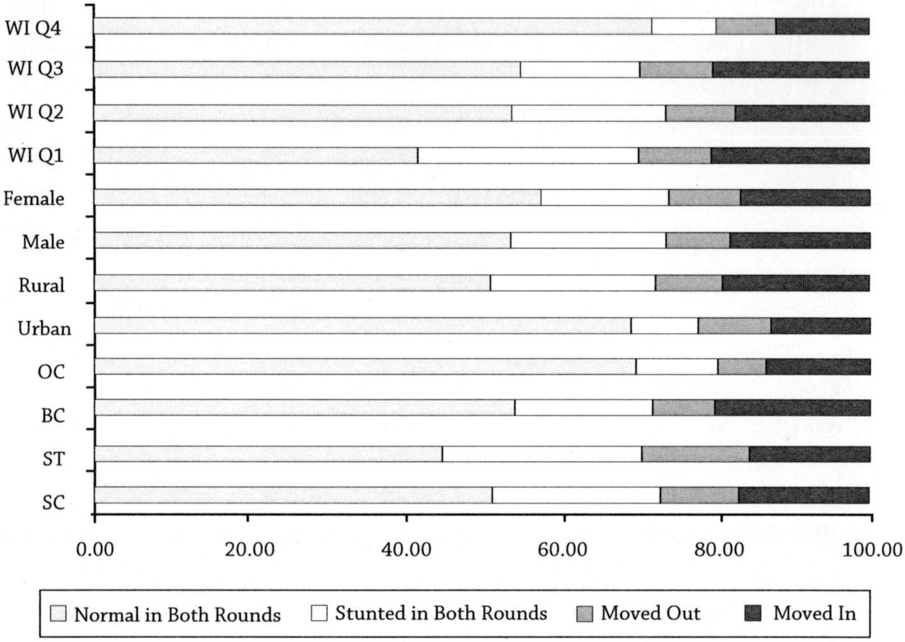

children have less resources to spend on children and are less likely to be food insecure than the households of children who slipped into stunting. Further, mothers of persistently stunted children are significantly shorter, younger and more likely to be workers than the mothers of children who move into being stunted. Persistently stunted children are more likely to be older and of higher birth order and from SC and ST social groups than the children who move into being stunted (Table 8.2).

Children who move out of being stunted are less likely to suffer from ill health than the children persistently stunted. Households of children who move out of being stunted are less probable to be food insecure and possess larger resource to spend on children than the households of persistently stunted children. Mothers of children who move out of being stunted are taller and more likely to be better educated and less probable to be worker than the mothers of children persistently stunted. Children who move out of being stunted are older, more likely to be going to formal school and more likely to be female child than the children persistently stunted (Table 8.2).

The percentage of children who are normal in both the rounds is 70; around 52; and 45 for other castes; STs and backward castes; and SCs in that order. The percentage of children who are persistently stunted (stunted in both the rounds) is the highest among STs (26) followed by SCs (22), backward castes (18) and other castes (11).

The other issue that needs to be examined is whether the state interventions like mid-meal and NREGS have any impact on the nutritional status of the children.

Analysis

The regression analysis helps us to find out the key predictors of the transition in the status of stunting of children. The following analysis captures the storyline of the predictors.

The eating of diverse diet by the children, household resources to spend on children, mothers height, timely antenatal care, completion of recommended cycle of immunisation for children, access to sanitation facilities, mother's awareness, children undergoing to formal schooling, households' participation in NREGS, being a girl child and age of mother are the key observable characteristics in Round 1 and Round 2 that exerted a positive significant influence on child's height for age z-scores in Round 2. Significant negative influences come from the long-term ill health of the child, household food insecurity, mothers being worker, birth order and coming from SCs and backward castes (column 2 of Table 8.3).

The significant positive key influences for a child remaining stunted through young childhood are child's age in Round 1, child's birth order, coming from SCs, backward castes and STs. This indicates that relatively older children among the one year old children are more likely to be persistently stunted and those of higher birth order are more prone to be persistently stunted. It is also clear that children from SCs, STs and backward castes are more liable to be persistently stunted. All these factors are related to biological production function of the households. The significant negative influences for a child remaining stunted through young childhood are eating diversified diet, mother's height, access to sanitation facilities, children undergoing formal schooling, being a male child and age of mother. Some of these negative influences also reflect the importance of the biological production function for the persistent stunting. For instance, they are mother's height, being male child and age of mother. This unfolds that child born to shorter mother and younger mother is more probable to be persistently stunted and also child being male. The significant negative factors also indicate the socio-economic factors that are likely to keep the children persistently stunted. They are diversified diet and access to sanitation facilities. This means that children who eat less diversified diet and do not have hygienic environment at home are more expected to be persistently stunted. Child going to formal schooling has also a negative significant socio-economic factor that influence child to be persistently stunted. This reveals that the child going to school does have mid-day meal entitlement. This might have high probability of preventing the children being persistently stunted. Thus the food intervention of the state has great potential to enable the children to escape from being persistently stunted, given the other factors that influence persistent stunting. All these indicate that adequate food and diversified diet in a healthy environment at home as socio-economic determinants have the potential to escape from being persistently stunted though the disadvantaged biological production function pushes into being persistently stunted (column 4 of Table 8.3).

The key contributing factors that helped a child move out of being stunted compared with the group of children who remain stunted in both rounds were eating diverse diet, mother's height, access to sanitation and age of the child. As noted earlier, these factors can be grouped in to two categories: factors related to biological production function (mother's height, age of the child) and factors related to socio-economic status of the households (diverse diet and access to sanitation). The relatively older children among the children of one year olds in Round 1 born to taller mother are more probable to move out of being stunted. Similarly, the children who eat more diversified diet in hygienic environment at home are more expected to escape from being stunted (column 6 of Table 8.3). The children who experience favourable biological production function and better socio-economic status are able to come back to normal when they grow five year old though they were stunned when they were one year olds.

The significant positive key influences for a children being moved into stunting (though they were normal when they were one year olds but turned out to be stunted when they grow five year old) compared with the group of children who were not stunted in both rounds are food insecurity and mother's participation in household decision-making. This unfolds that the children from the households who have experienced food insecurity are moving into stunting. But the mother's participation in household decision-making has not helped the children from slipping into stunting. The strength of this factor is found to be inadequate compared to other factors that push the children into stunting. The significant negative key factors that pushed the children into stunting are per capita consumer expenditure, immunisation, access to drinking water and sanitation facilities, timely introduction of supplementary food, going to formal school and households' participation in NREGS work in the village. This means that the children whose households have low resources to spend on children; and have not practiced safe motherhood and safe childhood practices; and do not have hygienic environment at homes and have no access to governments' mid-day meal and employment guarantee programme, have moved into stunting. All these factors are related to socio-economic factors. The factors related to biological production function have not turned up as determinants to push the children into stunting. But the descriptive data on the biological production function unfolds that the children who have slipped into stunting are in disadvantageous position compared with the children who are not stunted throughout the five year childhood. Thus the children, from among the normal set of children, who have experienced disadvantage with regard to both biological production function and socio-economic status have slipped into stunting when

Table 8.1

Patterns of Stunting and Mobility in Stunting According to Different Categories of Household

	Round 2		Round 1 and Round 2			
	Normal	Stunted	Normal in Both Rounds	Stunted in Round 1-Normal in Round 2	Normal in Round 1-Stunted in Round 2	Stunted in Both Rounds
All	1258 (64.51)	692 (35.49)	1086 (55.69)	172 (8.82)	338 (17.33)	354 (18.15)
SC	221 (61.73)	137 (38.27)	185 (51.68)	36 (10.06)	60 (16.76)	77 (21.51)
ST	169 (58.89)	118 (41.11)	129 (44.95)	40 (13.94)	44 (15.33)	74 (25.78)
BC	565 (62.36)	341 (37.64)	493 (54.42)	72 (7.95)	180 (19.87)	161 (17.77)
OC	303 (75.94)	96 (24.06)	279 (69.92)	24 (6.02)	54 (13.53)	42 (10.53)
Urban	374 (78.57)	102 (21.43)	330 (69.33)	44 (9.24)	61 (12.82)	41 (8.61)
Rural	884 (59.97)	590 (40.03)	756 (51.29)	128 (8.68)	277 (18.79)	313 (21.23)
Male	648 (61.89)	399 (38.11)	562 (53.68)	86 (8.21)	189 (18.05)	210 (20.06)
Female	610 (67.55)	293 (32.45)	524 (58.03)	86 (9.52)	149 (16.50)	144 (15.95)
WI Quartile 1	252 (51.22)	240 (48.78)	206 (41.87)	46 (9.35)	99 (20.12)	141 (28.66)
WI Quartile 2	307 (63.30)	178 (36.70)	263 (54.23)	44 (9.07)	83 (17.11)	95 (19.59)
WI Quartile 3	317 (64.30)	176 (35.70)	271 (54.97)	46 (9.33)	99 (20.08)	77 (15.62)
WI Quartile 4	380 (79.50)	98 (20.50)	344 (71.97)	36 (7.53)	57 (11.92)	41 (8.58)

Table 8.2

Determinants of Stunting and Mobility in Stunting in Andhra Pradesh

Discrimination of the Characteristics of the Children and Households	*Means and Proportions of Normal and Stunted Children in Round 2*			*Means and Proportions of Persistently Normal and Persistently Stunted Children*		
	Normal	*Stunted*	*Sig*	*Normal in Both the Rounds*	*Stunted in Both the Rounds*	*Sig*
No. of Observations	1319	692		1128	354	
Dietary Diversification Scores (Round 2)	5.67	5.47	**	5.77	5.22	***
Ill-health Scores (Last 24 hours) (Round 1)	0.22	0.29	***	0.23	0.29	**
Long Term Ill-health (Round 1)	0.04	0.05		0.04	0.06	@
Food Insecurity (Round 2)	0.06	0.15	***	0.06	0.13	***
Consumption Per Capita (Round 2)	823.55	658.86	***	836.96	640.49	***
Mother Education (>=10th Class=1/otherwise=0) (Round 2)	0.15	0.06	***	0.14	0.04	***
Mother is Worker (Round 2)	0.42	0.58	***	0.41	0.62	***
Mother's Height (Round 2)	151.00	148.78	***	151.08	147.74	***
First Antenatal Care (within 3 months=1/Otherwise =0) (Round 1)	0.61	0.52	***	0.61	0.51	***
Institutional Deliveries (Hospital=1/others=0) (Round 1)	0.68	0.59	***	0.70	0.60	***
Immunisation Doses (All) (Round 1)	0.73	0.70		0.72	0.71	

contd...

...contd...

Discrimination of the Characteristics of the Children and Households	*Means and Proportions of Normal and Stunted Children in Round 2*			*Means and Proportions of Persistently Normal and Persistently Stunted Children*		
	Normal	*Stunted*	*Sig*	*Normal in Both the Rounds*	*Stunted in Both the Rounds*	*Sig*
Immunisation Doses (All) (Round 2)	0.40	0.34	***	0.41	0.37	
Access to Drinking Water (Round 1)	0.20	0.11	***	0.21	0.14	***
Access to Sanitation (Round 1)	0.32	0.14	***	0.33	0.12	***
Breast Feeding (in months) (Round 1)	16.76	17.13	**	16.71	17.04	
Solid Introduction (Round 1)	0.85	0.78	***	0.86	0.80	***
No. of Groups (Round 1)	0.31	0.34		0.30	0.32	
Awareness Scores (Round 2)	5.20	5.23		5.27	5.09	*
Decision-making Score (Round 2)	0.83	1.05	***	0.83	1.05	***
Has Child Begun Formal School /accessing mid-day meal (Round 2)	0.47	0.39	***	0.47	0.43	
Participates in NREGS Work in Own Village (Round 2)	0.16	0.20	*	0.16	0.23	***
Age of Child in Months (Round 1)	11.89	11.70		11.66	12.57	***
Gender (Female=1/Male=0) (Round 1)	0.48	0.42	**	0.48	0.41	**
Birth Order (Round 2)	0.91	1.11	***	0.88	1.16	***

contd...

...contd...

Discrimination of the Characteristics of the Children and Households	Means and Proportions of Normal and Stunted Children in Round 2			Means and Proportions of Persistently Normal and Persistently Stunted Children		
	Normal	Stunted	Sig	Normal in Both the Rounds	Stunted in Both the Rounds	Sig
Age of Mother in Years (Round 1)	23.82	23.43	*	23.84	23.23	**
SC	0.18	0.20		0.17	0.22	**
ST	0.13	0.17	**	0.12	0.21	***
BC	0.44	0.49	**	0.45	0.45	
OC	0.25	0.14	***	0.27	0.12	***
Child Height (Round 1)	72.85	69.25	***	73.46	67.68	***
Child Height (Round 2)	105.39	99.25	***	105.40	98.90	***
Wealth Index (Round 1)	0.46	0.36	***	0.47	0.33	***
Wealth Index (Round 2)	0.52	0.43	***	0.53	0.41	***
Wealth Index Difference	0.07	0.07		0.06	0.07	

contd...

...contd...

Discrimination of the Characteristics of the Children and Households	*Means and Proportions of Moved out of being stunted and Persistently Stunted children*			*Means and Proportions of Moved into being stunted and Normal children*		
	Stunted in Both the Rounds	*Stunted in Round 1 and Normal in Round 2*	*Sig*	*Normal*	*Stunted in Round 2 but Normal in Round 1*	*Sig*
No. of Observations	354	191		1128	338	
Dietary Diversification Scores (Round 2)	5.22	5.06		5.77	5.73	
Ill-health Scores (Last 24 hours) (Round 1)	0.29	0.19	**	0.23	0.29	**
Long Term Ill-health (Round 1)	0.06	0.06		0.04	0.04	
Food Insecurity (Round 2)	0.13	0.05	***	0.06	0.17	***
Consumption Per Capita (Round 2)	640.49	738.87	**	836.96	678.10	***
Mother's Education (>=10th Class=1/otherwise=0) (Round 2)	0.04	0.18	***	0.14	0.07	***
Mother is Worker (Round 2)	0.62	0.50	***	0.41	0.52	***
Mother's Height (Round 2)	147.74	150.56	**	151.08	149.88	
First Antenatal Care (within 3 months=1/ Otherwise=0) (Round 1)	0.51	0.57		0.61	0.52	***
Institutional Deliveries (Hospital=1/others=0) (Round 1)	0.60	0.58		0.70	0.57	***
Immunisation Doses (All) (Round 1)	0.71	0.74		0.72	0.69	
Immunisation Doses (All) (Round 2)	0.37	0.35		0.41	0.30	***
Access to Drinking Water (Round 1)	0.14	0.12		0.21	0.09	***

contd...

...contd...

Discrimination of the Characteristics of the Children and Households	*Means and Proportions of Moved out of being stunted and Persistently Stunted children*			*Means and Proportions of Moved into being stunted and Normal children*		
	Stunted in Both the Rounds	*Stunted in Round 1 and Normal in Round 2*	*Sig*	*Normal*	*Stunted in Round 2 but Normal in Round 1*	*Sig*
Access to Sanitation (Round 1)	0.12	0.24	***	0.33	0.17	***
Breast Feeding (in months) (Round 1)	17.04	17.03		16.71	17.21	**
Solid Introduction (Round 1)	0.80	0.79		0.86	0.75	***
No. of Groups (Round 1)	0.32	0.32		0.30	0.36	*
Awareness Scores (Round 2)	5.09	4.84	@	5.27	5.38	
Decision-making Score (Round 2)	1.05	0.81	**	0.83	1.05	***
Has the Child Begun Formal School /accessing mid-day meal (Round 2)	0.43	0.51	*	0.47	0.35	***
Participates in NREGS Work in Own Village (Round 2)	0.23	0.20		0.16	0.16	
Age of Child in Months (Round 1)	12.57	13.23	**	11.66	10.79	***
Gender (Female=1/Male=0) (Round 1)	0.41	0.50	**	0.48	0.44	
Birth Order (Round 2)	1.16	1.08		0.88	1.05	***
Age of Mother in Years (Round 1)	23.23	23.66		23.84	23.63	
SC	0.22	0.24		0.17	0.18	
ST	0.21	0.21		0.12	0.13	

contd...

...contd...

Discrimination of the Characteristics of the Children and Households	*Means and Proportions of Moved out of being stunted and Persistently Stunted children*			*Means and Proportions of Moved into being stunted and Normal children*		
	Stunted in Both the Rounds	*Stunted in Round 1 and Normal in Round 2*	*Sig*	*Normal*	*Stunted in Round 2 but Normal in Round 1*	*Sig*
BC	0.45	0.41		0.45	0.53	***
OC	0.12	0.14		0.27	0.16	***
Child Height (Round 1)	67.68	69.24	***	73.46	70.94	***
Child Height (Round 2)	98.90	105.37	***	105.40	99.61	***
Wealth Index (Round 1)	0.33	0.40	***	0.47	0.38	***
Wealth Index (Round 2)	0.41	0.47	***	0.53	0.45	***
Wealth Index Difference	0.07	0.07		0.06	0.06	

Note: *** Indicates significant 1 per cent level

** Indicates significant 5 per cent level

* Indicates significant 10 per cent level

@ Indicates significant 15 per cent level

Table 8.3

Determinants of Stunting and Mobility in Stunting: A Multiple Regression Analysis

Independent Variable / *Dependent Variable*	*Height for Age Z -Scores (Round 2)*			*Persistently Stunted*		
	Coefficient	*Std Errors*	*Sig*	*Coefficient*	*Std Errors*	*Sig*
Dietary Diversification Scores (Round 2)	0.0334	0.0199	*	-0.0258	0.0092	***
Ill-health Scores (Last 24 hours) (Round 1)	0.0453	0.0684		-0.0170	0.0305	
Long Term Ill-health (Round 1)	-0.1977	0.1316	@	0.0488	0.0641	
Food Insecurity (Round 2)	-0.3266	0.1018	***	0.0499	0.0507	
Consumption Per Capita (Round 2)	0.0002	0.0001	***	0.0000	0.0000	
Mother's Education (>=10th Class=1/otherwise=0) (Round 2)	0.1635	0.1139		-0.0708	0.0527	
Mother is Worker (Round 2)	-0.1062	0.0654	@	0.0399	0.0305	
Mother's Height (Round 2)	0.0098	0.0027	***	-0.0024	0.0008	***
First Antenatal Care (within 3 months=1/Otherwise=0) (Round 1)	0.0844	0.0577	@	-0.0303	0.0267	
Institutional Deliveries (Hospital=1/others=0) (Round 1)	0.0209	0.0614		0.0185	0.0275	
Immunisation Doses (All) (Round 1)	0.0666	0.0666		-0.0091	0.0310	
Immunisation Doses (All) (Round 2)	0.2352	0.0694	***	-0.0272	0.0310	
Access to Drinking Water (Round 1)	0.1008	0.0840		-0.0341	0.0364	
Access to Sanitation (Round 1)	0.1969	0.1063	*	-0.0965	0.0453	*

contd...

...contd...

Dependent Variable / *Independent Variable*	*Height for Age Z -Scores (Round 2)*			*Persistently Stunted*		
	Coefficient	*Std Errors*	*Sig*	*Coefficient*	*Std Errors*	*Sig*
Breast Feeding (in months) (Round 1)	0.0058	0.0076		-0.0021	0.0037	
Solid Introduction (Round 1)	0.0002	0.0797		-0.0091	0.0378	
No. of Groups (Round 1)	0.0522	0.0528		-0.0029	0.0241	
Awareness Scores (Round 2)	0.0343	0.0230	@	-0.0006	0.0103	
Decision-making Score (Round 2)	0.0228	0.0303		-0.0153	0.0132	
Has the Child Begun Formal School/accessing mid-day meal (Round 2)	0.2552	0.0605	***	-0.0650	0.0271	**
Participate in NREGS Work in Own Village (Round 2)	0.1638	0.0866	*	-0.0092	0.0371	
Age of Child in Months (Round 1)	-0.0041	0.0088		0.0169	0.0042	***
Gender (Female=1/Male=0) (Round 1)	0.1910	0.0541	***	-0.0408	0.0246	*
Birth Order (Round 2)	-0.0838	0.0300	***	0.0329	0.0133	**
Age of Mother in Years (Round 1)	0.0144	0.0076	*	-0.0125	0.0036	***
SC	-0.2683	0.0960	***	0.1070	0.0540	**
ST	-0.1674	0.1259		0.1312	0.0705	**
BC	-0.1966	0.0766	***	0.0595	0.0385	@
Sentinel Site Dummy	Yes			Yes		

contd...

...contd...

Dependent Variable / *Independent Variable*	*Height for Age Z -Scores (Round 2)*			*Persistently Stunted*		
	Coefficient	*Std Errors*	*Sig*	*Coefficient*	*Std Errors*	*Sig*
Constant	-4.2532	0.5186	***			
No. of Observations	1579			1174		
R-Square	0.16			0.17		
Log Likelihood				-538.42		

...contd...

Independent Variable / *Dependent Variable*	*Moved out*			*Moved in*		
	Coefficient	*Std Errors*	*Sig*	*Coefficient*	*Std Errors*	*Sig*
Dietary Diversification Scores (Round 2)	0.0289	0.0186	@	0.0030	0.0096	
Ill-health Scores (Last 24 hours) (Round 1)	0.0392	0.0678		-0.0400	0.0299	
Long Term Ill-health (Round 1)	0.0625	0.1284		0.0288	0.0677	
Food Insecurity (Round 2)	-0.1237	0.0806		0.2010	0.0585	***
Consumption Per Capita (Round 2)	0.0000	0.0001		-0.0001	0.0000	*
Mother Education (>=10th Class=1/otherwise=0) (Round 2)	0.2201	0.1696		-0.0097	0.0536	
Mother is Worker (Round 2)	-0.0002	0.0661		0.0067	0.0304	
Mother's Height (Round 2)	0.0057	0.0029	*	0.0000	0.0009	
First Antenatal Care (within 3 months=1/Otherwise=0) (Round 1)	-0.0086	0.0543		-0.0161	0.0270	
Institutional Deliveries (Hospital=1/others=0) (Round 1)	-0.0714	0.0605		-0.0185	0.0284	
Immunisation Doses (All) (Round 1)	0.0727	0.0608		0.0326	0.0295	
Immunisation Doses (All) (Round 2)	0.0679	0.0687		-0.0619	0.0313	*
Access to Drinking Water (Round 1)	-0.2273	0.0651	***	-0.1284	0.0310	***
Access to Sanitation (Round 1)	0.1982	0.1201	*	-0.0981	0.0432	**
Breast Feeding (in months) (Round 1)	-0.0011	0.0078		-0.0008	0.0037	

contd...

...contd...

Dependent Variable / *Independent Variable*	*Moved out*			*Moved in*		
	Coefficient	*Std Errors*	*Sig*	*Coefficient*	*Std Errors*	*Sig*
Solid Introduction (Round 1)	-0.1450	0.0789	*	-0.0839	0.0413	**
No. of Groups (Round 1)	0.0200	0.0502		0.0156	0.0239	
Awareness Scores (Round 2)	-0.0036	0.0218		-0.0109	0.0111	
Decision-making Score (Round 2)	-0.0102	0.0278		0.0264	0.0142	*
Has the Child Begun Formal School/accessing mid-day meal (Round 2)	0.0465	0.0572		-0.1025	0.0276	***
Participate in NREGS Work in Own Village (Round 2)	0.0656	0.0816		-0.0797	0.0332	**
Age of Child in Months (Round 1)	0.0213	0.0087	**	-0.0053	0.0041	
Gender (Female=1/Male=0) (Round 1)	0.0559	0.0507		-0.0307	0.0252	
Birth Order (Round 2)	-0.0093	0.0269		0.0118	0.0147	
Age of Mother in Years (Round 1)	0.0032	0.0074		-0.0039	0.0036	
SC	-0.0257	0.0969		0.0187	0.0459	
ST	0.0125	0.1143		-0.0076	0.0617	
BC	-0.0704	0.0875		0.0171	0.0352	
Sentinel Site Dummy	Yes			Yes		
Constant						

contd...

...contd...

Dependent Variable / *Independent Variable*	*Moved out*			*Moved in*		
	Coefficient	*Std Errors*	*Sig*	*Coefficient*	*Std Errors*	*Sig*
No. of Observations	421			1171		
R-Square	0.16			0.11		
Log Likelihood	-227.05			-573.55		

Note: *** Indicates significant 1 per cent level

** Indicates significant 5 per cent level

* Indicates significant 10 per cent level

@ Indicates significant 15 per cent level

References

Behrman, J.R. and A.B. Deolalikar (1998). "Health and Nutrition"', in H. Chenery and T.N. Srinivasan (eds.), *Handbook of Development Economics* Volume 1. Amsterdam: North Holland

Cunha, F. and J.J. Heckman (2007). "The Technology of Skill Formation", *IZA Discussion Paper* No. 2550.

Engle, P., P. Menon and L. Haddad (1999). "Care and Nutrition: Concepts and Measurement", *World Development* 27(8): 1309-37, August.

Galab, S. and P. Prudhvikar Reddy (2010). *Impact Assessment of Andhra Pradesh Rural Poverty Reduction Project*. Hyderabad: Centre for Economic and Social Studies. May.

Galab, S., P. Prudhvikar Reddy and Rozana Himaz (2008). *Young Lives Round Survey Report: Initial Findings—Andhra Pradesh*. Oxford: Young Lives, Department of International Development, University of Oxford.

Himaz, R. (2009). "Persistent Stunting in Middle Childhood: The Case of Andhra Pradesh Using Longitudinal Data", *IDS Bulletin* 40(4), July.

Kabubo-Mariara, Jane, K.N. Godfrey and K.M. Domisiano (2009). "Determinants of Children's Nutritional Status in Kenya: Evidence from Demographic and Health Surveys", *Journal of African Economies* 18(3): 363-87

Nair, K.R.G (2007). "Malnourishment Among Children in India: A Regional Analysis", *Economic and Political Weekly*, 29 December.

Pridmore, Pat and Roy Carr Hill (2009). *Addressing the Underlying and Basic Causes of Child Undernutrition in Developing Countries: What Works and Why?*. Institute of Education, University of London.

Radhakrishna, R. and C. Ravi (2004). "Malnutrition in India: Trends and Determinants", *Economic and Political Weekly* 39(7), 14-20 February.

Radhakrishna, R. and K. Venkat Reddy (2004). *Food Security and Nutrition: Vision 2020*. A background paper prepared for Planning Commission.

Ruel, M.T. (2008). "Addressing the Underlying Determinants of Under-nutrition: Examples of Successful Integration of Nutrition in Poverty-reduction and Agricultural Strategies", *UN ACC/SCN News* (36): 18-21

Shiva Kumar, A.K. (2007). "Why are Levels of Child Nutrition not Improving?", *Economic and Political Weekly*, 14 April.

Strauss, J., and D. Thomas (1995). "Human Resources: Empirical Modeling of Household and Family Decisions", in J. Behrman and T.N. Srinivasan (eds.), *Handbook of Development Economics*. Vol. 3. Amsterdam: North-Holland.

Svedberg, P. (2008). "Why Malnutrition in Shining India Persists", Paper presented at *4th Annual Conference on Economic Growth and Development*. December 17-18. New Delhi: Indian Statistical Institute.

Thorat, S. and N. Sadana (2009). "Discrimination and Children's Nutritional Status in India", *IDS Bulletin* 40(4), July.

UNICEF (1990). "Strategy for Improved Nutrition of Children and Women in Developed Countries", *Policy Review Paper* E/ICEF/1990/1.6. New York.

World Bank (2006). *Repositioning Nutrition as Central to Development*. Washington DC.

...contd...

	Moved out			*Moved in*		
	Coefficient	*Std Errors*	*Sig*	*Coefficient*	*Std Errors*	*Sig*
Dietary Diversification Scores (Round 2)	0.0289	0.0185	@	0.0007	0.0095	
Ill-health Scores (Last 24 hours) (Round 1)	0.0393	0.0674		-0.0409	0.0296	
Long Term Ill-health (Round 1)	0.0547	0.1276		0.0193	0.0663	
Food Insecurity (Round 2)	-0.1253	0.0796		0.1810	0.0571	***
Consumption Per Capita (Round 2)	0.0000	0.0001		0.0000	0.0000	
Mother's Education (>=10th Class=1/otherwise=0) (Round 2)	0.2314	0.1698		-0.0058	0.0541	
Mother is Worker (Round 2)	-0.0018	0.0660		0.0085	0.0302	
Mother's Height (Round 2)	0.0057	0.0029	*	-0.0002	0.0009	
First Antenatal Care (within 3 months=1/Otherwise=0) (Round 1)	-0.0027	0.0540		-0.0237	0.0268	
Institutional Deliveries (Hospital=1/others=0) (Round 1)	-0.0696	0.0603		-0.0241	0.0280	
Immunisation Doses (All) (Round 1)	0.0848	0.0593		0.0303	0.0294	
Immunisation Doses (All) (Round 2)	0.0639	0.0680		-0.0566	0.0312	*
Access to Drinking Water (Round 1)	-0.2239	0.0650	***	-0.1257	0.0311	***
Access to Sanitation (Round1)	0.1991	0.1201	*	-0.0931	0.0436	**
Breast Feeding (in months) (Round 1)	-0.0011	0.0078		-0.0011	0.0037	
Solid Introduction (Round 1)	-0.1348	0.0777	*	-0.0960	0.0413	**
No. of Groups (Round 1)	0.0167	0.0498		0.0110	0.0237	

contd...

...contd...

	Moved out			Moved in		
	Coefficient	*Std Errors*	*Sig*	*Coefficient*	*Std Errors*	*Sig*
Awareness Scores (Round 2)	-0.0033	0.0216		-0.0100	0.0110	
Decision-making Score (Round 2)	-0.0067	0.0275		0.0207	0.0139	@
Participates in NREGS Work in Own Village (Round 2)	0.0700	0.0813		-0.0823	0.0328	**
Age of Child in Months (Round 1)	0.0212	0.0085	**	-0.0091	0.0040	**
Gender (Female=1/Male=0) (Round 1)	0.0525	0.0505		-0.0329	0.0250	
Birth Order (Round 2)	-0.0083	0.0268		0.0175	0.0146	
Age of Mother in Years (Round 1)	0.0032	0.0074		-0.0047	0.0036	
SC	-0.0143	0.0968		0.0193	0.0457	
ST	0.0224	0.1137		-0.0082	0.0614	
BC	-0.0618	0.0868		0.0135	0.0351	
Sentinel Site Dummy	Yes			Yes		
Constant						
No. of Observations	423			1184		
R-Square	0.14580			0.1001		
Log Likelihood	-232.8335			-584.8962		

Appendix Table A-8.2

Determinants of Stunting and Mobility in Stunting in Andhra Pradesh (Excluding Child Going Formal School and Participation in NREGS)

	Height for Age Z -Scores (Round 2)			*Persistently Stunted*		
	Coefficient	*Std Errors*	*Sig*	*Coefficient*	*Std Errors*	*Sig*
Dietary Diversification Scores (Round 2)	0.0335	0.0198	*	-0.0277	0.0091	***
Ill-health Scores (Last 24 hours) (Round 1)	0.0381	0.0681		-0.0156	0.0304	
Long Term Ill-health (Round 1)	-0.1891	0.1318		0.0540	0.0643	
Food Insecurity (Round 2)	-0.3026	0.1015	***	0.0498	0.0501	
Consumption Per Capita (Round 2)	0.0001	0.0001	**	0.0000	0.0000	
Mother's Education (>=10th Class=1/otherwise=0) (Round 2)	0.1584	0.1141		-0.0695	0.0529	
Mother is Worker (Round 2)	-0.1141	0.0653	*	0.0371	0.0304	
Mother's Height (Round 2)	0.0100	0.0027	***	-0.0025	0.0008	***
First Antenatal Care (within 3 months=1/Otherwise=0) (Round 1)	0.0958	0.0573	*	-0.0353	0.0265	
Institutional Deliveries (Hospital=1/others=0) (Round 1)	0.0288	0.0610		0.0154	0.0272	
Immunisation Doses (All) (Round 1)	0.0823	0.0661		-0.0112	0.0307	
Immunisation Doses (All) (Round 2)	0.2188	0.0691	***	-0.0213	0.0309	
Access to Drinking Water (Round 1)	0.1015	0.0837		-0.0440	0.0353	
Access to Sanitation (Round 1)	0.1822	0.1064	*	-0.0907	0.0455	*
Breast Feeding (in months) (Round 1)	0.0065	0.0076		-0.0030	0.0036	

contd...

...contd...

	Height for Age Z -Scores (Round 2)			*Persistently Stunted*		
	Coefficient	*Std Errors*	*Sig*	*Coefficient*	*Std Errors*	*Sig*
Solid Introduction (Round 1)	0.0282	0.0792		-0.0180	0.0380	
No. of Groups (Round 1)	0.0694	0.0526		-0.0078	0.0238	
Awareness Scores (Round 2)	0.0262	0.0228		-0.0002	0.0102	
Decision-making Score (Round 2)	0.0286	0.0299		-0.0186	0.0130	
Age of Child in Months (Round 1)	0.0047	0.0085		0.0153	0.0040	***
Gender (Female=1/Male=0) (Round 1)	0.1884	0.0539	***	-0.0406	0.0244	*
Birth Order (Round 2)	-0.0878	0.0298	***	0.0346	0.0133	***
Age of Mother in Years (Round 1)	0.0156	0.0076	**	-0.0130	0.0036	***
SC	-0.2288	0.0950	**	0.0970	0.0523	**
ST	-0.1483	0.1260		0.1249	0.0696	**
BC	-0.1928	0.0764	**	0.0529	0.0380	
Sentinel Site Dummy	Yes			Yes		
Constant	-4.2572	0.5184	***			
No. of Observations	1594			1187		
R-Square	0.15			0.17		
Log Likelihood				-543.36		

contd...

...contd...

	Moved out			*Moved in*		
	Coefficient	*Std Errors*	*Sig*	*Coefficient*	*Std Erros*	*Sig*
Dietary Diversification Scores (Round 2)	0.0295	0.0185	@	0.0019	0.0095	
Ill-health Scores (Last 24 hours) (Round 1)	0.0374	0.0673		-0.0387	0.0297	
Long Term Ill-health (Round 1)	0.0661	0.1276		0.0190	0.0664	
Food Insecurity (Round 2)	-0.1257	0.0796		0.1742	0.0567	***
Consumption Per Capita (Round 2)	0.0000	0.0001		0.0000	0.0000	
Mother's Education (>=10th Class=1/otherwise=0) (Round 2)	0.2286	0.1693		-0.0070	0.0540	
Mother is Worker (Round 2)	-0.0006	0.0658		0.0103	0.0303	
Mother's Height (Round 2)	0.0057	0.0029	**	-0.0002	0.0009	
First Antenatal Care (within 3 months=1/Otherwise =0) (Round 1)	0.0008	0.0538		-0.0249	0.0268	
Institutional deliveries (Hospital=1/others=0) (Round 1)	-0.0703	0.0602		-0.0218	0.0280	
Immunisation Doses (All) (Round 1)	0.0834	0.0594		0.0313	0.0293	
Immunisation Doses (All) (Round 2)	0.0608	0.0679		-0.0538	0.0313	*
Access to Drinking Water (Round 1)	-0.2228	0.0653	***	-0.1250	0.0313	***
Access to Sanitation (Round 1)	0.2125	0.1191	*	-0.0912	0.0438	*
Breast Feeding (in months) (Round 1)	-0.0012	0.0078		-0.0012	0.0037	

contd...

...contd...

	Moved out			*Moved in*		
	Coefficient	*Std Errors*	*Sig*	*Coefficient*	*Std Erros*	*Sig*
Solid Introduction (Round 1)	-0.1311	0.0775	*	-0.0996	0.0414	***
No. of Groups (Round 1)	0.0189	0.0497		0.0086	0.0237	
Awareness Scores (Round 2)	-0.0046	0.0215		-0.0105	0.0110	
Decision-making Score (Round 2)	-0.0049	0.0274		0.0183	0.0139	
Age of Child in Months (Round 1)	0.0217	0.0085	**	-0.0090	0.0040	**
Gender (Female=1/Male=0) (Round 1)	0.0507	0.0504		-0.0327	0.0250	
Birth Order (Round 2)	-0.0077	0.0269		0.0167	0.0146	
Age of Mother in Years (Round 1)	0.0028	0.0074		-0.0051	0.0036	
SC	0.0094	0.0946		0.0118	0.0451	
ST	0.0384	0.1132		-0.0025	0.0619	
BC	-0.0516	0.0862		0.0137	0.0352	
Sentinel Site Dummy	Yes			Yes		
Constant						
No. of Observations	423			1184		
R-Square	0.14			0.10		
Log Likelihood	-233.22			-587.50		

9

BHANOJI RAO

High Yielding Seed for Inclusive Growth

12 Years of Quality Schooling for All

Introduction

Three Constituents of Inclusive Growth

Building human capabilities as part of an inclusive growth strategy calls for measures aimed at ensuring that each person has a healthy and long life, and 12 years or more of world-class education. With good health and education, most will gain the capacity to derive reasonable purchasing power and stay out of poverty. In addition to health and education, inclusive growth requires a reasonable degree of equality in housing. A dwelling unit—minimum one room, toilet and kitchen—is critical for providing water and sanitation on a sustained basis and ensuring a healthy living environment. While the focus of this paper is on education, Annexure A-9.1 provides a short note on what could be done in regard to health and housing along with what has been said in Chapter 1 of the draft of Twelfth Five Year Plan on these two.

> The key for inclusive growth on a medium to longer term basis must rest with the movement towards perfect equality of opportunity in at least 12 years of education. This is also the key for development of capabilities.

About this Paper

The motivation for this paper stems from the belief, of the author and dozens of his friends and associates, in the criticality of the first 12 years of education in laying the communicational, analytical and devotional foundations on which rests the life time of welfare, material and spiritual, at the individual, family and societal levels. It is also based on the firm conviction founded on experience that a primary duty of the government is the provision of education at primary and secondary schools that could and should bring together children of diverse backgrounds and income levels under one roof and build solid bases for the unity of the nation.

Rest of the paper is organised as follows. The next section provides a short brief on inclusive growth. Inclusive growth as enunciated in the draft Twelfth Five Year Plan and its discourse on the first 12 years of education are the subject matter of Section 3. Section 4 comments on the ground reality in regard to primary and secondary education, and outlines in brief 'the high yielding seed for inclusive growth', namely, 12 years of quality schooling for all the children of India.

Growth *versus* Inclusive Growth

Even if the rates of economic growth are high, i.e., even if the economy is growing rapidly in size, nothing will trickle down to those who are not involved in the growth process either as entrepreneurs or employees, because of lack of appropriate capabilities. This is why the state has to intervene and orchestrate an inclusive growth path.

Achieving and maintaining a high rate of economic growth is not difficult if a sound investment climate is created by an appropriate policy framework. Domestic investment and FDI (foreign direct investment) together could boost the IR (investment rate) to levels in the region of 35 to 40 per cent of GDP (gross domestic product). Even if one assumes a relatively high ICOR (incremental capital output ratio) of 4, the IR could yield a 8-10 per cent rate of economic growth.

Removing all sorts of obstacles in the way of private investment, domestic and foreign, will do the trick with regard to attracting domestic investments and FDIs. This is precisely what the country has achieved since the 1991 economic liberalisation policies. Whether it is steel or power, road or air transport, land lines or mobile connections, private sector has begun to show its strength thanks to the positive encouragement it received at the hands of public policy.

The results have been impressive with the economy registering high investment rates and growth rates. During 2007-2012, for instance, despite regional and global economic turmoil, the average investment rate (investment as per cent of GDP) was 36 per cent as against the saving rate of 33 per cent. During the most recent six years (2007-08 through 2012-13), the average growth rate of GDP was a fairly high 7.5 per cent.[1]

Does it mean that the impressive economic performance since the nation achieved independence translated itself as equally impressive living standards for one and all? There is no evidence to say so. In fact, even on the basis of a relatively conservative poverty line, the percentage of people with income or expenditure below the poverty line was close to 30 per cent in 2009-10.[2] On the basis of the simple measure of poverty alone, one could surmise that economic growth has not 'trickled down' to the poor and vulnerable, and has not been inclusive.

As per *Economic Survey* (2012-13: 24): "Economic growth though important cannot be an end in itself. The Twelfth Five Year Plan, with its focus on 'Faster, More Inclusive and Sustainable Growth', puts the growth debate in the right perspective."

The Twelfth Plan's Inclusive Growth and Education

The Twelfth Five Year Plan (2012-2017) draft wears the subheading "Faster, More Inclusive and Sustainable Growth."[3] In the rest of this section, a summary is provided of the relevant parts of Chapter 1, followed by a summary of the pertinent segments of the education chapter (Chapter 21 of Volume 3 running into 77 pages).

1. The annual GDP growth rates for each of the years from 2007-08 through 2012-13 in percentage terms were 9.3, 6.7, 8.6, 9.3, 6.2 and 5.0—yielding an average growth rate of 7.5 per cent. See *Economic Survey, 2012-13*, Government of India, Ministry of Finance, February, 2013.
2. *Economic Survey 2012-13*, Government of India, Ministry of Finance, p. 25.
3. PDF document pages as indicated.

Inclusive Growth Outlined in Chapter 1 of Volume 1

The Twelfth Plan discourse on inclusiveness begins with explaining the meaning of inclusiveness, starting with the assertion on page 5 of Chapter 1: "Inclusiveness means many different things and each aspect of inclusiveness poses its own challenges for policy." Two paragraphs are devoted to inclusiveness as poverty reduction. The following two statements summarise the main point: first, ensuring an adequate flow of benefits to the poor/marginalised remains an important policy focus in the Twelfth Plan, given that poverty continues to be a high 29.8 per cent of the population amounting to some 350 million people in 2009-10.[4] Second, it would seem that there has been some reduction in poverty during the Eleventh Plan period and "it can be claimed that the Eleventh Plan has indeed delivered on inclusiveness" (Page 6 of Chapter 1, Volume 1).

As in respect of poverty reduction, two paragraphs (1.26 and 1.27, page 6) are devoted for inclusiveness as group equality. The growth process should be seen to be fair by different socio-economic groups in the society. The reference here is to groups such as SC, ST, OBC and other minorities: "...narrowing the gap between the SCs or STs and the general population must be part of any reasonable definition of inclusiveness..."

Paragraphs 1.28 and 1.29 are about Inclusiveness as Regional Balance. "In the Twelfth Plan, we must pay special attention to the scope for accelerating growth in the States that are lagging behind." It is pointed out that infrastructure improvement is an important component of the regionally inclusive development strategy.

Two more paragraphs are about inclusiveness and inequality. Paragraph 1.30 begins with the statement: "Inclusiveness also means greater attention to income inequality." The rest of the paragraph is

4. "Questions have been raised about the appropriateness of the Tendulkar poverty line... There is no doubt that the Tendulkar Committee poverty line represents a very low level of consumption and the scale of poverty even on this basis is substantial. An Expert committee under Dr. C. Rangarajan has been set up to review all issues related to the poverty line keeping in view international practices" (Volume 1, Chapter 1, Paragraph 1.24). It would have been nicer for a Plan document to avoid the content that resembles a research paper or a text for 12th graders.

about how income inequality is denoted by the Gini coefficient, etc. The following set of statements from the next paragraph (1.31, p.7) are a great consolation:

> Any given level of inequality of outcomes is much more socially acceptable if it results from a system which provides greater equality of opportunity. As a society, we therefore need to move as rapidly as possible to the ideal of giving every child in India a fair opportunity in life, which means assuring every child access to good health and quality education. While this may not be possible to achieve in one Plan period, the Twelfth Plan should aim at making substantial progress in this dimension.

Given the singular importance, for inclusiveness, of ensuring education of the highest quality for each and every child of the nation, all the rest of the discourse on inclusiveness is of really no consequence. For instance, paragraph 1.32 is about inclusiveness as empowerment. The best empowerment outcome stems from education and the least from the lack of it. The section on inclusiveness ends with several paragraphs on inclusiveness through employment programmes. It is all about Mahatma Gandhi National Rural Employment Guarantee Act (MGNREGA).

Chapter 1 page 9 provides a box on Eleventh Plan Achievements on Inclusive Growth, giving "important indicators showing the extent to which the Eleventh Plan succeeded in fulfilling the objective of inclusive growth". The indicators are: 8 per cent average GDP growth during the Eleventh Plan (2007–08 to 2011–12), 3.7 per cent agricultural GDP growth, decline in poverty rate (noted earlier in this paper), relatively higher growth rate of consumption per capita in rural areas, decline in the unemployment rate, higher rate of increase in rural real wages, a rise in the complete immunisation rate, and an improvement in the primary school enrolment rate. As if the readers are just a bunch of fools, the list of indicators included growth rates of GDP, average consumption and so on—these are part of growth no doubt, but what one is looking for in inclusive growth is the extent to which people could draw on that growth.

Education: Chapter 1 of the Plan

There are three paragraphs (1.51–1.53) on education in Chapter 1. The key points could be summarised as follows.

> The SSA has brought us close to the target of universalisation of primary education and the Right to Education Act (RTE) 2009 makes eight years of elementary education a fundamental right for all the children. The MDM Scheme has ensured that retention in schools has improved greatly. However, the learning outcomes for a majority of children continue to be disappointing. Addressing the quality issue in our schools is critical for the effective development of human capabilities and for achieving the objective of equality of opportunities. The quality of teachers and, even more important, their motivation and accountability will need to be improved (1.51).
>
> The success of the SSA has put pressure on expanding the capacity of secondary schools and the Rashtriya Madhyamik Shiksha Abhiyan (RMSA) addresses this issue. Although there is considerable focus on providing secondary school access, the dropout rates between elementary and secondary schools continue to be high, and between the secondary and post-secondary stage they are even higher (1.52).[5]

Finally, pages 35-36 of Chapter 1 provide a listing of 25 core indicators that "reflect the vision of rapid, sustainable and more inclusive growth." Three indicators (7-9) refer to education: 7. Mean Years of Schooling to increase to seven years by the end of Twelfth Five Year Plan. 8. Enhance access to higher education by creating two million additional seats for each age cohort aligned to the skill needs of the economy. 9. Eliminate gender and social gap in school enrolment (that is, between girls and boys, and between SCs, STs, Muslims and the rest of the population) by the end of Twelfth Five Year Plan.

So far the reference has been to Chapter 1, which is an overview and hence one should look for detail in the sectoral chapters. Rest of

5. Paragraph 1.53 is about higher education and here is the most pertinent issue and the relevant target: "Not even one Indian university figures in the latest list of the top 200 universities in the world. We should work towards ensuring that there are at least five by the end of the Twelfth Plan." Let us wait and watch with utmost interest to see which of our great institutions will ensure reaching the target.

this section aims at summarising the pertinent points in the Plan's chapter (chapter 21) on education.

Education: Notes From and Comments on Chapter 21

> Recognising the importance of education in national development, the Twelfth Plan places an unprecedented focus on the expansion of education, on significantly improving the quality of education imparted and on ensuring that educational opportunities are available to all segments of the society.[6]

The Twelfth Plan targets (page 51) with regard to school education are: ensuring universal access in tune with RTE provisions, that is, providing good-quality free and compulsory education to all children in the age group of 6 to 14 years; improving attendance and reducing dropout rates; increasing gross enrolment ratio (GER) at secondary level to over 90 per cent and senior secondary to 65 per cent; provision of at least a year of pre-school education in primary schools to all children; and improving learning outcomes with regard to reading and numeracy skills by class 2, and critical thinking, expression and problem solving skills by class 5.

Sarva Shiksha Abhiyan (SSA), Right to Education and Private Sector

SSA is the flagship programme for promoting universal elementary education. SSA has merged components of the National Programme for Education of Girls at Elementary Level (NPEGEL) and the residential school scheme, Kasturba Gandhi Balika Vidyalaya (KGBV), that have focus on girls' education (page 53). "Although the number of elementary schools has increased to 13.04 lakh, many schools lack the basic infrastructure facilities required under the RTE Act" (page 54).

Sad to say, the RTE provisions for schools are themselves quite meager. The Act seeks only 8 years of compulsory education. The Act's provisions simply call for (see the Act for full details) a PTR (pupil to teacher ratio) of 30-35; 1 class room per teacher, an office cum store

6. This is from paragraph 21.1, page 47 of Twelfth Five Year Plan (2012-2017), Social Sectors (Volume III). All page numbers in this section refer to Volume III.

cum head teacher room, kitchen for cooking MDMs (mid-day meals), playground, library, and equipment for teaching, learning and games.

Whither Primary and Secondary Education?

RTE Report Card

The *RTE Report Card 2011 for Rural India* from the *Annual Status of Education Report 2011* (ASER, prepared by an NGO) is one source that provides invaluable indicators. The following findings are based on the various tabulations in the report. Some 40 per cent of the schools do not have the PTR as per norms; a quarter of the schools do not have the desired one classroom per teacher; 40 per cent schools do not have a playground; a little over a quarter of schools do not have adequate drinking water; and around half the schools do not have usable toilets.

A little over 90 per cent of schools catering to primary education do not have computers, while the percentage is also high at 70 with regard to middle schools. As if to indicate the effect of inadequate facilities, attendance was mostly around 70 per cent of the enrolment.

The lack of facilities and inspiring teachers are reflected in the following: Over 60 per cent of children in standard III in government schools and over 40 per cent in private schools cannot read a standard I level text. Over 50 per cent of standard V students in government schools and close to 40 per cent in private schools cannot read standard II level text. As for arithmetic, 70 per cent of government school students in standard V and 60 per cent from private schools cannot perform division operations. The inadequacies in educational performance must not be allowed to continue as they can hurt the promotion of individual progress, national development, equal opportunities and social cohesion.

More on Ground Reality

There are three demographically large nations in the world: US known for its R&D (research and development), technology, and the status as a super power; China known today as a soon to be a super power with huge exports and reserves; and India, described by *The Economist* in a recent article[7] as an expected and not yet proven economic power. In an earlier article, the magazine questions why innovation is not shaping the education sector.[8]

Table 9.1 below shows the selected educational indicators for the three countries. We have a long way to go in establishing an educational profile for the population that befits the people of an independent and democratic country. DISE 2011-12[9] points to the following deficiencies among others: 44 per cent of schools have no playgrounds, 30 per cent have no functioning toilets, 11 per cent have only one teacher, a high 64 per cent have no electricity and the average number of class rooms per school was just about 3.3. Yes, we are moving forward, but with not much to celebrate perhaps.

Table 9.1

Selected Education Data for China, India and US, 2010

	China	*India*	*US*
Compulsory Education			
Starting age	6	6	6
Years of schooling	9	9	12
Secondary education			
Enrolment %	81	63	96
% in technical/vocational			
Secondary	21	1	NA
Upper secondary	46	2	NA
Pupil Teacher Ratio			
Lower secondary	15	31	13
Upper secondary	16	21	14

Source: World Development Indicators and UNESCO.

7. "India: Can India Become a Great Power?", *The Economist*, 30 March 2013.
8. "New Rules for Schools," *The Economist*, 23 March 2013.
9. *Elementary Education in India, DISE 2011-12: Flash Statistics*, New Delhi: National University of Educational Planning and Administration.

Incentivising Private Schools is not the Answer

In the US, which is the world's second largest democracy, the icon of the industrialised world and the seat of capitalist enterprise, private school enrolment in primary and secondary education put together was only 9.9 per cent of total enrolment in 2010. In contrast, in India, private sector shares were 31 per cent in the enrolments in classes I-V and 33 per cent in classes VI-VIII. Instead of planning to reverse this trend, the Twelfth Five Year Plan enshrines the private sector role as indicated in Box 9.1.[10]

Box 9.1

Increased Role of the Private Sector

Private providers (including NGOs and non-profits) can play an important role in elementary education. Their legitimate role in expanding elementary education needs to be recognised and a flexible approach needs to be adopted to encourage them to invest in the sector. The current licensing and regulatory restrictions in the sector could be eased and a single window approach should be adopted so that the process of opening new schools by private providers is streamlined... In all, private players would be encouraged to set up more schools, provided they are committed to, and held accountable for, providing high-quality education and are transparent in their operations.

Author's Comment: No child has taken special care to be especially born in a poor family and be condemned to a 'private' school that does not exist or a government school that does not teach. Shame on all of us—so called educated people for allowing a Plan to say the above in regard to elementary and secondary education. The planners cannot be speaking on the one hand about equality of opportunity and on the other about encouraging the private sector!

Source: *Twelfth Plan*, Volume III, p.64.

---

10. In Singapore, in the mid-1960s, at the time of separation from Malaysia, there used to be just one or two highly reputed schools along with others that were not so well-known. The government took it as a challenge to achieve equality of educational opportunity and it has done so extremely well. School buildings with good infrastructure and facilities, teachers who are well-paid and rewarded, adherence to GCE (O) and (A) examination system with global recognition etc., have served the city state well in the transformation of Singapore from 'the third world to the first'.

The Way Forward[11]

At the outset, it is important to recognise that the first 12 years of education has a key role to play in nation building and the achievement of progress on many fronts.

First, minimal inequality in schooling promotes cohesion, order, security and peace in society. That is not possible if from age 6 to 18, majority of children are condemned to study in less-endowed schools.

Second, owing to inter-linkages to the rest of personal achievements, school education (12 years) provides the basis for individual progress over the full life span and for development to be spread widely. This will happen if children at age 6 are not divided into those that could afford the posh private school and those that must languish in a street corner government school.

Third, quality education for all up to class 12 (and more) would imply an exceptionally well-informed and participative electorate, a major pillar of a vibrant democracy, which, in turn, is the grand finale of our political liberties.

Finally, all the caste-based and other reservations in tertiary education would mean very little unless each child is educated in an identically well-endowed school-setting to begin with.

India should aim for the highest possible level of equality in school education, with a high degree of uniformity of standards and just one national examination at the end of class 12, results of which are globally accepted, and which allows for a dignified exit to all and sundry entrance tests.

Following are the much needed initiatives: Building identically well-endowed schools in terms of physical infrastructure (class rooms, furniture and fixtures, dining halls, auditoria, gyms etc.); Pupil-Teacher Ratio of 20 or less; one computer per child; free textbooks that pass on from one batch to another; teacher salaries bearing a fixed ratio to the pay of university and college teachers;

---

11. This section draws on the following publications by the author: "Children have a Right to Free Education", *Times of India*, Hyderabad edition, 25 June 2012; "Gandhiji's Core Values and their Criticality for Human Progress", *GITAM Journal of Gandhian Studies* 1(1), January–June 2012; and "Inclusive Growth: Why, What and How?" *Business Standard*, 29 September 2011.

common 12th grade examination for the nation covering English, mathematics, science etc. but not local language and allied subjects; and possibility for students to opt for GCE (A) as well as IB along with the national 12th grade examination.

In Fond Memory of Mahatma Gandhi and Pundit Nehru

The immediate need is for launching a programme to build brand new and identically well-endowed government schools: Mahatma Gandhi Primary School (MGPS) and Jawaharlal Nehru Secondary School (JNSS), with distinguishing standard architectural design across the country. One recognises a temple/church/mosque from a distance. Such must be the case with MGPS and JNSS. They must have top-class libraries and computer labs, and excellent dining halls for MDMs. They should have book banks and first-class laboratories. Teacher salaries are to bear a relationship to university teacher pay: 75 per cent for secondary school teachers and 50 per cent for primary school teachers.

Our nation deserves the unveiling of a separate education development plan with the aim of setting up excellent government schools with well-paid teachers. If such a healthy development were to result in private schools experiencing a dearth of students and teachers, so be it. Till we get the MGPS and JNSS to endow our children with real equality of opportunity, we have no moral authority to proclaim any greatness for our nation.

Annexure A-9.1

Health and Housing Initiatives for Inclusive Growth

Schools that unify children and housing estates that unify citizens have important by-products: peace, security and harmony.

In this annexure, first we provide the list of core indicators in the Twelfth Plan relating to health and housing and then provide what could be some minimal initiatives.

Twelfth Plan's Core Indicators

Pages 35-36 of Chapter 1 of the Draft Plan provide a listing of 25 core indicators that "reflect the vision of rapid, sustainable and more inclusive growth." The following refer to those with at least have some bearing on inclusiveness with regard to health and housing.

Health: Reduce IMR (infant mortality rate) to 25 and MMR (maternal mortality rate) to 1 per 1,000 live births, and improve child sex ratio (0–6 years) to 950 by the end of the Twelfth Five Year Plan. Reduce under-nutrition among children aged 0–3 years to half of the NFHS-3 levels by the end of Twelfth Five Year Plan.

Housing: Ensure 50 per cent of rural population has access to 40 lpcd piped drinking water supply, and 50 per cent *gram panchayats* achieve Nirmal Gram Status by the end of Twelfth Five Year Plan.

What Needs to Be Done

Health: The first priority should be to ensure a fair degree of equity in maternal and child care across the population. Much can be accomplished if a significant number of deliveries take place in well-equipped hospitals. There is a need to build world-class polyclinics in place of the existing primary health centres, with sufficient provision of wards/rooms for deliveries, while ensuring they are well staffed with incentives for employees to stay put at the workplace. As for curative medical care, the best option is to move slowly but steadily in a time-bound manner towards universal national medical insurance.

Housing: Here is what the Father of the Nation wrote: "I shall work for an India...in which there shall be no high class and low class of people; an India in which all communities shall live in perfect harmony." Public housing, and private housing with appropriate homes for the poor in and around the same cluster, will go a long way towards fulfilling Mahatma Gandhi's dream. With regard to housing, it is vital not to use vote bank politics with slum dwellers: allowing them to stay put indefinitely, granting property rights for the slums, and so on. Such actions will surely create the moral hazard of continued expansion of slums. It will go down as the perpetuation of the culture of one of the grossest forms of visible inequality.

10

PRAJNA PARAMITA MISHRA

Gender Inequality at Work

Case of a Mining Community

Introduction

The India Development Policy Review 2006, titled "Inclusive Growth and Service Delivery: Building on India's Success", focuses on two major challenges facing the country today: improving the delivery of core public services and maintaining rapid growth while spreading the benefits of this growth more widely (World Bank, 2006). It is noted that the government policy is looking beyond just maintaining rapid growth to making growth more inclusive (Rao, 2006). The Approach Paper to the Eleventh Five Year Plan of India also aims towards faster and more inclusive growth, i.e., the growth must benefit one and all (Government of India, 2006). Despite strong economic performance of India over the years, a huge gap still remains between the rich and poor. To bridge the gap, employment plays a very vital role and in the provision of employment opportunities gender should play an important role as women constitute nearly half of the Indian population.

In this era of globalisation and privatisation, gender role at work participation is a significant issue. As per the 2001 Census, the work participation rate (WPR), which is a measure of economically active population to total population, shows that the WPR of male workers has been almost stagnating. Contrary to this, the work participation rate of female workers has registered an increasing trend. Regarding WPRs of women, it would be useful to have some discussion on changes in census definitions. In the censuses of 1891-1921, the main economic question related to livelihood or occupation or means of subsistence of each person. As a result, economically active population included the persons, who were not working but receiving income from land, property, interest etc. The concept of 'income' was introduced in the 1931 census and continued up to 1951 census. In 1961 census, the concept of 'work' was introduced as opposed to income, the population classified into workers and non-workers (Government of India, 2001). Housewives, who in addition to house work, engaged themselves in work for sale of product or in domestic service of others for wages were treated as 'workers'. At the 1971 census, a person was treated as a worker only if he had spent his time mainly in work or if he worked at least for a day in regular (non-seasonal) work during the preceding week, and therefore, the reference period for regular work was changed from one fortnight in 1961 to one week in 1971. As a result of changed definition and concepts, the WPR suffered in 1971. While the overall population increased from 439 million to 548 million, the number of workers declined from 188 million to 180 million and the number of female workers showed a decline from 59.5 million in 1961 to 31.5 million in 1971 (Government of India, 2001). The 1981 census classify the population into two groups: main workers—those who had worked for the major part of the year (6 months [183 days]) and marginal workers—those who had worked for less than 6 months (183 days). In the 1991 census, the definition of economic activity was enlarged to include all types of unpaid family work. The information was to be collected for all unpaid work in farm or family enterprise and specially the women who constitute the predominant part of unpaid workforce. After 1991 census, it was found out that WPR of women was low due to under reporting. The economic questions were reformulated and so that females, children and the aged, who work only during the peak season in farm and non-farm activities such as ploughing, sowing, harvesting, and collection of farm produce, were not missed by the census. Persons engaged in cultivation and growing of crops (except plantation crops) solely for domestic consumption and persons engaged in rearing of animals for production of milk for their own use, were decided to be treated as 'workers'.

The female WPR increased from 14.2 per cent in 1971 to 25.68 per cent in 2001 (Government of India, 2008). The increase has been more in rural areas (8.1%) in the last 20 years. This is more than double the increase in urban area (3.6%). It is important to emphasise that, this is despite the fact that in rural areas women are generally engaged in agricultural subsistence work, including unpaid work on farms and it is difficult to identify them separately (Government of India, 2008). The female WPRs in the country vary substantially across the geographical regions and even among the states of the same region. This may be due to different cultural traditions and socioeconomic condition of the women. Reported female work participation is also sensitive to changes in the wording of questions and the enumeration practices adopted in different censuses.

Women comprise the vast majority of world's unpaid informal workforce. They are the most discriminated, most vulnerable and least empowered members of many societies (Macdonald, 2003). Most of the time women are included as cheap labour in the informal sector. Discrimination of women also takes place outside the labour market such as unequal access to formal education, skill training, restricting their employment opportunities (Chakravarty, 2004). The Beijing Declaration, adopted at the Fourth World Conference on Women in 1995, recognises women's empowerment and their full participation on the basis of equality in all sphere of society, including participation in the decision-making process and access to power, as fundamental for the achievement of equality, development and peace. Similarly, Principle 20 of the Rio Declaration on Environment and Development, adopted at the Earth Summit in 1992, emphasises women's vital role in environmental management and development. Therefore, their full participation is essential to achieve sustainable development. Over the years a change in economy has brought about a visibility for the women worker which did not exist before (Jhabvala and Sinha, 2002). The term 'feminisation of labour' is now widely used as women are now visible in all areas of work.

With this background, this paper has tried to study the work participation of women in a coal mining area of India. In several parts of the developing world, women have worked in the past and continue to work as miners, either independently, as part of a family unit of labour, or as employees of others (Lahiri-Dutt and Macintyre,

2006). Mining has played an important role in the modernisation of the developing world. Most of the literature on mining has reflected on the negative impacts of mining on women. However, this paper has tried to look at the role of women in the WPR of a coal mining region.

This paper has tried to answer the following research questions.

(a) To what extent women are involved in mining, especially in Indian coal mining?

(b) What are the different economic activities in which women of mining community are involved except mining?

(c) Do they have more diversified livelihoods than the women of non-mining villages?

This paper has been organised as follows. Section 1 is an introduction to the study. The role of women in the context of Indian coal mine is discussed in section 2. Section 3 is about methodology and data collection. This section also gives a brief introduction of the study area. Section 4 discusses the role of women in the Ib Valley Coalfield of Odisha, India. It also compares their livelihoods activities with that of non-mining villages. Finally, section 5 concludes the study.

Coal Mining and Women Miners in India

Mining industry is generally perceived as a male dominated sector. Mining employs only 1 per cent of the global work force. Of the various types of mining, coal mining employed only 5 per cent of women (Lahiri-Dutt, 2000). India is the 3rd largest coal producing country. Coal India Limited (CIL) contributes around 85 per cent of coal production in India. According to CIL, it is the largest company in the world in terms of coal production and is the largest corporate employer in the country employing nearly 425,000 persons (Coal India Limited, 2009). However, the increasing reliance on open cast mining has brought a decline in coal mining jobs, even if coal mining rapidly expands and production is rising. Table 10.1 shows the employment in Indian coal mines by category and sex. After 1985, total employment declined over the years. In 1985, it had reached 551,000 and declined to 393,000 by 2004. Total employment of both

Table 10.1

Employment in Indian Coal Mines: By Category and Sex

Years	Below Ground	Open Cast Working			Above Ground			Total		
		Male	Female	Total	Male	Female	Total	Male	Female	Total
1961	229547	45510	14979	60489	98151	23078	121229	373208	38057	411265
1971	228345	34909	8109	43018	98852	12035	110887	362106	20144	382250
1981	302324	45594	9568	55162	134582	21290	155872	482500	30858	513358
1985	317023	57181	7609	64790	146891	22487	169387	521095	30096	551191
1990	312625	62956	3562	66518	150838	19114	169952	524619	22676	549095
1995	287240	64123	3781	67904	140446	17723	158169	492809	20504	513313
2000	248819	66854	1997	68851	127629	13088	140717	443304	15085	458387
2001	239457	67284	1737	69021	117965	11736	129701	424706	13473	438179
2004	210962	61332	1618	62950	108778	10824	119602	381070	12442	393514

Source: http://www.indiastat.com/

male and female member has declined. However, in case of open cast mining female employment has drastically reduced from 1961 to 1994. Number of women working above ground has also reduced over the years.

In many countries of the world, employment is falling as a result of mechanisation and privatisation. This process first displaced women workers as the surplus labour. Lahiri-Dutt (2000) has explained about the women WPR in Eastern Coalfield Limited (ECL).[1] In the initial phase of mining development in ECL, tribal and semi tribal people were employed in large number along with their women. The percentage of female worker was as high as 61 per cent in 1921. These people were leaving the coal mines during agricultural season to work in their own field. As a result, collieries began to bring male immigrants labour (Lahiri-Dutt, 2000). In the history of Indian coal mines, women work participation was not significant except in the coal mines of ECL (Lahiri-Dutt, 2000). Table 10.2 shows the insignificant participation of women in the subsidiaries of CIL. Percentage of female workers is highest in the CIL headquarters followed by CCL and ECL. Due to the Hindu dominated population and prevalence of patriarchy, women are not allowed to go and work.

The role of women in the mining industry has declined over the years but after nationalisation it has decreased at an alarming rate. In most of the countries, mining remains a male dominated sector. It is partly because of legislation prohibiting women from working underground; a ban contested on evidence that such work endangers women's health and also increasing mechanisation is reducing the workforce (MMSD, 2002). At the international level, a number of International Labour Organisation (ILO) conventions have restrictions for women's involvement in shift work and underground mines. The 1919 Convention on Night Work (Women) prohibited women from industrial work during the night. The 1935 Convention

1. CIL has nine subsidiaries. They are Eastern Coalfields Limited (ECL), Northern Coalfields Limited (NCL), South Eastern Coalfields Limited (SECL), Western Coalfields Limited (WCL), Mahanadi Coalfields Limited (MCL), Central Coalfields Limited (CCL), Bharat Coking Coal Limited (BCCL), North Eastern Coalfields Limited (NECL), and Central Mine Planning and Design Institute Limited (CMPDIL).

on Underground Work (Women) prohibited all female, whatever her age, to be employed on underground work in any mine. In 1901, the Indian Mines Act restricted the age of employment of children in mines. In 1935, the Act prohibited companies to employ women in underground mines. In 1952, there was a complete ban which stated that women miners will be employed only in surface work during the day shifts. The period of work got restricted from 16 to 8 hours for underground workers and 9 hours for surface workers (Lahiri-Dutt, 2001).

Table 10.2

Sex-wise Employees in CIL and its Subsidiaries in India

Company	*Total Workers*	*Female Workers*	*Male Workers*
ECL	100104	8397 (8.39)	91707
BCCL	84960	6902 (8.12)	78058
CCL	62973	5340 (8.47)	57633
WCL	66324	3103 (4.67)	63221
SCCL	85022	3529 (4.15)	81493
MCL	20770	988 (4.75)	19782
NCL	16811	534 (3.17)	16277
NEC	3251	263 (8.08)	2988
CMPDI	3170	159 (5.01)	3011
DCC	647	34 (5.25)	613
CIL HQ	1134	162 (14.28)	972
Total	445166	29411 (6.60)	415755

Note: Figures in parenthesis are in percentage.

Source: *http://www.indiastat.com/*

The various protective legislations developed for women miners, though probably designed to improve their working conditions, have acted as instruments to exclude them from formal mining sector. The nationalised company has been unwilling to recruit women because of their special and protected status on the one hand, and on the other hand the legislation has not included any means for the protection of employment opportunities and job security (Lahiri-Dutt, 2006). Table 10.3 shows the mine-wise man power of Ib Valley

Coalfield (a part of MCL). MCL was started in 1992, two decades after nationalisation, to take care of both the coalfields of Odisha. It is clear from the Table that female manpower is very very low in the Ib Valley Coalfield. This paper has concentrated on Ib Valley Coalfield and tries to find out the different economic activities in which the mining villages women are involved in and how diversified is their livelihoods in comparison to that of non-mining villages.

Table 10.3

Mine-wise Manpower of Ib Valley Coal Field

Mine Name	*Male*	*Female*	*Total*
Lajkura	553	06	559
Samaleswari	755	13	768
OC 1&2	N.A	N.A	1110
OC 3	N.A	N.A	1251
OC 4	N.A	N.A	568
HRC	N.A	N.A	981
HBM	N.A	N.A	1020
Belpahar	1003	24	1027
Lakhanpur	736	04	740
Lilari	264	02	266

Source: MCL Office.

Study Area, Data Collection and Methodology

This study concentrates on the Ib Valley Coalfield of Odisha. Odisha state has two coalfields. One is Talcher and the other is Ib Valley Coalfield. Ib Valley Coalfield is situated in Jharsuguda and Sundargarh district of Odisha between latitudes 21° 32’ to 22° 06’ N and longitudes 83° 32’ to 84° 10’ E covering an area of 1375 square kilometer. The coalfield is named after the river Ib, a tributary of the river Mahanadi. After nationalisation of coal mines, the mines came under WCL. Later on, it came under SECL and then under MCL after its formation in 1992. Now this coalfield has been divided into 5 areas comprising 5 underground and 7 opencast mines. The five areas are: Orient area, Ib valley area, Lakhanpur area, Basundhara area and

Garjanbahal area. The last two areas are new compared to the first three. Basundhara started operation after 1997, and Garjanbahal is yet to start operation. This study concentrated on the first three areas.

As coal mining started in this area nearly a century ago and it was difficult to go for a before and after comparison. Therefore, a with and without method is used. The sample consists of five villages situated near the coal mines (mining villages) and two villages, which are away from the coal mines (control villages) but belong to the same district. In the mining villages, three combinations of villages were taken to see the difference of impact between the underground mines and the opencast mines. They are: (a) two villages near underground mines, (b) two villages near opencast mines, and (c) two villages near both underground and opencast mines. Data were collected from January 2005 to May 2005. Information was gathered with the help of a structured questionnaire. The households were selected using the circular systematic sampling method. In total, 360 households were selected—260 from the mining villages and 100 from the control villages.

To compare the diversified livelihoods, a Herfindahl Index was used. In economics, the Herfindahl Index is a measure of the size of firms in relationship to the industry and an indicator of the amount of competition among them. It is defined as the sum of the squares of the market shares of each individual firm.

$$H = \sum (S_i^2) \quad (1)$$

Where S_i is the market share of firm i in market. The Herfindahl Index (H), also known as Herfindahl-Hirschman Index (HHI), has a value that is always smaller than one. A decrease in the Herfindahl Index generally indicates a loss of pricing power and an increase in competition, while an increase implies monopoly. This Herfindahl Index can be used in the diversification measurement issues (Barrett and Reardon, 2000). The diversification index is calculated as:

$$D_1 = 1\text{-}H \quad (2)$$

Generally in economics, the most common method of diversification is the Gini coefficient. The advantage of Herfindahl Index is its computational simplicity. Since its computation requires just simple arithmetic, it is easier to memorise than the discrete approximation to an integral that comprises the Gini (Barrett and Reardon, 2000). The Herfindahl requires only knowing positive values because the square of a zero share is always zero and therefore does not affect the sum. One does not have to identify the full range of admissible assets, activities or income sources in the population before one calculates the first Herfindahl Index. On the other hand, the Gini coefficient value varies with the number of zero-valued entries. So it is important to know the full range of possibilities before estimating the first household's Gini coefficient (Barrett and Reardon, 2000).

Gini is invariant to expansion or contraction of the number of options available to the decision-maker, in contrast to the Herfindahl index. A good measure of diversification should change with adjustments to either the absolute or relative shares, as the Herfindahl Index does, not just the relative shares, as in the Gini. For these reasons, Herfindahl Index is used to study diversification behaviours (Barrett and Reardon, 2000). Computation of Herfindahl indices of asset holdings, activities to which different assets (land, labour and livestock) are applied, and incomes, allows for multidimensional perspective on household diversification behaviours. These index measures, therefore, provide a good supplement to simpler measures of income levels and shares.

Ib Valley Coalfield: A Case

Livelihood diversification is a survival strategy of the rural households in developing countries, as agricultural activities are unable to provide sufficient means of survival (Hussein and Nelson, 1998). Ellis (1998) defines livelihood diversification as "the process by which households construct a diverse portfolio of activities and social support capabilities for survival and in order to improve their standard of living." Livelihood diversification is normal for most people in majority of rural areas of developing countries in both Asia and Africa (Adams, 1994; Schoonmaker, 1994), and non-agricultural activities are a critical component of such diversification.

Although livelihood diversification is an important strategy that rural people adopt in order to achieve sustainable livelihood, there are two other strategies, which play an equally important role. They are migration and agricultural intensification (Hussein and Nelson, 1998). As agriculture is not playing an important role in the livelihood of the community in Ib Valley Coalfield, cases of migration are also not seen among the rural population (as mining provides them employment) hence, these two points have not been taken into consideration, and the emphasis is on livelihood diversification.

There is a general belief that mining brings economic development to the local community by increasing their chance of getting a secure job, and that it also results in the expansion of other business activities, as the population of that area rises. This conveys the idea of livelihoods in which own farming has become a relatively small proportion of the overall activity portfolios of the farm families (Ellis, 2000). However, this benefit is received at the cost of abandoning all their agricultural lands and sometimes homesteads. This section will discuss the different livelihoods options that households of mining villages are having. It will show the contribution of mining (direct and indirect) to the livelihoods of the rural people. At the same time, it will also compare the livelihoods of the control villages, hence giving an idea of the general villages of the same district where mines are not present.

It has been confirmed by many researchers that rural people not only specialise in crop and fish production or livestock, but also depend on other activities (Dercon and Krishnan, 1996; Ellis, 1996; Unni, 1996). This is reflected in all mining villages and control villages (Table 10.4). In all mining villages and control villages, majority of the workers are working in the construction sector (Table 10.4). A village near to underground mine is the only exception. In this village, majority of the workers are engaged in mining. In other two types of villages, mining is taking second majority of workers, which is absent in control villages. Percentages of cultivators are less in all mining villages than the control villages. This is because most of them no more possess agricultural land. The company has taken their land for mining expansion. In control villages this percentage is not significant (15.81). But 26 per cent of the households depend on agriculture as a secondary source of income in control villages. Trade and commerce is taking more percentage of workers in mining villages while others sector has a majority share in control villages. This is because mining village population is comparatively rich economically than the control village population.

Table 10.4

Occupational Distribution of Workers

Activities	*Villages Near OC Mines*	*Villages Near UG Mines*	*Villages Near OC+UG Mines*	*Control Villages*
Agriculture	23 (13.77)	4 (5.55)	12 (8.21)	31 (15.81)
Mining	47 (28.14)	34 (47.22)	45 (30.82)	0 (0.00)
Construction*	57 (34.13)	19 (26.38)	55 (37.67)	103 (52.55)
Trade and Commerce	13 (7.78)	7 (9.72)	13 (8.90)	5 (2.55)
Others	27 (16.16)	8 (11.11)	21 (14.38)	56 (29.08)
Total	167 (100.00)	72 (100.00)	146 (100.00)	196 (100.00)

Notes: Figures in parentheses shows the percentage of workers to total workers in the respective villages.

* Agricultural labour is another occupational activity. In case of both mining and control villages, agriculture is seasonal (July-November). In the control villages 103 workers, who are working in construction sector 49 (47.57%) of them work as agricultural labourer during this season. As in another eight months they are working in construction sector, their primary source of income is coming from that. Therefore, they are included in construction sector. In mining villages this percentage is 13.1.

Source: Field Study.

Many livelihood diversification strategies are often gender specific. Literature confirms that though women may undertake a similar wide range of diversified activities as men (Chen, 1989), in many contexts men are able to avail themselves of diverse opportunities that are not open to women because of cultural constraints (Hussein and Nelson, 1998). This section discusses all the economic activities taking gender into consideration (Table 10.5). In the mining villages a job in mine is an important source of income for nearly 47.5 per cent of the households. But it is a male dominated sector. From the five mining villages, in three of them, not a single woman of the sample households is working in the mines. From the other two villages, only three women are working in the mines.

Table 10.5

Gender Inequality in Economic Activities

Economic Activities	Villages near to OC Mines		Villages near to UG Mines		Villages near to OC+UG Mines		Control Villages	
	Male	Female	Male	Female	Male	Female	Male	Female
Mines/ Govt. Job[#]	47 (28.14)	0 (0)	32 (44.44)	2 (2.77)	44 (30.13)	1 (0.68)	14 (7.14)	4 (2.04)
Cultivator	21 (12.57)	2 (1.19)	4 (5.55)	0 (0)	10 (6.84)	2 (1.36)	30 (15.30)	1 (0.51)
Labour	43 (25.74)	14 (8.38)	16 (22.22)	3 (4.16)	46 (31.50)	9 (6.16)	70 (35.71)	33 (16.83)
Business	13 (7.78)	0(0)	7 (9.72)	0 (0)	13 (8.90)	0 (0)	3 (1.53)	2 (1.02)
Others	19 (11.37)	8 (4.79)	8 (11.11)	0 (0)	17 (11.64)	4 (2.73)	28 (14.28)	11 (5.61)

Notes: Figures in parentheses shows the percentage of workers in the respective villages.

\# In case of mining villages, this is job in mines and, in case of control villages, this is central and state government job.

Source: Field Work.

According to Lahiri-Dutt (2001), in India from 1900 to 1935 women accounted for over 30 per cent of the workforce in opencast mining in the Eastern Indian Collieries, whereas now they represent approximately 6 per cent of total employment in mining in that region. This is reflected in Ib Valley Coalfield, where the women participation rate in mining is negligible (Table 10.5). Very few women are found to be working as cultivators both in mining and control villages. This is because, the dependence on agriculture is decreasing in the mining villages, while in the control villages, they work as casual labour in agriculture. It has been observed that farming is also a male-dominated activity in rural Odisha.

The first reason for the absence of women participation in mining is that most of the people have a job in mine as a result of compensation package. In the patriarchal society, men always receive rehabilitation packages. Without having any legal rights over land or natural resources, women are neither consulted nor compensated during displacement. All compensation goes to the men and the women are always left behind (Kushwaha, 2003). Gender needs have never been a concern for rehabilitation packages and programmes. From the three women of the study villages, who are working in mines two of them are working as sweepers.

In this case it is also interesting to know the role of women in other forms of economic activities. The number of women working in construction sector is less in the mining villages, compared to the control villages. The reasons are: in the mining villages, most male members are engaged in mines and hence they have a good source of income. While in the control villages, the male members are engaged in agriculture (which is seasonal and also very uncertain as it depends on monsoon) and casual labour, where they do not have a good source of income. Another reason is women belonging to higher castes are not allowed to go out for work. Most of them are housewives, though some work if they are highly educated or if they have a socially prestigious job. Even in the Tangarpali village, where female participation in economic activities is the highest, the participation of females from the other caste (OC) group is very low. Scheduled tribe (ST) women in this village work as casual labour in a nearby brick kiln. As Lahiri-Dutt (2006) rightly points out, cultural identity such as ethnicity, caste and religion have powerful influence on social and gender relationships within the labour force in India.

Women play no role in business in the mining villages. In one of the control villages—Saletikra—two women of the OC group were engaged in business. One had a grocery shop in her home, and the other ran a flour mill in her home. Participation of women in other activities is also less in the mining villages, while in Saletikra 10 scheduled caste (SC) women are engaged in *beedi* making. It is made from Tendu leaves. People collect these leaves and send it to a nearby godown. Again they bring the dried leaves from that godown and prepare *beedi*. It is a part of livelihoods mainly in forest areas. In the mining villages Charla, some SC households are engaged in collecting Tendu leaves. However, with mining their access to natural resources is declining day by day. Neither do they have their agricultural land to cultivate nor access to natural resources.

It can be inferred that the, important causes of low women participation in workforce are: mechanisation and banning of women to work in mines, taboo for higher castes woman to work, which is not socially prestigious and their education standards not being high enough to get a good job. In case of other castes most of them used to collect forest products, and as forests are being destroyed due to mining, this activity has decreased. With mining, the economic standard of the households has risen considerably, so now women do not prefer to go out for work. The situation is the same in the control villages with an exception of SC and ST category. Among those women who are engaged in economic activities, most of them belong to SC and ST category. These women work as their income level is very low.

To show the diversification of livelihoods, the Herfindahl Index is again taken into account. The Herfindahl Index for diversification of livelihoods is shown in Table 10.6. The Table shows that control villages have comparatively more diversified sources of livelihoods than all the mining villages. Even though women WPR is not high enough in both the villages, still the figures of control village reflects that they have a diversified livelihoods.

Table 10.6

Herfindahl Index for Livelihoods Diversification

Villages	*Herfindahl Index*	*Diversification*
Mining Villages	0.978739	0.021261
Control Villages	0.919444	0.080556

Source: Fieldwork.

In control villages, villagers are mostly dependent on agriculture. But agriculture is not a safe source of income as without irrigational facilities it depends on monsoon. And monsoon is uncertain in this area every year. Therefore, the villagers have to look for alternative sources of income in search of livelihoods.

Conclusion

An awareness of gender issues has come to the mining sector. There is a rising demand of gender equity and people are conscious about women past roles in the mines and their present contribution. Historically, women's participation in the labour force has given them greater economic autonomy and has been the basis for politicisation and demands for gender equity (Lahiri-Dutt and Macintyre, 2006). From the above discussion it is clear that coal mining, which is a good form of physical capital, is providing a good source of energy to the country. It is also a good source of revenue. People are getting direct and indirect employment. However, this sector is highly neglecting one section of society that is women. With mining, they have lost their socio-economic status and the patriarchal society is also to some extent working as a barrier.

Alternative livelihoods promoted in the mining areas are often unattractive for the people working there because income from mining is much higher. Credit schemes coupled with training measures are introduced by some development organisations to encourage women to pursue alternative livelihoods (Banchirigah, 2008). Increasing the levels of education amongst women could improve their skills and level of participation in farming, trading and small scale mining, thereby encouraging them to become more proactive in securing loans, developing businesses and improving health of their families. Mining can only be an effective vehicle of economic development if gender concerns are built into every aspect of project development.

References

Adams, R.H. (1994). "Non-farm Income and Inequality in Rural Pakistan: A Decomposition Analysis", *Journal of Development Studies* 30(1): 146-67.

Banchirigah, S.M. (2008). "Challenges with Eradicating Illegal Mining in Ghana: A Perspective from the Grassroots", *Resources Policy* 33(1): 29-38.

Barrett, Christopher C. and Thomas Reardon (2000). "Asset, Activity and Income Diversification Among African Agriculturists: Some Practical Issues", Unpublished Project Report to USAID BASIS CRSP. USA: Cornell University.

Chakravarty, D. (2004). "Expansions of Markets and Women Workers: Case Study of Garment Manufacturing in India", *Economic and Political Weekly* 39(45): 4910-16.

Chen, M. (1989). "Women and Household Livelihood Systems", *ARDA* 15(2-3).

Coal India Limited (2009). *About Us*. Available at *https://www.coalindia.in/en-us/company/aboutus.aspx* (Accessed on 15 July 2009).

Dercon, S. and P. Krishnan (1996). "Income Portfolios in Rural Ethiopia and Tanzania: Choices and Constraints", *Journal of Development Studies* 32(6): 850-75.

Ellis, F. (1996). "Policy Implications of Rural Livelihood Diversification". *Mimeo*. Overseas Development Group. Norwich: University of East Anglia.

Ellis, F. (1998). "Survey Article: Household Strategies and Rural Livelihoods Diversification", *The Journal of Development Studies* 35 (1): 1-38.

————. (2000). *Rural Livelihoods and Diversity in Developing Countries*. Oxford: Oxford University Press.

Government of India (2001). *Census of India*. New Delhi: Office of the Registrar General and Census Commissioner. Ministry of Home Affairs.

————. (2006). *Towards Faster and More Inclusive Growth: An Approach Paper to the 11th Five Year Plan*. New Delhi: Planning Commission. Government of India.

————. (2008). *Workers and Non-Workers*. An Analysis based on 2001 Census. New Delhi: Office of the Registrar General and Census Commissioner. Ministry of Home Affairs.

Hussein, K. and J. Nelson (1998). "Sustainable Livelihoods and Livelihoods Diversification", *IDS Working Paper* 69. Sussex: Institute of Development Studies.

Jhabvala, R. and S. Sinha (2002). "Liberalisation and the Women Workers", *Economic and Political Weekly* 37(21): 2037-44.

Kushwaha, R. (2003). "Women in Mining Areas Suffer Social, Physical, Mental Abuse", *Free India Media*, July 21. Available at *http://www.freeindiamedia.com/women/21_july_03_women1.htm*

Lahiri-Dutt, K. (2000). "Gender Dimension of Mining", *Mining Environmental Management* 8 (5):19-21.

————. (2001). "From Gini Girls to Scavenger: Women in Raniganj Collieries", *Economic and Political Weekly* 36(44): 4213-21.

————. (2006). "Kamins Building the Empire: Class, Caste, and Gender Interface in Indian Collieries", in Jaclyn J. Gier and Laurie Mercier (eds.), *Mining Women: Gender in the Development of a Global Industry, 1670 to 2005*. New York: Palgrave Macmillan.

Lahiri-Dutt, K. and Martha Macintyre (2006). *Women Miners in Developing Countries Pit Women and Others*. Hants, England: Ashgate.

Macdonald, I. (2002). "Introduction: Women's Rights Undermined", in Ingrid Macdonald and Claire Rowland (eds.), *Tunnel Vision Women, Mining and Communities*. Victoria, Australia: Oxfam Community Aid Abroad.

———. (2003). "Tunnel Vision: Women's Rights Undermined?", Paper presented in *Women in Mining Conference*. Madang. August 03.

Mining, Minerals and People (2003). "Women in Mining Struggles in India: The Invisibility of Gender Concerns in Mining Struggle", *Background Paper*, Indian Women and Mining Seminar. Delhi.

MMSD (2002). *Breaking New Ground: Mining, Minerals, and Sustainable Development*. London: Earthscan Publications Ltd.

Rao, B. (2006). "An Inclusive Policy for All", *Business Line*, December 12.

Schoonmaker, F.K. (1994). "Challenges in the Collection and Use of Information on Livelihood Strategies and Natural Resource Management", in I. Scoones and J. Thompson (eds.), *Beyond Farmer First*. London: Intermediate Technology Publications. pp.124-33.

Unni, J. (1996). "Diversification of Economic Activities and Non-agricultural Employment in Rural Gujarat", *Economic and Political Weekly* 31(33): 2243-50.

World Bank (2006). "Inclusive Growth and Service Delivery: Building on India's Success", *Development Policy Review. Report* No. 34580-IN. Washington D.C.

11

SHAHEEN

Millennium Development Goals and Muslim Minorities in India

A Status Report

Introduction

The Millennium Development Goals (MDGs) emerged from Millennium Declaration with 189 signatory countries during the United Nations Millennium Summit, in September 2000. Through the MDGs, the United Nations (UN) reaffirmed its commitment to the right to development, peace, security, gender equality, eradication of poverty and sustainable development. Globally minorities are among the poorest of the poor. The UN Declaration on the Rights of Persons Belonging to National or Ethnic, Religious and Linguistic Minorities (UNDM) says "States should consider appropriate measures so that persons belonging to minorities may participate fully in the economic progress and development in their country" (Article 4.5). In the UN's Millennium Declaration (2000), states expressed their commitment to including minority rights into national framework.

India has an important role to play in the achievement of the MDGs, and the broader global objectives of the Millennium Declaration, as India alone accounts for nearly one-fourth (364 million) of the world's poor, largest number of maternal deaths in the world and dismal rates of infant mortality and maternal mortality. India is also home to the highest number of undernourished people in the world, and one-third of the world's under-weight children. The progress made by India will significantly determine whether the world will be able to meet some of the most critical targets of the MDGs such as infant mortality rates (IMR), maternal mortality rates (MMR), school enrolment and retention, as well as universal access to water and sanitation. On the other hand, India as the world's largest democracy has an important contribution to make to the future global agenda through significant technical, intellectual, financial and historic contributions. India being one of the 189 signatory countries of the UN Millennium Declaration has adopted MDGs as a measure of their progress on key development indicators galvanising large scale support for its achievement.

India provides a wonderful kaleidoscope of the country's rich social composition. India is the birthplace of several religions, Hinduism, Buddhism, Jainism, and Sikhism, and has been a home for different communities (Jews, Zoroastrians, Muslims and Christians) for thousands of years. Minorities in India, as per the National Commission of Minorities Act, 1992, are Muslims, Christians, Buddhists, Sikhs and Parsis. Muslims constitute the second largest religious group in India and the largest religious minority. Sachar Committee Report (2006) outlines that Muslims as a community, in India are deeply impecunious and suffer from huge illiteracy, high drop-out rate, below average work participation rate (WPR), poor credit flow, poor water and sanitation facilities, and high IMR and MMR. Asghar (2007) in his article pointed out the problems associated with minority communities especially Muslims. He argued that in India, Muslims are a very large minority and hence their exclusion from social, cultural, economic and political processes poses much greater problems. Mistry (2005) presents a demographic history of Indian Muslims, including the growth and distribution of the Muslim population across Indian states over the past century. Comparative fertility and mortality rates are presented for various religious communities to explain the differential growth of the Muslim population. Khalidi (2006), providing statistics to back his point, argues that while in recent years a few Muslims have undoubtedly witnessed some degree of improvement in their economic conditions, the majority of Muslims still remain mired in poverty. Shariff (1998) argues that the WPR among the Muslims is the least, both for males and females, suggesting a relatively higher unemployment rate as compared to other communities defined by religion. Hasan (2003) presents that educational backwardness among the Muslims, is the product of poverty and neglect by the state. Due to structural location in the economy and the perception of discrimination, only few Muslims can afford or aspire for the higher education. He stresses the need for affirmative action. Nayar (2007) states that poverty and social exclusion are important socioeconomic variables which are often taken for granted while considering ill-health effects. In the Indian context, Nayar argues that caste may be considered broadly as a proxy for socio-economic status and poverty. In his review, he examined broad linkages between castes and some select health utilisation indicators, and also examined data on prevalence of anaemia, treatment of diarrhoea, IMR, utilisation of maternal health care and childhood vaccinations among different caste groups in India. Nayar pointed out that the linkages between caste and some health indicators show that poverty is a complex issue which needs to be addressed with a multi-dimensional paradigm.

Against this backdrop, this paper is conceptualised to assess the progress of marginalised Muslim minorities in India against the MDGs. It also measures the performance of the signatory country India towards meeting the targets in 2015.

The paper is organised as follows. Starting with the introduction, the second section provides a detailed summary of the MDGs from the Millennium Declaration. The third section provides a summary of a comprehensive analysis of the progress of India with reference to the goals and targets. The fourth section relates to the review of performance of Muslim minorities in India against the targets identified in the MDGs.

For the purpose of this study, the research parameters are confined to pan-India patterns. The paper is based on the relevant secondary data collected from various reports of government agencies, civil society organisations, individual works by researchers and institutions associated with religious minorities, UNDP, UNICEF and other international and national sources.

Millennium Development Goals: A Snapshot

In September 2000, the Millennium Declaration was adopted at the Millennium Summit, held in the 55th General Assembly of the UN. MDGs and targets come from the Millennium Declaration, with 189 signatory countries, including 147 heads of the State and Government. The MDGs comprise 8 goals, 21 targets and 60 indicators as quantitative benchmarks for attaining the goals (UNDG, 2003). Some objectives are set in proportional terms while other objectives are set out as statements of intentions. The goals from the declaration include:

Goal 1—Eradicate extreme poverty and hunger: The first set of MDGs aims to reduce extreme poverty by half in the period between 1990 and 2015. It also aims to bring down the share of population suffering from national hunger in the same period by 50 per cent. The indicators for measuring success are: the percentage of population earning below 1.25 dollar a day; the poverty gap ratio; and the share of the poorest quintile in national consumption. Other indicators include: prevalence of underweight children under five years of age and proportion of population below minimum level of dietary energy consumption.

Goal 2—Achieve universal primary education: Education is a key indicator in how a country is developing. This is to be achieved by ensuring that by 2015 children—boys and girls alike—will be able to complete a full course of primary school. Net enrolment ratio in primary education, proportion of pupil starting at grade I who reach grade V, and literacy rate of 15-24 age group are the indicators proposed to measure success in achieving the set goal.

Goal 3—Promote gender equality and empower women: It lays emphasis on eliminating gender disparity in primary and secondary education, and at all subsequent levels of education. Ratio of girls to boys in primary, secondary and tertiary education, ratio of literate women to men in the 15-24 age groups, share of women in wage employment and proportion of seats held by women in the national legislature are the indicators for measuring success in instituting gender equality scheme.

Goal 4—Reduce child mortality: Under-five mortality rate (U5MR), IMR, and proportion of 1-year old children immunised against measles are indicators that measure success in reaching MDG targets by 2015.

Goal 5—Improve maternal health: The target includes reducing by three-quarters, the MMR in the period between 1990 and 2015. The indicators include MMR and proportion of births attended by skilled health personnel. The MMR is a measure of the number of women aged 15-49 years dying from maternal causes per 100,000 live births. The major causes of maternal death are excessive bleeding during childbirth (common in home deliveries), obstructed and prolonged labour, infection, unsafe abortion, disorders related to high blood pressure and anaemia. Furthermore, what also contributes to MMR is the lack of complete antenatal care.

Goal 6—Combat HIV/AIDS, malaria and other diseases: The MDG envisages halting the spread of preventable diseases such as HIV-AIDS, malaria and tuberculosis, and reversing the trend by the year 2015—crucial to the general health of the population. The relevant indicators designed to measure the success of the goal are: HIV prevalence among young pregnant women aged 15-24 years, condom use rate under the contraceptive prevalence rate (CPR), condom use at last high-risk sex, CPR, ratio of school attendance of orphans to school attendance of non-orphan aged 10-14 years, prevalence of deaths associated with malaria and tuberculosis, proportion of population in malaria risk areas using effective malaria prevention and treatment measures, and proportion of tuberculosis cases detected and cured under directly observed treatment short course (DOTS).

Goal 7—Ensure environmental sustainability: Much of the focus in this goal is regarding physical environmental concerns. The targets are proportion of land area covered by forest, ratio of area protected to maintain biological diversity to surface area, energy use per $1 GDP (PPP), carbon dioxide emissions per capita and consumption of ozone depleting chlorofluoro carbons (CFCs), proportion of population using solid fuels, proportion of population with sustainable access to an improved water source—urban and rural, proportion of population with sustainable access to an improved sanitation—urban and rural, proportion of households with access to secure tenure. The tangible targets are to bring down by half the proportion of population without sustainable access to safe drinking water and sanitation, and to improve the lives of the slum-dwellers by 2020.

Goal 8—Develop a global partnership for development: Developing countries struggle to compete against developed countries because of the world's unfair trade rules which allow developed countries to heavily subsidise their industries and corporations as well as placing high tariffs on the exports from developing countries. The targets are unemployment rate of young people aged 15-24 years—each sex and total, telephone lines and cellular subscribers per 100 population, personal computers in use per 100 population/Internet users per 100 populations.

The collective aim is to use these goals as the framework for national and international development activities to 2015. There is no compulsion for any country to work towards meeting the MDG targets. However, MDGs have become the most widely acknowledged yardstick to measure development efforts for judging the nations progress. Failure to comply reflects poorly on nation's capability and will also bring in international pressure. The year 1990 has been considered as the base year and the year 2015 as the end period for this purpose.

Millennium Development Goals: National Status and Progress

As we draw closer to 2015, India being one of the 189 countries pledging to adopt the MDGs in their respective national planning frameworks, an assessment of progress in meeting the stated objectives and targets of MDGs is called for. It is important to evaluate group-specific performance in assessing its achievements and relevance because of India's entrenched social hierarchy and complex cultural diversity. In the Indian context, an ideal exercise with MDG indicators needs to capture the depth and spread of the catchment population that forms the problem spheres (*Millennium Development Goals—India Country Report, 2011*). India's MDG framework is as per the UNDG's framework and it consists of 8 goals, 12 targets (target 1 to 11 and target 18) and 35 indicators. While MDGs are general in nature, the targets under the same are more specific. Indicators for measuring the progress of these targets are defined in concrete terms. Some of the targets are relative to base value; some of the targets are absolute, while others aim at trend reversal.

The rationale of the MDGs is to focus policies and programmes that have maximum beneficial effect. The goals and targets embodied in the MDGs have found reflection in India's development priorities. The effort to meet and better the MDGs in India is a stated objective in many of the key policy documents of the country, including the Twelfth Five Year Plan. In quantifiable terms, the inclusive growth strategy involved identifying 27 targets at the national level that were placed in 6 major categories namely: income and poverty, education, health, women and children, infrastructure and environment. Government of India (GoI) through its planned implementation of countrywide welfare programmes (Sarva Shiksha Abhiyan [SSA] (Education for all), the National Rural Health Mission [NRHM], the Expanded Midday Meal Scheme, the Integrated Child Development Mission [ICDM], Sampoorna Grameen Rozgar Yojana [SGRY]) with enhanced budget allocation, demonstrated its commitment to achieve the MDGs by 2015. The global economic crisis during 2008-09 has impacted the social development initiatives. Food crisis during drought and fuel crisis have impacted the development process, despite the resilience shown by Indian economy.

Towards Achieving Millennium Development Goals India 2013 report (MoSPI, 2013) presents a snapshot of the status of India's progress and likely achievements *vis-à-vis* the targets. It reveals that the recent trend of sharper decline in poverty headcount ratio (PHR), IMR and U5MR, and MMR are rays of hope which indicates near achievement of the respective MDG targets. Despite noteworthy progress made, all the MDGs will not be met by 2015.

The MDGs that grew as agreements and resolutions of several UN World Conferences have been accepted as framework for measuring development progress of a nation. First seven goals directed at reducing poverty are mutually reinforcing. Eighth goal, global partnership for development, refers to the means for attaining the first seven.

Goal 1: Eradicate Extreme Poverty and Hunger

Reducing poverty is the key factor for inclusive growth for any country, which is also followed by India (MoSPI, 2011). In India, the standards for measuring poverty differ from international definition. Planning Commission data reveals decline in PHR from 36 per cent in 1993-94 to 27.5 per cent in 2004-05. As per the poverty estimates of 2011-12, PHR is 21.9 against the target of 23.9 for 2015. Poverty gap ratio (PGR) indicating the depth of poverty is recorded as 5.05 for rural and 2.70 for urban India in 2011-12 as shown in the Table 11.1. If there is an improvement in the rate of decline in poverty, India is expected to achieve its target by 2015. Share of poorest quintile in national consumption is recorded as 9.75 in rural India and 7.11 in urban India in 2009-10. National Sample Survey (NSS) results reveal that calorie consumption in rural India has consistently declined since 1987-88 from 1683 kcal to 1624 kcal in 2004-05. Malnutrition is a significant indicator of food insecurity which continues to be a major hurdle. Prevalence of underweight children under 3 years of age is recorded as 43.5 per cent in 2011 against 52 per cent in 1990, which shows that India is going slow in eliminating the effect of malnourishment. It is expected to reach 33 per cent by 2015 against target value of 26 per cent. Goal 1 may fall short of the target though the pace of reduction of poverty and hunger has accelerated. Table 2.1 summarises the progress of indicators against MDG1.

Table 11.1

Status of Indicators for MDG 1

Indicator	*Achievement*	*Target for 2015*
PHR (2011-12)	21.9	23.9
Prevalence of underweight children under 3 years of age (2011)	43.5%	26%
Indicator	*Rural*	*Urban*
PGR (2011-12)	5.05	2.70
Share of Poorest Quintile in National Consumption (2009-10)	9.75	7.11

Source: MoSPI, 2013.

Government Policies/Initiatives

Some specific initiatives have been designed to help India meet its goal of eradicating extreme poverty and hunger, and ensuring employment for socially excluded. Nations commitment to fight poverty and hunger include.

1. National Rural Employment Guarantee Act (NREGA) renamed by an Amendment as the Mahatma Gandhi National Rural Employment Guarantee Act (MGNREGA), 2005 provides legal guarantee for 100 days employment in every financial year to adult members of any rural household at the statutory minimum wage.
2. SGSY organises the poor and build their capacities systematically to take up self-employment opportunities and link them to sustainable livelihood opportunities. SGSY has been renamed as National Rural Livelihood Mission (NRLM).
3. Indira Awas Yojana (IAY) provides financial assistance to the BPL (below poverty line) households in rural areas for construction of a dwelling unit.
4. Jawaharlal Nehru National Urban Renewal Mission (JNNURM) initiates steps to bring about improvement in the existing service levels in a financially sustainable manner.
5. Important Twelfth Plan programmes addressing MDGs include National Food Security Mission, Rashtriya Krishi Vikas Yojana, MGNREGA, IAY, NRLM, National Urban Livelihood Mission and Rajiv Awas Yojana.

Goal 2: Achieve Universal Primary Education

Net enrolment ratio (NER) in primary education is universally taken as the major indicator to assess countries development against the 2015 target (MoSPI, 2011). NER of 40 per cent of India's population is 18 years and under. Money, policies and structures are now developed around them. Challenges for attaining this goal are lack of infrastructure, low amount of GDP invested into education and high absenteeism. District Information System on Education

(DISE) 2010-11 shows that NER at primary level is 99.89 as shown in Table 2.2. Achieving universal primary education is round the corner ahead of 2015. DISE shows proportion of pupils starting grade I who reach last grade of primary (Apparent Survival Rate) for 2010-11 as 82. India is likely to attain 100 per cent youth literacy rate by 2015. Table 11.2 summarises the progress of indicators against MDG2.

Table 11.2

Status of Indicators for MDG 2

Indicator	*Achievement*	*Target for 2015*
Net Enrollment Ratio at primary level (2010-11)	99.89	100
Proportion of pupils starting grade I who reach last grade of primary (2010-11)	82	

Source: MoSPI, 2013.

Government Policies/Initiatives

In 2002, The 86th Constitutional Amendment Act (CAA) was passed which is one of most significant development towards MDG goal. It made primary education a Fundament Right for all children in the age group of 6-14 years. GoI in partnership with State governments designed different schemes and programmes.

1. SSA (2000): programme for achievement of Universalisation of Elementary Education (UEE).
2. Mid Day Meal (MDM): largest school feeding programme for primary and upper primary school children to enhance enrolment, retention and attendance and simultaneously improve nutritional levels among children.

Goal 3: Promote Gender Equality and Empower Women

Education will lead to empowerment, and empowerment is possible only with access to education. Gender parity index (GPI) is the ratio of enrolment of female students to enrolment of male students in primary, secondary and tertiary levels. Gender parity has already been achieved in primary education by 2007-08 and the disparity in secondary education is set to disappear by 2015. According to the 2011 Census, 65.5 per cent females and 82.1 per cent of males—a gap of nearly 17 per cent points—were considered as literates. Due to an improvement in female literacy, the gender gap in literacy closed by nearly 5 per cent points in the period 1991-2001. However in the ensuing decade of 2001-2011, the gender gap reduced by only a further 3 per cent points indicating a slowing down of the process. The percentage share of women in wage employment in the non-agricultural sector was at 18.6 in 2009-10 (NSS) (19.6 in urban and 17.6 in rural areas). The proportion of seats held by women in National Parliament was 11.21 per cent in 2013 against the target of 50 per cent in 2015. The target has been achieved for primary grade and the progress is on track for secondary grade. Table 11.3 summarises the progress of indicators against MDG3.

Government Policies/Initiatives

To achieve targets set under this MDG, primary education is made free and compulsory for girls by state and Central governments.

Table 11.3

Status of Indicators for MDG 3

Indicator	*Achievement*	*Target for 2015*
Ratio of girls to boys in primary education (GPI of GER) (2010-11)	1.01	1.00
Ratio of girls to boys in secondary education (GPI of GER) (2010-11)	0.88	1.00
Ratio of girls to boys in tertiary education (GPI of GER) (2010-11)	0.79	1.00
Literacy rate of 15-24 years (2007-08)	86	100
Female to male literacy rate of 15-24 years (2007-08)	0.88	1.00
% Share of women in wage employment in the non-agricultural sector (NSSO, 2009-10)	18.6	50
Percentage of seats held by women in National Parliament (2013)	11.21	50

Source: MoSPI, 2013.

1. SSA (2000)—programme for achievement of UEE.
2. Early Child Care and Education (ECCE)—supports girls education, especially at elementary school stage.
3. ICDS—promote pre-school education and provide for training of anganwadi workers, primary school teachers, and health workers.
4. National Programme for Education of Girls at Elementary Level (NPEGEL)—provides additional provisions for enhancing the education of underprivileged/disadvantaged girls at elementary level.
5. Kasturba Gandhi Balika Vidyalaya (KGBV)—for setting up residential schools at upper primary levels for girls.
6. Important Twelfth Five Year Plan programmes addressing this MDG include Rashtriya Madhyamic Shiksha Abhiyan, Rashtriya Uchhtar Shiksh Abhiyan and National Mission for Empowerment of Women including Indira Gandhi Matritav Sahyog Yojana.

Goal 4: Reduce the U5MR by Two-thirds between 1990 and 2015

High prevalence of neonatal and infancy deaths still looms on the country leading to high child mortality in the last two decades. With 1 in 10 children dying before the age of five and almost 2 million children dying every year, India has an embarrassingly high child mortality rate. As per MDG targets, U5MR was to be reduced to 42 per thousand live births by 2015. India is likely to attain a 50 per thousand live births by 2015, missing the target by 10 percentage points. IMR is also likely to miss the 2015 target. IMR is 44,000 live births in 2011 against 27,000 live births. Proportion of 1 year (12-23 months) children immunised against measles was at 74.1 per cent in 2009 (UNICEF and GoI). India is expected to cover 89 per cent by 2015 with a likely fall of 11 percentage points from the target. Table 11.4 summarises the progress of indicators against MDG4.

Table 11.4

Status of Indicators for MDG 4

Indicator	*Achievement*	*Target for 2015*
U5MR (per 1000 live births) (2011)	55	42
IMR (per 1000 live births) (2012)	42	27
Proportion of 1 year old children immunised against measles	74.1	

Source: MoSPI, 2013.

Government Policies/Initiatives

1. ICDS—largest and unique programme for early childhood development.
2. Navjat Shishu Suraksha Karyakram (NSSK)—two day training programme on basic new born care and resuscitation.
3. Ministries and Departments of Government of India (GoI) in the Twelfth Five Year Plan designed specific programmes to specially address the MDG like National Health Mission, including NRHM.

Goal 5: Improve Maternal Health

Unsafe motherhood affects the health of the women, their families and communities which is mostly avoidable. Currently, there are states in India which number amongst the worst performing regions in the world, and India as a whole has more maternal deaths than any other country. The MMR was 200 per 1 lakh live births in 2010 against 109 (per 1 lakh live births) in 2015. Measures are to be initiated to bridge gaps in ensuring safe motherhood. Proportion of births attended by skilled health personnel has been increasing. With the increased rate of deliveries by skilled personnel 52 per cent was recorded in 2007-08 (NFHS) against a target of 100 per cent. Sixty-two per cent is the target likely to be achieved which is far short of the targeted coverage. Table 11.5 summarises the progress of indicators against MDG3.

Table 11.5

Status of Indicators for MDG 5

Indicator	*Achievement*	*Target for 2015*
MMR (per 100,000 live births) (2007-2009)	212	109
Proportion of births attended by skilled health personnel (%) (2007-08)	52.0	100

Source: MoSPI, 2013.

Government Policies/Initiatives

1. The Reproductive and Child Health Programme (RCHP)—addresses the issue of reduction of infant mortality rate.
2. Janani Suraksha Yojana (JSY)—led to a huge increase in institutional deliveries.
3. Accredited Social Health Activist (ASHA)—quality of antenatal and postnatal care is being strengthened.
4. Indira Gandhi Matritva Sahyog Yojana (IGMSY)—a conditional maternity benefit scheme.
5. Ministries and Departments of GoI designed goal specific important programmes in Twelfth Five Year Plan like National Health Mission including NRHM, ICDS, and National Mission for Empowerment of Women including Indira Gandhi Matritav Sahyog Yojana.

Goal 6: Combat HIV/AIDS, Malaria and Other Diseases

HIV epidemic in India is to a large extent confined among the high risk groups (MoSPI, 2011). It is estimated that 2.6 million people in India live with HIV/AIDS (UNAIDS). The disease is almost certain to spread due to the lack of knowledge about the disease, testing and prevention. Trend reversal in prevalence of HIV/AIDS continues since 2005 even though the reduction in prevalence has become less noticeable after 2007. Condom use rate of the contraceptive prevalence rate was 5.2 (NFHS) in 2005-06. Condom use at last high risk sex was 74 per cent (NACO [National AIDS Control Organisation]) in 2010. Percentage of population aged 15-24 years with comprehensive correct knowledge of HIV/AIDS was 32.9 (NACO) in 2006. The stability in reversing the trends in prevalence of malaria and TB is yet to be achieved. Prevalence of TB shows an increase since 2009. Death rates associated with malaria in 2010 was recorded as 0.06 (NVBDCP [National Vector Borne Disease Control Programme]). Deaths due to TB per 100,000 population was 26 (WHO report 2011) in 2010. Proportion of TB cases detected and cured under DOTS was 87 per cent (RNTCP [Revised National TB Control Programme]) in 2010. Table 11.6 summarises the progress of indicators against MDG6.

Table 11.6

Status of Indicators for Goal 6

Indicator	*Achievement*
HIV prevalence among pregnant women aged 15-24 years (%) (2010-11)	0.39
Condom use rate of the contraceptive prevalence rate (%) (2005-06)	5.2
Condom use at last high risk sex (2010)	74
% of population aged 15-24 years with comprehensive correct knowledge of HIV/AIDS (2006)	32.9
Annual parasite incidence rate (malaria) (2010)	1.3
Prevalence of TB (including HIV) per 100,000 population (2010)	256
Deaths due to TB per 100,000 population (2010)	26

Source: MoSPI, 2013.

Government Policies/Initiatives

Some specific initiatives have been designed to help India meet its goal of combating HIV/AIDS, malaria, tuberculosis and other diseases. The initiatives undertaken for meeting the target by 2015 include:

1. National AIDS Control Programme (NACO) aims at halting and reversing HIV epidemic in India.
2. RNTCP—decrease mortality due to TB and cut transmission of infection until TB ceases.
3. Ministries and Departments of GoI designed specialised programmes in the Twelfth Five Year Plan to address MDG6 like NVBDCP, RNTCP, and National AIDS & STD Control Programme.

Goal 7: Ensure Environmental Sustainability

Environment comprises all entities, natural or manmade which provide value, now or perhaps in future, to humankind (MoSPI, 2011). There was an increase in the forest cover by about 1128 sq. km between 2007 and 2011. Protected areas cover about 5.02 per cent of the country's total land area. The consumption of ozone depleting products (CFCs) has gone down. Trend shows that the per capita carbon-dioxide emissions (MT) has been increasing year by year and was recorded at 1.39 in 2012. Target of halving the proportion of households without access to safe drinking water by 2015, has already been achieved by 2007-08. Current trend predicts attaining 100 per cent coverage of safe drinking water for both rural and urban sectors by 2015. An improved sanitation facility still eludes half of the households. Target is to reduce the proportion of households having no access to improved sanitation to 38 per cent by 2015, while likely reduction by 2015 seems to be only about 43 per cent. As per Census 2001, the share of slum population as percentage of urban population living in slums was 23.1 in 2001. Conditions of slum dwellers in India's urban areas shows signs of marginal improvement in terms of roads, water supply, electricity connection, sanitation, education, medical facilities etc. Table 11.7 summarises the progress of indicators against MDG7.

Table 11.7

Status of Indicators for MDG 7

Indicator	*Achievement*
Area covered under forests as % of geographical area (2011)	21.05
Ratio of area protected to maintain biological diversity to surface area (%) (2013)	5.02
Energy use per GDP (₹) (2011-12)	0.1453 kWh
Carbon dioxide emissions per capita (2012)	1.30 MT
Consumption of ozone-depleting CFCs (ODP tonnes) (2007)	998.5

Source: MoSPI, 2013.

Government Policies/Initiatives

The government has put in place few programmes to advance towards meeting the target value in 2015 against MDG7. Few of them include:

1. Green India Mission—objective of this mission is to increase forest and tree cover.
2. National Rural Drinking Water Programme (NRDWP)—supports states/UTs with financial and technical assistance to implement drinking water supply schemes in villages.
3. India's National Action Plan for Climate Change (NAPCC)—emphasises on the need for sustainable development through clean energy technology.
4. Other programmes include: Urban Infrastructure Development Scheme for Small and Medium Towns (UIDSSMT), VAMBAY, National Slum Development Programme (NSDP) 1996-97, National Urban Renewal Mission, 73rd Constitutional Amendment—Decentralised planning, implementation and management of water supply, Community-based Water Quality Monitoring and Surveillance Programme, Sector Reform Project (1999) scaled up as Swajaldhara Programme, District Water & Sanitation Committee, State Water & Sanitation Mission, and Communication & Capacity Development (CCD) Units, which are the measures taken by the Government to reach the goal by target year 2015.
5. Ministries and Departments of GoI have designed specific programmes to address MDG7 in Twelfth Five Year Plan. They include National Afforestation Programme (National Mission for Green India), National Rural Drinking Water Programme, Nirmal Bharat Abhiyan, and JNNURM.

Goal 8: Develop a Global Partnership for Development

Goal 8 of MDGs is unique and it essentially focuses on government commitments and achievements, towards developing global partnership. Internationally, India has a sufficient range of products and adequate safeguard mechanisms to protect the interests of its farmers, assuming appropriate and effective domestic policy. Indian telecom market is one of the fastest growing markets. Information by Telecom Regulatory Authority of India (TRAI) shows that teledensity has increased significantly. Number of internet subscribers also increased significantly to about 13.54 million subscribers in 2009. Fixed telephone lines per 100 inhabitants was 24 per 100 people in 2012. Mobile cellular subscriptions per 100 inhabitants was 72 in 2011. Percentage of internet users per 100 inhabitants was 10 in 2011. Table 11.8 summarises the progress of indicators against MDG8.

Table 11.8

Status of Indicators for MDG 8

Indicator	*Achievement*	*Target for 2015*
Proportion of population using solid fuels (%) (2011)	67.4	
Households with sustainable access to an improved water source (%) (2008-09)	91.4	83
Households without access to sanitation (%) (2008)	49.2	38
Telephone per 100 population (2013)	73	
Internet subscribers per 100 population	1.2	
Personal computers per 100 population	Not available	

Source: MoSPI, 2013.

Government Policies/Initiatives

1. India has taken some positive steps to develop a global partnership for development to help India meet its goal. Important Twelfth Five Year Plan programmes addressing MDG8 include National e-Governance and Action Plan.

Annexure A-11.1 presents the summary of the progress of India against the MDGs. Out of the 60 indicators for the 8 goals, 35 were found relevant to India. Some of the variants of the measures being followed by India, with conceptual disparity with international definitions, in assessing the countries progress against the MDGs listed by United Nations are clearly presented in the annexure.

Millennium Development Goals: Muslim Minorities Status and Progress in India

India is among the most diverse societies in the world in terms of religious minorities. Religion in Indian census provides a wonderful kaleidoscope of the country's rich social composition. The country is the birthplace of several religions, Hinduism, Buddhism, Jainism and Sikhism, and home for thousands of years to Jewish, Zoroastrian, Muslim and Christian communities. Minorities in India, as per the National Commission of Minorities Act, 1992, are Muslims, Christians, Buddhists, Sikhs and Parsis. It has people from all the major religions in the world—Hindus, Muslims, Christians, Sikhs, Buddhists, Jains and Zoroastrians (Parsis). Religious composition of Indian population, as revealed in 2001 census, is: Hindus: 81.4%, Muslims: 12.4%, Christians: 2.3%, Sikhs: 1.9%, Buddhists: 0.8%, Jains: 0.4%, and others: 0.7%.

There is an absence of a comprehensive understanding of the poverty of minorities and its manifestations in the social, economic, cultural and political spheres. The MDGs have been criticised for ignoring specific vulnerabilities that minorities are facing which impact their material life such as access to welfare schemes, modern education, employment opportunities and political offices. Failing to make any specific mention of minorities in any of the 8 development goals, 21 targets and 60 indicators, the stated goals have remained distant to them. Prevailing conditions of injustice, insecurity and social exclusion against religious minorities might adversely affect a country's capability to meet MDG goals.

In the UN's Millennium Declaration (2000), states expressed their commitment "to strengthen the capacity of all countries to implement the principles and practices of democracy and respect for human rights, including minority rights." In this regard, few studies were taken up to measure and assess the prevailing socio-economic and educational conditions of religious minorities in India. The report of the Prime Ministers High Level Committee on 'Social, Economic and Educational Status of Muslims' popularly known as the Justice Sachar Committee Report and report of the 'National Commission for Religious and Linguistic Minorities' (NCRLM) constituted by GoI has created a great hope amongst the religious minorities who have been suffering from discrimination and under representation in the Nation's economic growth. Based on the recommendations, Prime Minister's 15-point programme addresses welfare of the minorities which include enhancing opportunities for education, ensuring an equitable share in economic activities and employment, improving the conditions of living of the minorities and prevention and control of communal disharmony and violence.

This paper studies the performance of India's Muslim minority community on indices of social development and asses their plausibility of meeting the MDGs by the target year 2015. For the purpose of this study, the research parameters are confined to pan-India patterns.

Goal 1: Eradicate Extreme Poverty and Hunger

The Sachar Committee (2006) estimated a poverty ratio of 31 per cent for Muslims with 365 days reference period in the year 2004-05. Table 11.9 depicts the poverty figures among urban and rural Muslims, which are found to be higher than the national average of 22.8 per cent and 22.7 per cent respectively. 38.4 per cent are deemed to be living in poverty amongst urban Muslims, and accounts for 26.9 per cent in rural Muslims. Rural-urban differential is highest for the Muslims compared to any other socio-religious category (SRC).

Table 11.9

Urban to Rural Poverty: India and Muslims

(in %)

India		*Muslims*	
Urban	*Rural*	*Urban*	*Rural*
22.8	22.7	38.4	26.9

Source: PMHLC Report, 2006.

The goal of reducing extreme poverty by half as envisaged in the MDG seems doubtful in the case of Muslims. Decline in incidence of poverty is observed in both urban and rural areas during 2004-05 to 2009-10 amongst Muslims. Observing the rate of decline in poverty in Table 11.10 which is slow, maintaining the same pace seems to be a challenging task.

Table 11.10

Head Count Ratio (%): India and Muslims

India				Muslims			
2004-05		*2009-10*		*2004-05*		*2009-10*	
Rural	*Urban*	*Rural*	*Urban*	*Rural*	*Urban*	*Rural*	*Urban*
28.0	25.8	21.9	20.8	33.0	40.6	20.5	34.3

Source: Thorat and Dubey, 2012.

The Monthly Per Capita Expenditure (MPCE) of Muslims, amongst the poorest, is shown in Table 11.11. In the rural areas, 26.2 per cent of all Muslims fall in the poorest quintile. Muslims count amongst the poorest with 40.7 per cent of them occupying the poorest slot.

Table 11.11

Distribution of Muslim Population by MPCE Quintiles

	1	*2*	*3*	*4*	*5*	*Total*
Rural MPCE	26.2	26.3	19.5	16.8	11.2	100
Urban MPCE	40.7	27.0	16.7	10.1	5.5	100

Source: NSSO, 2009-10.

Goal 2: Achieve Universal Primary Education

A substantial proportion of 18 per cent Muslim males and 15.4 per cent Muslim females have attained only primary education. Meanwhile at the higher levels of education, upper primary and above, Muslim proportion is significantly lower. Table 11.12 shows the literacy rate in Muslims as proportion of Muslim population by age groups. It is observed that there is a decline in the number of literates as we move to higher age groups. The literacy rate among Muslims in 2001 was 59.9 per cent far below the national average of 65.1 per cent.

Table 11.12

Literates as Proportion of Population by Age Group: Muslims

Age Group	*Proportion of Population*
6-13 Years	74.6
14-15 Years	79.5
16-17 Years	75.5
18-2 Years	70.5
23 Years & above	46.1
Total	59.9

Source: PMHLC Report, 2006.

In Table 11.13 it is observed that, educational attainment worsens in all the religious minorities, as we move from lower to higher levels of school education. Proportion of children completing middle school after primary education is only 65 per cent for Muslims. About 50 per cent of the Muslims who have completed middle school are likely to complete secondary school. High drop-out rate is observed among Muslim students. It is inferred from the figures presented in Table 11.13, that Muslims have the least literacy rate among all religious communities.

Enrolment rate (ER) and mean years of schooling (MYS) are more relevant for ensuring compulsory primary education for children. The Muslim children account to 83 per cent of MYS and 65 per cent of ER. Table 11.14 shows that the educational deprivation of Muslims is further compounded by the fact that even in the current school going age group (6-14 years), enrolment of Muslims remains poor as more than one-fifth i.e., 20.7 per cent were estimated to be out of school. The All India Survey of Out-of-School Children found a very high proportion of 7.67 per cent of Muslim children in the age group 6-13 reporting out of school.

Table 11.13

Educational Levels of Notified Minority Communities

Community	*Upto Primary Level*		*Middle*		*Secondary*		*Senior Secondary*		*Diploma*		*Graduation*	
	Male	*Female*	*Male*	*Female*	*Male*	*Female*	*Male*	*Female*	*Male*	*Female*	*Male*	*Female*
Muslims	62.2	69.8	15.8	14.2	12.0	9.5	5.0	3.9	0.5	0.2	4.4	2.4
Christians	45.4	46.2	17.6	16.6	17.7	17.2	8.0	9.5	1.9	3.7	8.8	8.6
Sikhs	44.3	49.9	17.5	16.1	22.6	18.8	7.7	7.4	1.0	0.8	6.9	7.0
Buddhists	51.0	59.9	17.6	17.4	15.2	12.5	8.6	6.3	0.5	0.1	7.0	3.8

Source: NCRLM Report, 2007.

Table 11.14

Proportion of Children Aged 6-14 years Enrolled in 2004-05: India and Muslims

India	*Muslims*
85.3	81.8

Source: PMHLC Report, 2006.

Goal 3: Promote Gender Equality and Empower Women

Among all the religious minorities in India, gender disparity at various levels of education appears insuperable. Recent NSSO, 2007-08 data on education further confirmed a high proportion of Muslims as illiterates. Census 2001 records female literacy rate in Muslim women as 50.1 per cent, closely followed by the national average of 53.7 per cent, though they lagged behind Muslim men by a margin of 17.5 per cent. 47.3 per cent of the Muslim women count amongst the most illiterate segments of the society while a mere 1.5 per cent continue more than higher secondary education as indicated in Table 11.15. At higher levels of education, upper primary and above, Muslim proportion was significantly lower than that among all other religious minorities. The probability of dropping-out was a 4 per cent lower among Muslim girls. Going by the current figures, it is unlikely that gender disparity at various levels of education will be mitigated by the target year 2015.

Table 11.15

Educational Levels of Muslim Minorities by Gender

	Muslims	
Education Level	*Male*	*Female*
Not Literate	34.7	47.3
Below Primary	23.1	20.0
Primary	18.0	15.4
Upper Primary/Middle	11.4	8.7
Secondary/Higher Secondary	10.0	7.1
More than Higher Secondary	2.8	1.5

Source: NSSO, 2007-08.

In Table 11.16, it is observed that Muslim girls, both in urban and rural areas, are a very high proportion of those who never attended school or any educational institution. The gender gap in Muslims is 8 per cent points. Nearly one-third of the Muslim minority children dropped-out after having enrolled for formal education. The drop-out rate was a significant 4 per cent points lower among Muslim girls. Further, the difference between male and female enrolment is only 5 per cent in primary education (or above). Only 47.7 per cent of Muslim males and 42.1 per cent of females were enrolled in primary level of education and above.

Table 11.16

Educational Status of Muslim Minorities by Gender

	Muslims	
Current Education Status	*Male*	*Female*
Never attended	16.5	24.7
Dropped out	34.5	31.9
Currently attending informal education (including pre-primary)	1.2	1.3
Primary and above	47.7	42.1

Source: NSSO, 2007-08.

Although gender disparity persists among Muslims in educational indicators, but they do better on other indicators of the status of women. Census 2001 indicates that 56.9 per cent of the Muslim girls are married only after attaining 18 years which is higher than the national average of 56.5 per cent and the incidence of child marriages is only 2.2 per cent.

Table 11.17 shows the distribution of Muslim women workers by their category of employment. The Muslim women have a big share in the occupations like agriculture, dairying, small animal husbandry, fisheries, social and agro-forestry, *khadi* and village industries, handlooms, handicrafts and sericulture. Most of the jobs in these sectors are low paid and are performed by women. Muslim women have almost no presence in decision-making positions from *Gram Panchayat* to Parliament.

Table 11.17

Distribution of Women Workers by Category of Employment

Cultivators in Own Land (CL)	*Agricultural Labourers (AL)*	*Household Industry (HHI)*	*Other Workers (OW)*	*Total*
20.7	22.0	8.1	49.1	100

Source: Census Survey Report, 2001.

Goal 4: Reduce the U5MR by Two-thirds between 1990 and 2015

Sachar Committee report reveals that the infant mortality (under-one year) and child mortality (under-five years) are lower in Indian Muslims than the national average. According to the NFHS-II, the IMR was reported as 59 per 1000 for Muslims against the national average of 73 per thousand. 25 per thousand children born in Muslims have a probability of dying between 1 and 5 years of age. As shown in the Table 11.18, NFHS-III data confirms the continuation of lower infant and child mortality among the Muslims of India compared to the national average. The IMR and U5MR of Muslim children declined from 77.0 and 106.0 in 1992-93 to 52.4 and 70.0 in 2005-06, a decline of 31.9 per cent and 33.9 per cent respectively.

Table 11.18

Infant, Child and Under-5 Mortality Rate

Neonatal Mortality	*Post Neonatal Mortality*	*Infant Mortality*	*Child Mortality*	*Under-5 Mortality*
34.1	18.2	52.4	18.5	70.0

Source: NFHS III, 2005-06.

India needs to reach an IMR of 29.6 and an U5MR of 39.6 by the 2015 survey. As far as meeting the target of MDG is concerned, decennial decline is observed to be very slow in Muslims and going by the current pace of decline, it is unlikely that India will be able to meet the MDG goal by 2015.

As presented in the Table 11.19, only 49.6 per cent of the Muslim children in the age group of 12-23 months have been vaccinated for measles against the national average of 58.8 per cent. Vaccination of Muslim children for all basic vaccines was also reportedly poor with only 36.3 per cent of them having benefitted as against 43.5 per cent being the national average. Table 11.20 presents the percentage of Muslim children aged 6-50 months classified as having anaemia by status of hemoglobin level.

Table 11.19

Per cent of Children Aged 12-23 Months With Specific Vaccination

	DPT				Polio						
BCG	*1*	*2*	*3*	*At birth*	*1*	*2*	*3*	*Measles*	*Basic Vaccines*	*No Vaccine*	*No. of Children*
69.7	67	58.3	47.8	45	90	84.5	77	49.6	36.3	7.3	1,814

Source: NFHS III, 2005-06.

Table 11.20

Per cent of Muslim Children Aged 6-50 Months Having Anaemia

Mild	*Moderate*	*Severe*	*Any Anaemia*	*No. of Women*
38.3	15.1	1.3	54.7	15,340

Source: NFHS III, 2005-06.

Goal 5: Improve Maternal Health

Under-nutrition is also a major factor responsible for the high morbidity and high mortality among the Indian women apart from children. The nutritional status of Muslim women is given in the Table 11.21. The Reproductive and Child Health Survey-II (RCHS-II) indicated a slightly lower percentage of maternal deaths for Muslims against the national average.

The total fertility rate for Muslims is higher than the national average as indicated in Table 11.22; the mean number of children born to women in the age group of 40-49 years is also higher for Muslims compared to the national average of 4.00. Table 11.23 indicates the prevalence of anaemia among the Muslim women in India.

Table 11.21

Nutritional Status of Women

Height			*Weight*				
Mean Height (cm)	*Percentage Below 145 cm*	*Number of Women*	*Mean Body Mass Index (BMI)*	*Percentage with BMI Below 18.5 Kg/m²*	*Percentage with BMI Below 25 Kg/m²*	*Percentage with BMI Below 30 Kg/m²*	*Number of Women*
151.5	12.3	10,108	20.5	34.1	12.4	2.8	9,207

Source: NFHS II, 1998-99 National Report.

Table 11.22

Total Fertility Rate (TFR)

TFR		*Mean No. of Children Ever Born to Women (Age 40-49 Years)*	
India	*Muslims*	*India*	*Muslims*
2.68	3.09	4.00	4.60

Source: NFHS III, 2005-06.

Table 11.23

Percentage of Women with Anaemia

Mild Anemia	*Moderate Anaemia*	*Severe Anaemia*	*Number of women*
34.2	14.2	1.3	9,545

Source: NFHS II, 1998-99.

Table 11.24 reveals that Muslim women lagged behind in receiving antenatal care from a recognised health care provider.

Table 11.24

Per cent Distribution of Muslim Women with Recent Live Birth by Antenatal Care

Doctor	*ANM/ Nurse/ Midwife/ LHV*	*Other Health Personnel*	*Dai/ TBA*	*Angan wadi/ ICDS Worker*	*Other*	*No One*	*Missing*	*Total*	*No. of Women*
48.2	21.3	2.2	0.7	0.5	0.2	26.8	0.1	100	6,486

Source: NFHS III, 2005-06.

Seventy-three per cent of Muslim women received antenatal care. Visit to the doctor was found to be only 48 per cent in Muslims which is the least when compared to women of other communities. Thirty-three per cent of the births in Muslims are least likely to take place in a health facility.

Goal 6: Combat HIV/AIDS, Malaria and Other Diseases

Table 11.25 presents information regarding the awareness of HIV-AIDS among the men and women in the age group 15-49 years. It is noticed that the awareness of HIV was least among the Muslim men and women. Only 55 per cent of the Muslim women interviewed had heard of the disease. The awareness was considerably higher among Muslim men with 82.2 per cent of them confirming knowledge. Only 4 out of 10 women and 7 out of 10 men knew of the prevention methods.

Table 11.25

Percentage of HIV Positive Women and Men Age 15-49

Women		*Men*		*Total*	
% HIV+	*No. of Women*	*% HIV+*	*No. of Men*	*% HIV+*	*Total*
0.06	7,285	0.21	5,626	0.1	12,912

Source: NFHS III, 2005-06.

The NFHS III data revealed a 0.06 per cent of occurrence of HIV among Muslim women, which is negligible against the national average of 0.22 and 0.22 per cent in Muslim men which is very low prevalence against the average of 0.36. However owing to the very small size of the sample that tested positive, religious differentials need to be spelt with a degree of caution. Table 11.26 lists the sources of knowledge about AIDS amongst Muslim minorities.

Muslims displayed the lowest CPR of 37 per cent against the national average of 48 per cent as outlined in the Table 11.27. Table 11.28 and 11.29 indicate the current use of contraception methods by Muslims. The use of condoms as a means of contraception seemed less preferred in Muslims. However 6.8 per cent of the Muslims preferred the use of condoms as a means of contraception against the national average of 5.2 per cent.

Table 11.26

Knowledge About AIDS

Source of Knowledge about AIDS	*Percentage*
Radio	37.2
Television	75
Cinema	4.9
News Paper, Magazine	23.5
Poster, Hoarding	8.4
Health Worker	2.9
Adult Education Programme	0.7
Friend, Relative	30
School Teacher	1.1
Other Sources	3.1

Source: NFHS II, 1998-99.

Table 11.27

Contraceptive Prevalence Rate (CPR)

India	*Muslims*
48	37

Source: NFHS II, 1998-99.

Table 11.28

Per cent Distribution of Currently Married Women by Modern Contraceptive Method

Any Method	*Any Modern Method*	*Modern Method*					
		Female Sterilisation	*Male Sterilisation*	*Pill*	*IUD*	*Injectibles*	*Condom/ Nirodh*
45.7	36.4	21.3	0.6	5.7	1.8	0.3	6.8

Source: NFHS III, 2005-06.

Table 11.29

Per cent Distribution of Currently Married Women by Traditional Contraceptive Method

Any Traditional Method	Traditional Method			Not Currently Using	Number of Women 100%
	Rhythm	Withdrawal	Folk Method		
9.3	5.6	3.4	0.3	54.3	12,288

Source: NFHS-III, 2005-06.

Table 11.30 shows the prevalence of disorders among women and men of Muslim minorities aged 15-49 per 100,000 population. It is noticed that Muslim men suffer from more disorders than the Muslim women. Table 11.31 shows the status of family planning among married Muslim women in three categories.

Table 11.30

Number of Women and Men Aged 15-49 per 100,000 With Disorders

Women				Men			
Diabetes	Asthma	Goitre	Total	Diabetes	Asthma	Goitre	Total
1,037	2,024	1,090	16,936	1,237	2,218	481	8,747

Source: NFHS III, 2005-06.

Table 11.31

Need for Family Planning Among Married Muslim Women

Unmet Need for Family Planning			Met Need for Family Planning			Total Demand for Family Planning		
For Spacing	For Limiting	Total	For Spacing	For Limiting	Total	For Spacing	For Limiting	Total
8.6	10.2	18.8	6.8	38.9	45.7	15.4	49.2	64.6

Source: NFHS III, 2005-06.

Goal 7: Ensure Environmental Sustainability

NSSO 60th highlighted the absence of tap water facility in a large proportion of Muslim homes. Poor Muslims live in hovels without electricity. Only 19 per cent of the Muslim household have piped water supply. Poor roads and lack of proper transport, sanitation, water, electricity and public health facilities pervade Muslim localities. Only 2.1 per cent Muslim farmers have tractors. Just 1.0 per cent own hand pumps. Villages with a concentration of Muslims are not well served with *pucca* approach roads and local bus stops. Muslim households have reported poor use of clean fuel. Muslim population seems to be close to average in terms of housing structure and better placed in terms of toilet facilities but ranks poorly in water availability, electrification and cooking fuel facilities. The availability of piped water, electricity and modern fuel (LPG/electricity) is lower among Muslims.

Annexure A-11.2 presents the summary of the progress of Muslim minorities of India against the MDGs along with the nations progress. The scarcity of development data of Muslim minorities on all the indicators of the MDGs holds up comparative analysis.

Conclusion

With roughly two years left for India in reaching the MDGs, the country managed to show significant progress in 10 out of 35 indicators. Recent challenges, including the economic crisis, food and fuel price volatility, ongoing climate change, mark a threat in reaching the desired targets. India has made a head-way with impressive gains in reducing poverty, improving primary education enrolment rate, decrease in gender gap in literacy, access to drinking water, noticeable decline in MMR, infant and child mortality rates, increasing forest cover and stability in prevalence of AIDS. There is still much left to be achieved in meeting the MDG targets by 2015. Biggest challenges much ahead are improved sanitation, food security, and gender equity standards. As per the latest statistics for MDG indicators of India, despite noteworthy progress made, all the MDGs will not be met by 2015. Audit of the Muslim minority community against meeting the MDG goals does not show a bright scenario either. Initiatives and efforts to achieve the MDGs like poverty reduction, reduction of IMR and MMR, environmental sustainability have benefitted minorities, but more coherent efforts and targeted strategies are required to address directly the plight of disadvantaged Muslim minorities.

Meaningful progress towards sustainable development, social inclusion, and stability of Muslim minorities in India can be achieved through holistic and sustained approaches, from understanding the impact of discrimination on Muslim minorities to ensuring effective participation of Muslim minorities to achieve equality.

Caste and gender based discrimination, inequality and social exclusion have always been inadequately addressed. In this context, in the post 2015 agenda, the Indian government in the forefront should make MDGs more socially just, equitable, sustainable and inclusive, focusing on the structural aspects leading to poverty, exclusion and inequality. Equitable, non-discriminatory and high quality public services like basic public health care with safe and sustainable water supply and sanitation, basic education, food and nutrition security with focus on children and women, employment and livelihood needs, peace and conflict with special attention to women and minorities should be ensured in the post 2015 development agenda. Governments and development agencies need to review MDG policies immediately to ensure that the rights and needs of Muslim minorities are fully considered. They also need to assess Muslim minority community's development progress against meeting the MDGs.

References

Anwar, Sardar, Muhammad Mukhtar Alam, Anulekha Bhattacharya, Wajida Tabassum and Ashok Bharti (2008). *Millennium Development Goals and Muslims: A Status Report 2008.* Delhi: Tehreek-E-Pasmanda Muslim Samaj (TPMS) and National Conference of Dalit Organizations (NACDOR).

Asghar, Ali Engineer (2007). *Identity and Social Exclusion-Inclusion: A Muslim Perspective.* Mumbai: Centre for Study of Society and Secularism.

Bhat, P.N. Mari and A.J. Zaviera (2005). "Role of Religion in Fertility Decline: The Case of Indian Muslims", *Economic & Political Weekly* 40(5): 385-402.

Central Statistical Organisation (CSO) (2005). *Millennium Development Goal India Country Report 2005.* New Delhi: Ministry of Statistics and Programme Implementation, Government of India. Available from: *www.mospi.nic.in*

———. (2011). *Millennium Development Goals: India Country Report 2011.* New Delhi: Ministry of Statistics and Programme Implementation, Government of India.

Das N.P., Urvi Shah and Rajnikant Patel (2009). *Emerging Causes and Determinants of Maternal Mortality in India: Based on Large Scale Surveys since the 1990s.* Baroda: Population Research Centre, M.S University. p.8.

Hasan, Mushirul (2003). *Making Sense of History: Society, Culture and Politics*. New Delhi: Manahor Publications.

International Institute for Population Sciences and ORC Macro (2000). *India: National Family Health Survey (NFHS-2), 1998-99.*

International Institute for Population Sciences (2007). "Key Findings", *National Family Health Survey-3, 2005-06.* Mumbai: IIPS. pp.194 and 393.

Kadrolar, Vilas M. (2013). "Millennium Development Goals A Glimpse on Status and Progress", *Indian Journal of Applied Research* 3(1).

Khalidi, Omar (2006). *Muslims in Indian Economy.* New Delhi: Three Essays Collective.

Kothari, A. (2013). "Development and Ecological Sustainability in India: Possibilities for the Post-2015 Framework", *Oxfam India Working Paper Series (OIWPS)* XVI, March. Delhi: Oxfam India.

Lanjouw, Peter and R. Murgai (2011). *Perspectives of Poverty in India: Stylized Facts from Survey Data.* Washington DC: International Bank for Reconstruction and Development/The World Bank. p.168.

Mahadevia, D. (2013). "Urban Poverty and the Post-MDG Framework: India", *Oxfam India Working Paper Series (OIWPS)* XVII, April. Delhi: Oxfam India.

Mistry, Malika B. (2005). "Muslims in India: A Demographic and Socio-economic Profile", *Journal of Muslim Minority Affairs* 25(3): 399-422.

Ministry of Health and Family Welfare (2008). *Annual Report 2007.* New Delhi: Ministry of Health and Family Welfare, Government of India. pp.119-22, 209, 238, 323, 326.

Ministry of Minority Affairs (2007). *Report of the National Commission for Religious and Linguistic Minorities 2007 (Ranganath Misra Report).* May. New Delhi: Government of India.

Ministry of Statistics and Programme Implementation (MoSPI) (2011). *Statistical Year Book India, 2011.* New Delhi: Govt. of India.

———. (2013) *Towards Achieving Millennium Development Goals India 2013.* New Delhi: Social Statistics Division, Ministry of Statistics and Programme Implementation, Government of India.

Minority Rights Group International (2003). *Minorities and Indigenous Peoples Rights in the Millennium Development Goals 2003.* May. London.

Nayar, K.R. (2007). "Social Exclusion, Caste and Health: A Review based on the Social Determinants Framework", Review Article, *Indian J Med Res* 126: 355-63.

Planning Commission (2012). *Press Note on Poverty Estimates 2009-10.* New Delhi: Government of India.

Rustagi, Preet, Abhay Kumar , Balwant Singh Mehta , Sunil Kumar Mishra and Payel Dutta Mazumdar (2008). *Socio-Economic Status of the Notified Minority Communities (Other than Muslims) 2008.* New Delhi: National Commission of Minorities.

Sachar, Rajindar, Saiyid Hamid, T.K. Oommen, M.A. Basith, Rakesh Basant, Akhtar Majeed and Abusaleh Shariff (2006). *Social, Economic and Educational Status of the Muslim Community of India (Sachar Committee Report).* New Delhi: Prime Minister's High Level Committee, Cabinet Secretariat, Government of India.

Shariff, Abusaleh (1998). *Relative Economic and Social Deprivation of Indian Muslims.* New Delhi: Institute of Objective Studies. pp.16-34.

Tanweer, Fazal (2013). "Millennium Development Goals and Muslims of India", *Oxfam India Working Paper Series (OIWPS)* XIII. January. Delhi: Oxfam India.

Thorat, S. and A. Dubey (2012). "Has Growth Been Socially Inclusive during 1993-94 and 2009-10?", *Economic & Political Weekly* XVII(10): 43-54.

UNDP (2010). *Marginalized Minorities in Development Programming: A UNDP Resource Guide and Toolkit 2010.* May. New York: Democratic Governance Group , Bureau for Development Policy.

United Nations (2008). *Millennium Development Goal Report 2008.* New York.

United Nations Development Group (UNDG) (2003). *Country Reporting on the Millennium Development Goals: Second Guidance Note.* United Nations.

United Nations International Children's Emergency Fund and World Health Organization, (2012). *Progress of Drinking Water and Sanitation.* New York: UNICEF and WHO. pp.45-47.

Wada Na Todo Abhiyaan (2007). *Measuring India's Progress on the Millennium Development Goals: A Citizens Report 2007. New Delhi.*

———. (2010). *Millennium Development Goals in India, 2010: Civil Society Report 2010.*New Delhi.

———. (n.d.). *Civic Society Constituency-National Report India: Post 2015 Development Agenda.* United Nations.

World Bank (2013). *World Development Indicators 2013.* Washington D.C.: The World Bank

Annexure A-11.1

India's Progress Against the Millennium Development Goals (MDGs)

GOAL 1 | Eradicate extreme poverty and hunger

Target 1: Halve, between 1990 and 2015, the percentage of population below the national poverty line	Target 2: Halve, between 1990 and 2015, the proportion of people who suffer from hunger

GOAL 2 | Achieve universal primary education

Target 3: Ensure that by 2015 children everywhere, boys and girls alike will be able to complete a full course of primary education

GOAL 3 | Promote gender equality and empower women

Primary Education	Secondary Education	Higher Education
Eliminate gender disparity in primary and secondary education, preferably by 2005, and in all levels of education, no later than 2015	Eliminate gender disparity in primary and secondary education, preferably by 2005, and in all levels of education, no later than 2015	Eliminate gender disparity in primary and secondary education, preferably by 2005, and in all levels of education, no later than 2015

GOAL 4 | Reduce child mortality

Target 5: Reduce by two-thirds between 1990 and 2015, the under-five mortality rate

GOAL 5 | Improve maternal health

Target 6: Reduce by three quarters between 1990 and 2015, the maternal mortality ratio (MMR)

GOAL 6 | Combat HIV/AIDS, malaria and other diseases

Target 7: Have halted by 2015 and begun to reverse the spread of HIV/AIDS	Target 8: Have halted by 2015 and begun to reverse the incidence of malaria and other major diseases

GOAL 7 | Ensure environmental sustainability

Target 9: Integrate the principles of sustainable development into country policies and programmes and reverse the loss of environmental resources	Target 10: Halve, by 2015, the proportion of people without sustainable access to safe drinking water and basic sanitation	Target 11: By 2020, to have achieved a significant improvement in the lives of at least 100 million slum dwellers

GOAL 8 | Develop a global partnership for development

Target 18: In cooperation with the private sector, make available the benefits of new technologies, especially information and communication

Note: Target already met or expected to meet by 2015.

Progress insufficient to reach the target with prevailing trends.

No progress or deterioration.

Sources: MoSPI India 2013 report; NSSO; UN, *MDG Country Progress Snapshot: India*, *Bestcurrentaffairs.com*. Compiled by the author.

Annexure A-11.2

Millennium Development Goals: Progress Chart

MDGs	Target	Target Indicators			Target 2015	Achievement (%) India		Achievement (%) Muslim Minorities	
		UNDP Framework	Indian Framework			Value	Year	Value	Year
Goal 1 Eradicate extreme poverty and hunger	Target 1.A Halve, between 1990 and 2015 the proportion of people whose income is less than $1 a day	Poverty HCR (% of population below the national poverty line)	Proportion of population below poverty line (%)	Rural	23.9	21.9	2009-10	20.5	2009-10
				Urban		20.8	2009-10	34.3	2009-10
		Poverty gap ratio	Poverty gap ratio (%)	Rural	26	5.05	2011-12		
				Urban		2.70	2011-12		
		Share of poorest quintile in national consumption	Share of poorest quintile in national consumption	Rural		9.75	2009-10	26.2	2009-10
				Urban		7.11	2009-10	40.7	2009-10

contd...

...contd...

	Target 1.B Achieve full and productive employment and decent work for all, including women and young people	Growth rate of GDP per person employed	GDP per person employed (constant 1990 PPP $)		8,401	2010		
		Employment to population ratio	Employment to population ratio, ages 15-24, total (%)		34	2010		
		Proportion of own-account and contributing family workers in total employment	Proportion of own-account and contributing family workers in total employment		81	2011		
		Malnutrition prevalence, weight for age (% of children under five)	Proportion of underweight children below 3 years (%)	26	43.5	2011		
	Target 1.C Halve, between 1990 and 2015, the proportion of people who suffer from hunger	Prevalence of underweight children under five years of age	Prevalence of underweight children under 3 years of age (%)		43.5	2011		
		Proportion of population below minimum level of dietary energy consumption	Proportion of population below minimum level of dietary energy consumption (%)	26.76	17.5	2011		

contd...

...contd...

Goal 2 Achieving universal primary education	Target 2.A Ensure that, by 2015, children everywhere, boys and girls alike, will be able to complete a full course of primary schooling	Net enrolment ratio in primary education	Net enrolment rate in primary grade (%)	100	99.89	2010-11		
		Proportion of pupils starting grade I who reach last grade of primary	Proportion of pupils starting grade I who reach grade V	100	82	2010-11		
		Literacy rate of 15-24 year olds, women and men	Literacy rate of 15-24 year olds, women and men	100	86	2007-08		
			Illiterates (%)		35.6	2007-08	40.8	2007-08, Sachar Committee
			% (6-14) out of school (%)		12.6	2007-08	20.7	2007-08, Sachar Committee
			Drop-outs (5-29)		34.3	2007-08	33.3	2007-08, Sachar Committee

contd...

...contd...

Goal 3 Promote gender equality and empower women	Target 3.A Eliminate gender disparity in primary and secondary education, preferably by 2005, and in all levels of education no later than by 2015	Ratio of girls to boys in primary, secondary and tertiary education	Ratio of girls to boys in primary education (Gender Parity Index of GER)	1.0	1.01	2010-11		
			Ratio of girls to boys in secondary education (Gender Parity Index of GER)	1.0	0.88	2010-11		
			Ratio of girls to boys in tertiary education (Gender Parity Index of GER)	1.0	0.79	2010-11		
			Female: Male literacy rate of 15-24 year olds	1.0	0.88	2007-08		
		Share of women in wage employment, in the non-agriculture sector	Share of women in wage employment, in the non-agriculture sector (%)	50	18.6	2009-10		
		Proportion of seats held by women in national parliament	Proportion of seats held by women in national parliament (%)	50	11.21	2013		

contd...

...contd...

Goal 4 Reduce child mortality	Target 4.A Reduce by two-thirds, between 1990 and 2015, the under-five mortality rate	U5MR	Under-five mortality rate (per 1000 live births)	42	55	2011	70	2005-06
		IMR	Infant mortality rate (per 1000 live births)	27	42	2012	52.4	2005-06
		Proportion of 1 year-old children immunised against measles	Proportion of 1 year-old children immunised against measles	100	74	2012	49.6 (children aged 12-23 months)	2005-06
Goal 5 Improve maternal health	Target 5.A Reduce by three quarters, between 1990 and 2015, the maternal mortality ratio	MMR	Maternal mortality ratio(per 100,000 live births)	109	200	2010		
		Proportion of births attended by skilled health personnel	Proportion of births attended by skilled health personnel (%)	100	52	2007-08		
	Target 5.B Achieve, by 2015, universal access to reproductive health	Contraceptive prevalence rate in women	Contraceptive usage CPR (%) — Women		56.0	2005-06	45.7	2005-06
			Contraceptive usage CPR (%) — Men		50.1		46.2	
		Adolescent fertility rate	Total Fertility Rate		2.68	2005-06	3.09	2005-06
			Births attended by skilled health staff (% of total)		53	2010		

contd...

...contd...

		Antenatal care coverage (at least one visit and at least four visits)	Antenatal care (%)		77.0	2006	73.1	2005-06
		Unmet need for family planning specially for married women (aged 25-34 years)	Unmet need for family planning among married women (%)		20.5 (women aged 15-49 married/ in union)	2008	18.8	2005-06
Goal 6 Combat HIV/ AIDS, malaria and other diseases	Target 6.A Have halted by 2015 and begun to reverse the spread of HIV/AIDS	Proportion of pregnant women aged 15-24 years with HIV/AIDS	HIV prevalence among pregnant women aged 15-24 years (%)		0.39	2010-11		
		Condom use at last high-risk sex	Condom use at last high-risk sex (%)		74	2010		
		Prevalence of HIV (% of population ages 15-49)	AIDS prevalence (%)	Women	0.22	2005-06	0.06	2005-06
				Men	0.36		0.22	
			Awareness of AIDS (%)	Women	57.0	2005-06	55.0	2005-06
				Men	83.6		82.2	
	Target 6.B - Achieve, by 2010, universal access to treatment for HIV/AIDS for all those who need it Data not available							

contd...

...contd...

		Incidence and death rates associated with malaria	Malaria annual parasite incidence (%)		1.3	2010		
		Proportion of children under 5 with fever who are treated with appropriate anti-malarial drugs	Proportion of population in malaria risk area using effective malaria prevention and treatment measures (%)		8.2	2006		
	Target 6.C Have halted by 2015 and begun to reverse the incidence of malaria and other major diseases	Incidence, prevalence and death rates associated with tuberculosis	Incidence rate and death rates associated with tuberculosis	No. of new cases per 100,000 population	185	2010		
				No. of deaths per 100,000 population	26.0	2010		
		Proportion of tuberculosis cases detected and cured under directly observed treatment short course	Prevalence of TB (Per 100,000 population)		256	2010		
			Proportion of TB cases detected (%)		70	2007-08		
			Proportion of TB cases cured under DOTS (%)		87	2010		

contd...

...contd...

Goal 7 Ensure environmental sustainability	Target 7.A Integrate the principles of sustainable development into country policies and programmes and reverse the loss of environmental resources	Proportion of land area covered by forest as percentage of geographical area	Area covered under forests as % of geographical area		21.05	2011		
		CO_2 emissions, total, per capita and per $1 GDP (PPP)	CO_2 emissions (metric tons per capita)		1.3 MT	2012		
		Consumption of ozone-depleting substances (CFCs)	Consumption of ozone-depleting CFCs (ODP tons)		998.5	2007		
	Target 7.B Reduce biodiversity loss, achieving, by 2010, a significant reduction in the rate of loss	Proportion of total water resources used	Improved water source (% of population with access)	100	92	2010		
		Energy use per GDP (₹)			0.143kwh	2011-12		
		Proportion of terrestrial and marine areas protected	Ratio of area protected to maintain biological diversity to surface area (%)		5.02	2013		
			Marine protected areas (% of territorial waters)		2	2010		

contd...

...contd...

	Target 7.C Halve, by 2015, the proportion of people without sustainable access to safe drinking water and basic sanitation	Proportion of population using an improved drinking water source	Proportion of population using improved water sources (%)	83	92	2010		
		Reduce the proportion of having no access to improved sanitation facility	Proportion of population using an improved sanitation (%)	38	34	2010	50	2006
	Target 7.D By 2020, to have achieved a significant improvement in the lives of at least 100 million slum dwellers	Proportion of urban population living in slums	Proportion of urban population living in slums (%)		29.4	2009		
Goal 8 Develop a global partnership for development	Target 8.A - Develop further an open, rule-based, predictable, non-discriminatory trading and financial system Target 8.B - Address the special needs of the least developed countries Target 8.C - Address the special needs of landlocked developing countries and small island developing States Target 8.D - Deal comprehensively with the debt problems of developing countries through national and international measures in order to make debt sustainable in the long term Target 8.E - In cooperation with pharmaceutical companies, provide access to affordable essential drugs in developing countries Are not relevant for India							

contd...

...contd...

	Target 8.F In cooperation with the private sector, make available the benefits of new technologies, especially information and communications	Fixed telephone lines per 100 inhabitants	Telephone lines per 100 population		73	2013		
		Mobile cellular subscriptions per 100 inhabitants	Mobile Cellular subscribers per 100 population		61	2010		
		Internet users per 100 inhabitants	Internet subscribers per 100 population		1.2	2013		

Sources: MoSPI India 2013 report; NSSO; Vilas and Kadrolkar, 2013; UN, MDG Country Progress Snapshot: India; RNTCP Status Report 2009; Thorat and Dubey (2012), *Bestcurrentaffairs.com*, Tanweer (2013), Sachar Committee Report, UNICEF (2012).

12

SOMA DE SILVA, R.S. GOYAL, NAZMUL KALIMULLAH AND ANAND AKUNDY

Teaching Evaluation in South Asia[1]

Collaboration among Voluntary Organisation for Professional Evaluation, Academia and Development Partner

Introduction

Evaluation is a very natural phenomenon. People evaluate things all the time. However, formal evaluation has a disciplined and methodical approach to this natural and common sense activity. Many people are mystified by the claim that it is a profession (Grob, 2009). This is largely because, unlike most physical or social sciences, evaluation has emerged as a distinct profession only recently. In several aspects, it is still evolving.

This paper discusses the role of academic institutions in promoting the culture and field of evaluation in South Asia. It focuses on the experience and lessons learned from the programme "Teaching Evaluation in South Asia" (TESA), which is designed to strengthen evaluation professionalisation in South Asia by institutionalising evaluation training in academic institutions. The programme is a collaborative effort between three partners: a consortium of academic institutions, a voluntary organisation for professional evaluation

1. This chapter is a reprint from "Teaching Evaluation in South Asia. Collaboration among Voluntary Organizations for Professional Evaluation (VOPEs), VOPEs, Academia and Development Partners", of Part 1: EvalPartners and the Roles of Voluntary Organizations for Professional Evaluation (VOPEs) in Rugh, Jim and Marco Segone (eds.) (2013). *Voluntary Organizations for Professional Evaluation (VOPEs): Learning from Africa, Americas, Asia, Australasia, Europe and Middle East*. Published by UNICEF, EvalPartners and IOCE in partnership with Cooperacion Espanola, Ministry for Foreign Affairs of Finland, United Nations Evaluation Group and UN Women.

(VOPE), which is the Sri Lanka Evaluation Association (SLEvA) and a development partner which is the International Development Research Centre (IDRC).

General Status of Evaluation Teaching in South Asia

In South Asia, as in many other regions, there has been an increasing demand, at various levels of government, for effective and focused evaluation of development efforts. Governments in developing countries are increasingly seeking accountability in the development process. At the same time, development partners and donors are also demanding good governance and effective use of increasingly scarce development resources towards achieving better outcomes. Mechanisms and systems in place are unable to meet the new challenges and hence these expectations and changes have made evaluation an important instrument for accountability, performance management and organisational learning.

Development of a culture of evaluation or what Hay (2011) has holistically described as "evaluation field building" particularly in the developing countries, has several challenges. It not only requires a political will and institutional design to internalise evaluation, but also involves capacity (building) and professionalisation to effectively carry out the evaluation function.

The South Asia region suffers from a dearth of professional evaluation expertise and the absence of an adequately developed evaluation culture to support national development processes. Evaluation practitioners have limited access to high-quality academic courses and practical training in evaluation, which consequently has hindered the evaluation capacity in the region. Most countries do not have well-established professional associations or networks that can facilitate exchange of academic advances and practical experiences. While the importance of evaluation in the achievement of national development results have been increasingly recognised in the public sector, among CSOs (civil society organisations), within the United Nations (UN) system and in multilateral and bilateral development partners, adequate systematic opportunities do not exist to generate capacity in the countries in the region. This is especially so in the mainstream educational programmes at colleges, universities and institutes of higher learning.

To aid the discussion about the realities on the ground, we draw upon what Grob (2010) has described as the fundamental pillars for a national evaluation system. These are:

1. Understanding evaluation types and methods and how policy makers and managers use them
2. Appreciating the relationships among evaluation and related professions
3. Establishment of government agencies that evaluate public programmes
4. Freedom and encouragement for growth of non-government evaluation organisations
5. Evaluation education and training programmes; and
6. Professional standards.

A close look at these expectations reveals that capacity building and professionalisation is at the core of this framework. Other authors such as Carden (2007) have also emphasised the importance of capacity building and professionalisation of evaluators to bridge the gap between them and the users of evaluation. But where do we stand in terms of evaluation capacity and professionalisation in South Asia? Shiva Kumar's (2010) observations in the context of India broadly depict the scenario in South Asia.

> At a macro-level, India has a reasonable (even impressive) capacity to undertake evaluations. Indeed, many well-established universities, policy think-tanks, social science research institutions and colleges—both within and outside government—have a pool of experienced evaluators. However, on closer examination, we find that there simply aren't enough institutions with the capacity to conduct evaluations for a country of India's size and diversity. Also, evaluation capacity is unevenly spread across the country...few states have evolved a strategy to develop adequate capacity to carry out evaluations at the state, district and village levels.

He further adds that: "...professionals carrying out evaluations in South Asia...tend to be good social science researchers, not trained evaluators."

Hay (2011) also notes that:

> Much evaluation in South Asia is certainly led by 'craftsmen' but a great deal is also led by researchers who, despite in some cases spending a large portion of their time leading or as part of evaluation teams—do not identify as evaluators (whether of the professional or specialist variety). Thus, while they draw on the theories, tools, and approaches from their various disciplinary backgrounds they are less likely to be aware of, draw from, and contribute to the field of evaluation whether as rooted within particular disciplines (such as education or public health) or development evaluation more broadly.

These words clearly indicate the gaps and grey areas for further improvement.

Teaching Evaluation in South Asia: A Response

It is in response to this situation that a group of academic institutions in South Asia came together to form a Consortium of Academic Institutions for Teaching Evaluation in South Asia (TESA). The members of the consortium are those who responded to a call for expression of interest by UNICEF Regional Office for South Asia through the print media, and who met the feasibility criteria of an assessment carried out by the World Bank Independent Evaluation Group. The consortium was of the view that for sustainable professional growth of evaluation competencies it is essential to make regular academic and professional training available at the higher academic institutions within the countries of South Asia. The consortium, in collaboration with UNICEF South Asia, experimented through the teaching of a short executive level course based on a common curriculum. The curriculum was developed jointly by London Metropolitan University and Carlton University. The faculty, who are members of the consortium, having been familiarised with the curriculum, conducted executive level courses at their respective institutions. Spurred by this experience, the consortium in collaboration with IDRC moved a step further to establish evaluation training at a post graduate diploma level, as a regular programme in their respective institutions.

The members of the consortium included IbnSina Institute of Public Health and Management Sciences (IPHMS), Kabul, Afghanistan; the Administrative Staff College of India (ASCI), Hyderabad, India; Indian Institute of Health Management Research (IIHMR), Jaipur, India; University and Industry Alliance, University of Dhaka, Bangladesh; Lahore University of Management Sciences, Pakistan and University of Sri Jayewardenepura, Sri Lanka. Based on the knowledge and experience of similar efforts, that formalising new structures could take a great deal of time and effort, the consortium decided instead to function as an informal network. However, it needed a mechanism for coordination and operational management. This role is played by the Sri Lanka Evaluation Association.

Since the establishment of the consortium, two institutions have discontinued and two others joined on invitation. To provide a sense of the collaborating institutions a brief introduction to the Consortium members is of value. The current members are as follows:

- The IPHMS is a higher education and professional training institute under the IbnSina Public Health Programme in Afghanistan. The institute provides training in management and public health to participants from Afghanistan and other countries.
- The ASCI is a think tank and a pioneer of evaluation practice in India. It is one of the leading institutions in India providing training, research and consultancy services to government, industry and international agencies.
- The IIHMR is an institute that established health management as an important discipline in India. The research conducted by the institute has contributed to strengthening and facilitating health sector reforms and a range of planning and policy level interventions.
- The University and Industry Alliance, a well-placed institution in Bangladesh, promotes evaluation teaching and practice. It is in a position to promote networking among universities and practitioners in public and private sector organisations.

- The University of Sri Jayewardenepura is one of the leading universities in Sri Lanka. It is committed to professionalise evaluation by introducing evaluation training through its Faculty of Medical Sciences.
- Himgiri Zee University, Uttarakhand, India, is a research-based multi-faculty and interdisciplinary university sponsored by the TALEEM Research Foundation, Ahmadabad.
- Institute of Public Enterprise (IPE), Hyderabad, India.

The long-term purpose of TESA is to build evaluation capacity by training and research in member institutions to expose and encourage students to undertake higher levels of learning in evaluation. The expected outcome is that the participating academic institutions will establish capacities to deliver academic evaluation programmes in their respective institutions. This is expected to contribute significantly to the strengthening of an evaluation culture through the presence of academically qualified professionals in the countries. Three outputs are considered necessary and sufficient to yield this outcome. These three outputs to be produced in the programme are:

i) a curriculum designed, tested and agreed upon to be used as a common pedagogy for all institutions;
ii) a core group of faculty members with capacity to teach the curriculum; and
iii) administrative arrangements in place to conduct the post graduate diploma.

TESA has now successfully completed the first output by producing the curriculum. Work on administrative arrangements for institutionalising the evaluation course is at various levels of progress in the different institutions. Work is ongoing and further efforts are needed to achieve the third output, which is to establish a group of faculty members with competency to teach evaluation topics.

The curriculum is designed to give the students a level of awareness of the fundamentals of evaluation not only in terms of the methodologies but also in terms of some of the soft skills. For this purpose, the curriculum consists of eight modules: Introduction to evaluation and the development context of South Asia; Evaluation design; Evaluation approaches; Quantitative methods in evaluation;

Qualitative methods in evaluation; Norms, standards and ethics in evaluation; Communication in evaluation; and Managing evaluation. The curriculum development was driven by the need to integrate capacity development into the process. A process of co-production was therefore adopted where senior faculty members of participating institutions worked in collaboration with evaluation professionals and teachers from the North. The resource persons provided some technical inputs, access to appropriate resources and primarily reviewed the draft materials produced by the consortium members. A Teachers' Guide was provided, which gives step-by-step guidance on delivering the modules from the basic material. Supplementary materials such as PowerPoint presentations, case studies and exercises have also been added. The process was time consuming but was well appreciated by the consortium members as it has led to a sense of ownership.

A key component of the course is the practicum. The practicum is designed to be an application of the theoretical knowledge of the modules in a guided and systematic manner. It is also expected to be a product of the institution that contributes to the research and knowledge-base of the country, based on expressed needs at national or sub-national levels. The faculty would develop a plan for evaluations in consultation with relevant government and other institutions. From this research plan, appropriate and feasible components would be assigned to students as their practicum. Each student would develop a complete evaluation design for the assigned component. This would be done in stages as the student completes the modules. The practicum is integrated into each module. In the first module, for example, the students would examine the relevance and importance of the assigned evaluation in the development context of the country. In the second module, they would develop the evaluation design, and in the third and fourth modules they determine and develop the most appropriate method mix. In the remaining modules, as part of their practicum, they would identify ethical issues, the plans to address them, decide how to ensure evaluation standards and also decide on an effective form of communicating the evaluation process and findings. Each stage is to be completed under supervision or assessed to ensure that the evaluation meets the quality standards. Upon approval of the written evaluation proposal, students would carry out the field work and develop the communication materials. The faculty would arrange for the students' evaluation findings to be consolidated and provided as a contribution to specific sectors or programmes, as relevant.

The practicum is therefore designed to yield an evaluation that meets quality criteria, has utility and adds to the institution's research contribution to the country. TESA expects research to be an integral part of the course. An aim of TESA is to develop an innovative and contextualised research and training programme where both students and staff can engage in meaningful and relevant research. Possibilities of thematic research across different countries with comparable research designs will be explored so that findings can be consolidated. Promoting the use of findings will be a main focus. Rather than the traditional projects carried out by students as an examination requirement, which tend to have a narrow focus and be isolated, students will be required to make specific contributions within an overall research design. Additionally, in close collaboration with governmental and international organisations, TESA will explore opportunities for students and staff to contribute to ongoing evaluations in South Asia or outside. Sufficient time will be allocated for this work whilst integrating the practical sessions to develop the evaluation design within the theoretical modules.

The TESA evaluation course is not limited to a diploma course at post graduate level. It can also be taught in modular form and it can be modified to suit workshops of short durations of one to two days. It can be used in this form by non-degree awarding institutions and VOPEs. Modules have already been used in this form by SLEvA. They have also been used as resource materials for evaluation workshops designed for specific purposes and audiences such as government officers. ASCI, IHMR, University and Industry Alliance and IbnSina have used the modules in this way.

The consortium of academic institutions has benefited from several resource persons who are evaluation professionals and academia from the University of Toronto, Canada; Gallaudet

University, Washington DC, USA; and, the Centre for Public Programme Evaluation, Virginia, USA. Two of the resource persons were engaged in co-production of the modules with Consortium members. Other resource persons have provided comments at workshops and reviewed several modules. One resource person set up a temporary website to help with the exchange of information during the module development stage.

Role of Sri Lanka Evaluation Association

A key feature of TESA is that a VOPE has played a central and strategic role in the evolution and functioning of TESA. SLEvA not only was an architect of the TESA concept at its inception, it also provided the operational hub for TESA. SLEvA organised all meetings and carried out the administrative and financial implementation. With this collaborative arrangement, TESA members, even though functioning as an informal network, could effectively focus on developing the curriculum and capacity development etc. SLEvA was able to play this critical partner role since it has reached a relatively stable position where a tradition of regular voluntary activities has been established. Equally importantly, a core group of members have evolved to continue the traditions. SLEvA has gained sufficient stature to attract members who are influential and committed to keep the establishment running and progressing. The collaboration has been smooth and productive and an objective review would most likely view it as a successful and mutually beneficial partnership.

SLEvA's contribution to TESA is not confined to coordination. It has also made a significant contribution to the curriculum development by developing one module and testing several others through workshops. SLEvA intends to have a programme of professional development workshops for its members and others based on the modules. SLEvA has also undertaken the management of the website.

Contribution of the Funding Agency

The operationalisation of the TESA concept was made possible by the IDRC through its acceptance of the concept of TESA and encouragement through catalytic funding support. IDRC recognising that the very limited evaluation training and evaluation research in universities in South Asia poses a major challenge to evaluation practice in the region, is strongly supportive of this effort to develop high quality evaluation training and to establish postgraduate diploma programmes in evaluation in South Asia. IDRC has also offered other very catalytic support in terms of access to its on line library facilities for TESA members. It has also supported networking by enabling TESA participation and representation at important evaluation events. Through this process TESA collaborated with the South Asia Community of Evaluation Conclaves, held in 2010 and 2013, and that collaboration has continued.

With the agreed activities under IDRC funding completed in 2012, and with the IDRC phase-out of evaluation field building activities, TESA now needs to look for strategic support for its next phase. This next phase is the actual implementation of the teaching, which requires capacity for teaching the curriculum, for undertaking assessments and to have in place the necessary quality assurance systems.

Good Practices, Challenges and Future Directions

TESA considers as one of its good practices, the approach it used to develop the curriculum, which was through co-production and collaboration. Senior academic staff of the consortium took the responsibility to develop the modules while the resource persons provided feedback and technical inputs where needed. This approach of co-production rather than adopting an externally developed curriculum enabled the potential teaching staff to take ownership of the curriculum design and content. It also served as a capacity development strategy of learning by doing. This co-production mode was supported by collaboration among consortium members. The consortium members provided comments on one another's work and quite importantly tested in workshops the modules developed by other members. The presentations at review meetings, feedback from invited experts in the field, testing and piloting of the modules were good capacity development strategies that also served to enhance ownership. While enhancements will continue, an eclectic experience of institutions in developing and writing the curriculum materials has helped to complete them, and also shaped their delivery structure.

Another endearing practice of TESA is that the members of the consortium worked entirely on a voluntary basis. The senior academic staff gave of their time and expertise to develop the curriculum in a spirit of a contribution from the institution. The funding that was available was for the purpose of meetings, to engage the services of a few experts and for basic material costs. It was of great satisfaction to the consortium that the members did work their way through this task despite their own heavy work place schedules, even though the speed of the process could have been greater. It can be argued that what sustained this contribution are the firm commitment of the core consortium members and the confidence of the sponsors, IDRC. This core group remained steadfast and worked through the constraints that surfaced. There is also the expectation that institutionalising evaluation would, in the medium term, bring benefits to the institutions in terms of having a well-accepted course for which there would be a growing demand.

The voluntary basis of work by the consortium members and a VOPE functioning as a secretariat have the much discussed limitations as well as positive spinoffs. The voluntary nature of the work means that constraints of time and resources reduce the speed of work. With respect to one main product, which is the development of the curriculum, this was not a major hindrance. The collaborative spirit that evolved and the ownership that was established did more than offset the disadvantage of a somewhat slow speed. However, it is a challenge to maintain a high level of motivation of the members of the consortium and to make the concept attractive to institutions. The tendency of institutions is to seek quick gains as part of their business processes. A programme that requires initial investments in terms of staff time in the expectation of fairly medium term gains pose challenges in creating a high level of commitment.

Reaching out for partnerships and networking has proved to be helpful. TESA has already received some external recognition that has inspired its work and helped sustain its momentum through networking. One such network is with the Community of Evaluators (CoE) South Asia. This networking was initiated and supported by the TESA consortium members, being active members of the CoE. The facilitating role of IDRC that has sponsored both CoE and TESA reinforced the connections. TESA was represented in the CoE during 2012 and had a strong presence at the second Conclave in February 2013. TESA has also been able to network with SLEvA, not just as its coordinator but also as a well-established national evaluation association in the region. Some TESA members have joined SLEvA membership. A partnership with CLEAR South Asia has been explored and it is expected to be operational as further work, especially teaching, unfolds. TESA now looks forward to being an active member of EvalPartners and build peer to peer partnerships with other regional evaluation training programmes.

The major challenge for TESA is to set in place the competencies needed to teach the evaluation course. The faculty members from the academic institutions are experienced professionals in their own fields. Yet, a systemic orientation is needed for the evaluation curriculum so that all would be at a known adequate level of competencies. This is also needed to ensure a degree of uniformity across the institutions. As a step in achieving these competencies, currently, the faculty is encouraged to select the modules they are interested in teaching and, as preparation for the formal training, to review the selected modules; supplement examples; develop case studies; adapt the presentations; and to devise exercises for student assessments. A formal introductory programme, where the faculty members demonstrate the teaching of these modules and feedback is given by both peers and experienced teaching professionals, is the next major step in operationalising TESA. This introduction is to be scheduled as a series of sessions, each session focusing on a number of modules lasting about a week. During these sessions, expert professionals would co-teach to demonstrate the approach. In the medium-term TESA plans to identify emerging bright scholars who perform well on the diploma course and who are also creative and committed to become successful teachers for further academic training in appropriate universities. For this process, TESA is seeking collaboration and catalytic support from the international community and universities.

In the academic arena there are several issues to address. One issue is reaching agreement on what exactly it means to place evaluation in the South Asian context. What bearings do social norms, values and ethnicity play in evaluation methodologies, ethics, norms and standards? As TESA gains deeper understanding of these issues through its teaching, the teaching methodology will be modified.

As the next phase, simultaneously with the staff development activities, TESA is currently engaged in expanding its membership and partnerships. A number of institutions have expressed interest in joining TESA and have already participated in some events. These include Sharda University, India; the S.P. Jain Institute of Management and Research, Mumbai, India; Guru Ghasidas University, Bilaspur, India; the University of Kelaniya, Sri Lanka; etc. TESA will be delivered not only as a postgraduate diploma but in several other modes. These include evaluation modules within other academic programmes such as Masters in Business Management offered by universities and professional development workshops offered by VOPEs. TESA is considering developing online programmes as short training programmes based on the modules. An e-learning programme in partnership with EvalPartners on *www.MyMandE.org* is already being discussed.

The TESA programme is designed as a sustainable solution to the lack of professionalisation of evaluation. The programme is for the purpose of generating a steady flow of evaluation professionals from local institutions of higher learning who could promote a culture of evaluation in support of more effectively achieving development results for people. TESA has reached its early milestones. It is seeking partnerships, both South-South and North-South, for two purposes. Firstly, to take the next steps of achieving a broad-based and relevant tertiary education in evaluation in South Asian countries, and to do this in an efficiently and collaborative way. Secondly, and equally important, it looks forward to sharing the experience and knowledge it has gathered with similar regional initiatives for teaching evaluation. TESA looks forward to EvalPartners which would be a forum to bring peers with similar interests enabling partnerships to be forged in pursuit of common goals.

References

Carden, F. (2007). "The Real Evaluation Gap", *Alliance Magazine* 12: 4. December.

Grob, George F. (2010). "The Pillars of Public Programme Evaluation", in Bobs Williams and Meenakshi Shankar (eds.), *Evaluation South Asia.* UNICEF.

Hay, Katherine (2011). "Building the Field of Evaluation in South Asia: A Framework and Ideas", *Working Paper Series* No-3. Community of Evaluators.

Shiva Kumar, A.K. (2010). "A Comment on Evaluation Field Building in South Asia: Reflections, Anecdotes, and Questions," *American Journal of Evaluation* 31(2).

13

HEMNATH RAO HANUMANKAR

Converging a Wage Employment Based Anti-Poverty Programme with Natural Resource Management

A Holistic Case Study of the Kandhamal District in Odisha, India

The Mahatma Gandhi National Rural Employment Guarantee Programme

The Government of India (GoI) in the Ministry of Rural Development (MoRD) notified the Mahatma Gandhi National Rural Employment Guarantee Act (MGNREGA) on the 2 February 2006, heralding the advent of rights based legal framework for enhancing the livelihood security of rural households. The Act guarantees 100 days of wage employment in a financial year to any rural household whose adult members volunteer to do unskilled manual work at wage rates linked to the statutory minimum wage in each state. In the long history of wage employment programmes that India has had in pursuit of poverty alleviation, MGNREGA stands out for its emphasis on development of natural resources and assets at community and household levels through a process of participatory decision-making in GPs (*gram panchayats*)[1] for strengthening the livelihood resource base of the rural poor. Yet, the primary objective of the Act is to provide wage employment on demand to self targeted households.

The evidence for reduction in levels of rural poverty with rise in both agriculture and non-agriculture based employment, originally brought out in the studies of the Planning Commission of India for

1. *Gram Panchayats* are village councils which constitute rural India's primary level of local self-government.

developing the *National Human Development Report* (2001) and later corroborated by Chadha (2008) and others, deepened the interest among Indian policy makers in a self-selecting wage employment programme like the MGNREGA. An attempt at integration of employment generation with development programmes was seen as early as during the Sixth Five Year Plan period when the National Rural Employment Programme (NREP) and Rural Landless Employment Guarantee Programme (RLEGP) were launched. In these programmes, development projects and employment generation were closely intertwined and employment was viewed as an integral component of development. RLEGP was similar to NREP in most respects with special emphasis on the landless poor.

Beginning with the 200 most backward districts of the country in the first phase, 130 additional districts were covered under the MGNREGA in the second phase during 2007-08. Currently, the Act is implemented in 624 districts across India. In regard to the progress in the implementation of the Act since inception, 8 billion person days of employment have been generated through 4.55 million works by the end of March 2011. Besides the physical and financial progress reported by the GoI, independent studies by institutions of repute have suggested that the implementation of the Act has primarily benefited the rural poor with enhanced wage bargaining power leading to buoyancy in the rural labour market. Other benefits include improved purchasing power of the rural poor; reduced distress migration to urban areas; augmented productivity of small and marginal farm holdings; regeneration of natural resources; empowerment of women; and stronger democratic processes of governance in PRIs (panchayati raj institutions) responsible for local self-government (Hanumankar, 2011). While the potential for harvesting the above benefits under MGNREGA is not in doubt, a plethora of shortcomings and constraints have been identified in the programme implementation processes, as pointed out in various media reports. The gap between expected and actual levels of performance, notwithstanding, the MGNREGA has contributed significantly to the renewal of the country's depleting natural resources base.

MGNREGA Integrated Natural Resource Management (INRM) Convergence in Kandhamal District

The scope for leveraging MGNREGA to generate a positive impact on Natural Resource Management (NRM) had been recognised by the programme management teams at the national and regional levels in the very early phase of implementation of MGNREGA. That 4 out of the 8 categories of works approved for employment generation under Schedule 1 of the Act, bears this out. Yet, very few studies have attempted investigating the processes and dynamics that influence the selection of projects in the Gram Sabha meetings with focus on developing natural resources that have potential to generate sustainable livelihoods. Kandhamal district in India's eastern state of Odisha, had seen very little progress in the implementation of MGNREGA despite being one of the most backward districts of Odisha selected in the first Phase of the programme. As per the 2001 Census, 69 per cent of the district's total population belonged to two ethnic groups namely the Kandho (scheduled tribe [ST]) and Pano (scheduled caste [SC]),[2] the former accounting for 52 per cent and the latter for 17 per cent of the district's population of 0.65 million. Only around 15 per cent of the geographical area of 764,900 hectares is cultivable. In spite of a low population density of 80 persons per square kilometre as against the state's average of 236, the average net sown area per rural family is a meagre 0.5 hectares which explains the very poor quality of cultivable land. The district's average annual rainfall of 1525 mm is a saving grace.

Difficult topography of land apart, the district has borne the brunt of ethno-communal conflicts for many years. In December 2007, a major skirmish was witnessed between two social groups but the worst riots erupted in August 2008 which impaired normal life in the district due to unprecedented violence. Serious distrust and hatred amongst different sections of the society was palpable. The following details of damage to life and property emerged at the end of the riots.

2. The Constitution of India provides for special privileges in matters of human resource development to certain socially disadvantaged groups of people recognised as belonging to SCs and STs.

- More than 25,000 persons rendered shelter less.
- More than 4,800 houses were damaged.
- More than 50 deaths reported.
- Livelihood disrupted as agricultural operations were suspended.
- 118 shops and commercial establishments were damaged.
- 229 places of religious worship were damaged.
- 12 public institutions and some police outposts were bombed.

This case study examines the role and contribution of the pilot project for developing sustainable rural livelihoods through convergence of MGNREGA with management of natural resources in partnership with an NGO (non-governmental organisation).

Pilot Project for MGNREGA Convergence with Natural Resource Regeneration

The United Nations Development Programme (UNDP), New Delhi and MoRD, GoI, supported the Professional Assistance for Development Action (PRADAN), an NGO with a pilot project for capacity building of GPs in implementing Integrated Natural Resource Management (INRM) practices as part of the MGNREGA works for a six month period from October 2007 to March 2008. The pilot project was aimed at experimenting if INRM could facilitate a transition for MGNREGA from being an unskilled wage-employment programme to a programme for promotion of sustainable livelihoods for the poor rural households through creation of natural resource based productive assets. Kandhamal was one of the five districts selected across the country for implementation of the pilot project. Ten GP were identified from three blocks (Balliguda, Dairingabadi and K. Nuagaon) for implementing the pilot project in twenty five villages/habitations spanning the ten selected GPs in the district.

The activities envisaged under the pilot project are listed in Box 13.1. These activities were planned to promote INRM based on models and methods that PRADAN has developed over the years from its experience of working in different states of India (Nath, 2011). The INRM practices involve participatory planning among rural communities to enhance land productivity through soil conservation, rainwater harvesting and diversified cropping patterns.

Though progress during the pilot project was hindered by law and order problems that cropped up in the district during December 2007, the initial results were encouraging enough for PRADAN to launch a separate pilot project in Gunjagaon GP of Kandhamal district with funding support from Oxfam later in 2008.

Based on the progress demonstrated in Gunjagaon in integrating INRM with MGNREGA, the UNDP, Bhubaneswar, supported another project in five GPs for enhancing the capacity of village communities to plan and implement MGNREGA works utilising the INRM models developed by PRADAN. This second project was also approved for six month duration, from October 2009 to March 2010. In the meantime, the District Level Peace Committee constituted by the Government of Odisha in the aftermath of the riots of August 2008, saw a great opportunity to leverage the MGNREGA-INRM works to initiate the process of dialogue and reconciliation between the conflicting groups. The Committee in its guidelines formulated under the aegis of the Special Administrator stated that: "... in each of the affected villages one labour intensive work under MGNREGA will be started. In this 'Work for Peace', both the communities should participate for creation of community assets of their choice. This will also provide minimum wage employment to all the families." Even as the second UNDP project got off to a start in the five GPs, the Kandhamal District Administration decided in November 2009 to involve seven other field NGOs with PRADAN as the nodal NGO for expanding the scope of MGNREGA-INRM 'Work for Peace' to six other blocks.

Outcomes from the Pilot Projects

The most significant outcome from the two pilot projects supported by the UNDP and MoRD has been an increase in awareness and capacity of the rural communities in villages where the pilot projects were implemented, to exercise their rights under the MGNREGA and participate in the Gram Sabhas (village council meetings). In the three hamlets/villages sampled for this case study—Limarpadar from Mahasingh GP, Gasukia from Sirtiguda GP of K. Nuagaon Block and Nadapatanga from Barkhama GP of Balliguda Block—the wage seekers shared during the focus group discussions that the job cards were previously in the possession of local labour contractors. Participation in the orientation courses organised as IEC (information, education and communication) events under the UNDP-MoRD pilot projects for members of Self-Help Groups (SHGs) and Village and GP level committees enabled the wage seekers to recover their job cards and demand employment. The social outcomes in this regard are summarised in Table 13.1.

Box 13.1

Activities Planned Under MGNREGA-INRM Pilots

1. Orientation of the project personnel at district, block and GP levels on INRM based livelihoods for rural poor and opportunities for their convergence with MGNREGA.
2. Awareness of gram sabha members on their entitlements under MGNREGA.
3. Identification, training, deployment and monitoring of a large cadre of LRPs (local resource persons) to serve as facilitators for participatory planning.
4. Helping adult members of rural households to understand their right to unskilled manual work for 100 days in a year under MGNREGA.
5. Capacity building of gram sabha in planning INRM based shelf of projects for providing wage employment under MGNREGA.
6. Preparation of GP wise INRM-MGNREGA project plans.
7. Organising workers for implementation and monitoring of the MGNREGA works.
8. Ensuring transparent processes for quality in execution of MGNREGA works.
9. Guiding the rural communities in the effective use of the assets created.
10. Documentation of experiences, learning and sharing progress.

Following improved awareness of their rights and provisions under MGNREGA, the village communities torn apart by the social conflicts of 2007 and 2008 began coming together to demand, plan and participate in the MGNREGA works. Job cards were issued to households that did not have the same or reissued to those who lost the job cards in arson during the ethnic conflict. The outcome was a growth in the person days of wage employment generated as may be seen from the progress shown in Table 13.2 for two GPs of the K. Nuagaon block. In focus interviews, the wage seekers from the hamlets sampled from these GPs articulated that MGNREGA provided an opportunity for them to put behind their hostilities and work hand in hand at MGNREGA work sites. In recognition of having leveraged MGNREGA for restoring communal harmony, the district was selected for an award for the year 2009-10.

Table 13.1

Social Outcomes from Pilot Projects

Social Unit	*Pre-Intervention Status*	*Focus of Intervention*	*Outcome*
Family	Vicious cycle of migration. No light at the end of the tunnel syndrome. Unaware about NREGA and other govt. schemes. Most villagers did not attend *palli-sabha*.	Visioning exercise for family to aspire for a better life and plan towards it by accessing what is due under MGNREGA and other development schemes. Helping families especially women to attend *pallisabaha* and demand execution of their plans.	Family is aware of the provisions under MGNREGA and seek access to wage employment. Family prepares plan taking into consideration its resource and skill base. Plans have been finalised and approved for 48 villages and INRM work has been initiated in around 20 villages which has instilled confidence amongst the villagers.
SHG	Most women have come together for well-being of their families but not aware of all options.	SHG level orientation and awareness of Rights and entitlements under MGNREGA.	SHG is able to help its members work towards enhancing their wage employment under MGNREGA and prepare plans for developing INRM on their farm land.
Village/GP Committees	Lacked people's trust and could not involve them in planning MGNREGA shelf of projects.	Village and *panchayat* level orientation on MGNREGA and INRM.	Members of GP understand the aspirations of families and village communities and realise how MGNREGA-INRM can help improve socioeconomic status of the villages across the GP.

Table 13.2

MGNREGA Performance in Two GPs of K.Nuagaon Block

G.P.	*Mahasingh*				*Sirtiguda*			
Year	2007-08	2008-09	2009-10	2010-11	2007-08	2008-09	2009-10	2010-11
No of Villages	27	27	27	27	18	18	18	18
No of House-holds	1,702	1,702	1,702	1,702	1,479	1,479	1,479	1,479
No of Job cards	1,073	1,220	1,365	1,480	970	1,320	1,485	1,618
Person-days of Employ-ment	16,170	27,742	33,049	54,900	12,000	32,000	47,000	56,000

Source: PRADAN'S Database

As may be seen from Table 13.3, the INRM models demonstrated by PRADAN were integrated with MGNREGA in developing mango orchards in the upland farm holdings of nine tribal farmers who were also encouraged to cultivate vegetables as an inter-crop in the Limarpadar hamlet of Mahasingh GP. While the table shows a sample of nine farmers who participated actively in MGNREGA, the mango plantation was actually taken up in 22 acres by 22 households at the rate of 1 acre per household in this hamlet of 60 households at the planting rate of 160 saplings per acre. The excavation of pits for planting the saplings, fencing against grazing cattle and the mango saplings were all provided under the MGNREGA with guidance from PRADAN's LRPs. Returns from the freshly planted mango orchards will have to wait for three more years but cauliflower cultivation as an inter-crop or as a second crop in addition to the traditional rainfed paddy has already generated additional income for the farmers. This approach to planting fruit trees in uplands, pulses and vegetables in midlands aided by INRM models of water conservation and paddy in low lands following the System of Rice Intensification (SRI) has been very well received by *jhooming* tribal farmers, as it helps them enhance farm income without risking food security.

Table 13.3

Limbarpadar: Beneficiaries of MGNREGA-INRM Works

S. No.	*Name*	*Job Card No*	*No. of Mango Plantation*	*No. of Farm pond*	*Wage days under MGNREGA*	*Type of crop*	*Additional Income (₹)*
1	Madhuka Mallick	8332	160	3	100	Cauliflower	35,000
2	Raghunath Pradhan	8357	160	-	100	Peas	5,000
3	Prehma Mallick		160	1	100	Cabbage, Cauliflower	10,000
4	Kanu Mallick	8371	160	8	100	Cauliflower	30,000
5	Ratnakar Mallick	8336	160	-	100	Cauliflower	10,000
6	Nimanti Mallick	8325	160	-	80	Brinjal pea	7,000
7	Kunime Mallick	8358	160	7	100	Cauliflower	30,000
8	Sajahe Mallick	8377	160	4	80	Potato	6,000
9	Parsuram Pradhan	8372	160	-	100	Cereals	7,000

Source: Culled from PRADAN'S field diary.

Through field visits arranged for groups of small and marginal farmers to PRADAN's INRM demonstration sites in Keonjhar district within the state as well as IEC efforts, the pilot projects have motivated the village communities to develop participatory plans for implementing INRM practices through MGNREGA works on individual and community lands. In the early months of MGNREGA, the focus of work was almost entirely on road connectivity between villages and hamlets within each GP. With the capacity developed among the village communities to deploy participatory planning tools like resource mapping and asset planning, some villages where pilot projects were implemented now feel empowered to continue the planning process on their own without external support. This confidence was demonstrated particularly by women members of

SHGs in the Nadapatanga village of Barkhama GP where 100 out of 120 job card holding families have planned and implemented atleast one INRM model such as the 5 per cent pit, 30 X 40 model,[3] dug wells or land levelling all of which has doubled the cropping intensity in the village which predominantly drew livelihood support in the past from collection of non-timber forest produce and *jhooming* cultivation of red gram and turmeric.

Growing awareness of INRM models and confidence in the communities to plan their future livelihood security is prompting entrepreneurship in the villages. Farmers are converting their small landholdings into fish ponds even at the risk of not having enough land to grow food grains. Despite the fact that paddy yields have almost tripled from adopting SRI in paddy cultivation, the prospect of cost intensive multi-purpose farm ponds of the Type 3 (150 X 100 X 8 feet) being sanctioned by the *Palle/Gram Sabhas* under MGNREGA is being seen as an opportunity by enterprising small farmers to foray into fish culture. As may be seen from Table 13.4, four farmers in the Gasukia hamlet of Bondaguda village of the Sirtiguda GP have been the beneficiaries of such ponds each costing around ₹ 1.5 lakh. Their sense of entrepreneurship is commendable and is a positive outcome as one of them has already purchased out of personal resources and introduced 2000 fingerlings in the pond. Yet, in the absence of convergence with any scheme of the Fisheries Department and with no formal technical support, such investments could prove too risky for small tribal farmers. The risks could arise out of weather conditions, incidence of disease, market price fluctuations etc., and hence the need to address the issues of risk management and food security.

---

3. 30 X 40 Model: A method of *in situ* soil and water conservation, it involves dividing uplands into small plots of 30 x 40 ft (30 ft along the slope and 40 ft across the slope), digging pits at the lowest point in each plot and bunding the plot using the soil dug out of the pits. By plotting unterraced and unbunded lands and creating water collection pits in each plot, run-off water is checked and collected.

Table 13.4

Gasukia: Enterprising Farm Pond Beneficiaries

S. No.	*Name*	*Job Card No*	*Asset*
1	Lungu Mallick	7301	Farm pond type-3
2	Nuari Mallick	7265	Farm pond type-3
3	Prantajini Mallick	7288	Farm pond type-3
4	Rusma Mallick	7294	Farm pond type-3
5	Rajani Mallick	7248	5 per cent
6	Rangita Mallick	7281	5 per cent
7	Ratnabati Mallick	7241	5 per cent
8	Kadambati Mallick	7312	5 per cent
9	Kasmati Mallick	7278	5 per cent
10	Kimburi Mallick	7309	5 per cent

Source: Culled from PRADAN'S field diary.

A very encouraging outcome from the MGNREGA-INRM pilots in the Kandhamal district has been the heightened sense of voluntarism among single member households in the villages to dedicate their assets for the welfare of the community. The beneficiary of a dug well in Nadapatanga village, Jambuvathy Patel, a widow, revealed that she has dedicated the well provided to her under MGNREGA to the village community after her death. Another beneficiary, Parvathy Pande had been recommended for a similar well by the palle sabha in her individual landholding but she has located the well in such a way that the entire village draws water for their regular household consumption. It transpired during the focus interviews that the process of participatory planning has brought a sense of cohesiveness among the households in the village and a deeper appreciation of the need to leverage natural resources for the wider benefit of the village community. This sense of voluntarism has also contributed to social harmony.

The bottom line of the outcomes discussed above has been a distinct improvement in the socio-economic status and micro-level human development in the villages where the pilot projects were implemented. Rural households are encouraged to increase spending on the education of their children, health and food as participants of the focus group discussion in the Gasukia hamlet shared, where 80 per cent of the job card holders have availed of 100 days of employment under the MGNREGA. Many households have acquired additional assets such as goats and bullocks with the increased income, both from wages and higher farm yields. Rusma Mallick from Gasukia gestured during the discussion that her silver jewellery mortgaged several years back has now been redeemed from the better earnings that MGNREGA-INRM brought to her. Santosh Kumar Pande, Gram Sanjojak (mate) emphatically said during the focus interview that most communities in tribal dominated villages recognise that their lives revolve around four natural resources—forests, farm land, water and animal husbandry. The MGNREGA-INRM pilots have raised the capacity of the village communities to efficiently manage natural resources. This view was endorsed strongly by the members of the Barkhama G.P., Santhilata Nayak and Ganeswar Digal who reminded that the focus of MGNREGA would have been confined to roads and ponds, if not for the pilot projects on INRM.

Though the unit of analysis for this case study has been the rural poor who have benefited through MGNREGA-INRM works, an unmistakable outcome is the enhanced credibility of the NGOs with the district and state administration. The evidence comes from the decision to involve other field NGOs like SWATI, Sewa Bharathi, Jagruthi and a few others as field NGOs to replicate the results from the pilot projects in other blocks of the District, with PRADAN as the lead organisation. The District Collector, Krishna Kumar, expressed firmly that the micro-watershed based INRM practices was the way forward for MGNREGA works in the district to progress, with an active role for NGOs like the PRADAN. This view was supported by all other officers in the district including the Project Officer, District Rural Development Agency (DRDA), Dilip Ray, who believes that the pilot projects have shown how wage employment can make way for livelihood security by enhancing productivity of land and natural resources.

References

Planning Commission of India (2001). *National Human Development Report*. New Delhi: Government of India. pp.36-37.

Chadha, G.K. (2008). "Employment and Poverty in Rural India: Which Way To Go Now?", *Working Paper Series* 14. New Delhi: Sub-Regional Office for South Asia, ILO Asia-Pacific.

Hanumankar, H.R. (2011). *Study of MGNREGA: A Case in Implementation of an Anti-Poverty Programme in Andhra Pradesh, India*. London: VDM Verlag. pp.8-10.

Nath, N. (2011). "NREGA as an Opportunity to Promote INRM based Livelihood", in N. Ranjan, *NREGA: Design, Process and Impact*. New Delhi: GoI-UNDP. p.147.